THE SABUROV MEMOIRS

OR

BISMARCK & RUSSIA

PETER ALEXANDROVITCH SABUROV

THE SABUROV MEMOIRS

OR

BISMARCK & RUSSIA

BEING
FRESH LIGHT ON THE LEAGUE
OF THE THREE EMPERORS
1881

by

J. Y. SIMPSON

CAMBRIDGE
AT THE UNIVERSITY PRESS
1929

CONTENTS

Chapter

ILLUSTRATIONS

PREFACE

THE League of the Three Emperors (1881) was a nineteenth-century political event of capital importance in the international life of Europe which has not yet received in itself that measure of investigation which it merits. Even to-day, apart from certain passages in Prof. A. F. Pribram's classical work on *Die politischen Geheimverträge Österreich-Ungarns* (1920), well-known in the English translation entitled *The Secret Treaties of Austria-Hungary*, certain passages in Volume III of the revealing German Foreign Office publication entitled *Die grosse Politik der europäischen Kabinette 1871–1914*, Edward von Wertheimer's *Graf Julius Andrassy: sein Leben und seine Zeit* (3 vols. 1910–13), and an admirable brochure, *L'Alliance des Trois Empereurs*, by Prof. K. Kratchounof of Sofia (1924), there is strangely little in the way of serious studies devoted mainly to the great issues involved.[1] The principal reason is that first-hand material bearing on the negotiations that led up to the League has hitherto been scarce.

In May, 1917, M. Saburov gave me a signed copy of his work in French entitled *Ma Mission à Berlin 1879–1884*, which had been printed for private circulation (*na pravakh rukopisi*) in St Petersburg a few months before the outbreak of the War. He expressed his desire to have it made available some time to the

---

[1] Reference may also be made to Prof. J. V. Fuller's work entitled *Bismarck's Diplomacy at its Zenith*.

Western world, as he believed that it had value as a record of events. Two articles containing excerpts from these Memoirs were contributed by me to *The Nineteenth Century* in the months of December, 1917, and January, 1918, under the title "Russo-German Relations and the Saburov Memoirs" References to these selections in such works as *Die grosse Politik*, vol. III, pp. 113 n. and 133 n., and Sir C. Grant-Robertson's *Bismarck*, seemed to indicate that M. Saburov's too modest estimate of his own work deserved further consideration.

Accordingly, the main part of this volume constitutes a complete translation of *Ma Mission à Berlin*.[1] The Memoirs are preceded by an editorial Introduction in two sections, the first of which is of a more biographical nature, while the second represents a translation of an article entitled "Russie, France, Allemagne (1870–1880)" contributed by M. Saburov to *La Revue de Paris* (15 March, 1912). This article is included here as forming a peculiarly suitable introduction to the Memoirs themselves. The latter are followed by an editorial Postscript, the earlier portion of which is devoted to the light shed on the negotiations as furnished in the relevant communications to and from Prince Bismarck set forth in Volume III of *Die grosse Politik der europäischen Kabinette* 1871–1914. The second part is devoted to some general conclusions. The notes throughout, unless when expressly indicated to the contrary, are editorial.

[1] Extracts and short résumés from the original work have appeared in the Russian publication, *Krasny Archiv*, I, 64 ff. (1922).

For much assistance in connection with these and the introductory biographical section, I am indebted to M. Peter Petrovitch Saburov, to Baron Alexander Felixovitch Meyendorff, who has kindly read the work in proof and supplied several important details in addition to those acknowledged in the text, and to M. Alexander Onou, late Russian Consul-General in London, whose personal relationship to Baron Jomini has made him an invaluable commentator on contemporary personalities and events. I wish further to acknowledge the courtesy of M. M. E. Sablin in granting permission for the examination of certain documents in the archives of the Russian Embassy in London, as also to thank Principal Sir C. Grant-Robertson, and Sir J. W. Headlam-Morley, K.B.E., friend and former colleague, for help ungrudgingly given. To the Editors of *Die grosse Politik* I wish to make acknowledgment of their generous permission to make use of such portions of the third volume of their monumental work as bears upon the present undertaking. Lastly, I would express my thanks to Miss Mona Fisher and Miss E. McNeil for their careful revision of the translations from the French and German respectively.

J. Y. SIMPSON

25 CHESTER STREET
EDINBURGH

July 1929

ABBREVIATIONS

D.G.P. *Die grosse Politik der europäischen Kabinette 1871–1914.*

P.S.T. A. F. Pribram's *The Secret Treaties of Austria-Hungary.*

INTRODUCTION

I

BIOGRAPHICAL

PETER ALEXANDROVITCH SABUROV, the author of these Memoirs, was born on 22 March/3 April, 1835, on the estate of Veryaevo, in the district of Elatma in the Government of Tamboff. He was a member of a distinguished family. His brother Andrew held for several years the portfolio of the Minister of Public Instruction, while family marriage ties linked him with Prince Anatole Gagarine, one of the more considerable landed proprietors in Russia: a sister was the well-known head of a school for girls at Voronezh. As a youth he attended the Imperial Alexander Lyceum, St Petersburg, where he completed his studies in December, 1854, gaining the first gold medal. His outgoing dissertation on *The Commercial Routes of the Ancient Greeks in the Black Sea* was published shortly after in St Petersburg. Thus early had his mind been directed to the regions around South Russia, and their many related political and economic problems.

After a brief interval he entered the Ministry of Foreign Affairs as an Assistant Secretary in the Chancelry. From 1857 to 1859 he served as Secretary in the Russian Legation at Munich. Thence he was sent to England, where he remained for nearly eleven years, first as Second Secretary, then as First Secretary, and finally as Counsellor of the Russian Em-

bassy in London, under Baron Brunnow.[1] Here he
had the opportunity of making the acquaintance of
the leading British statesmen—Disraeli, Gladstone,
Salisbury and others. Having great social gifts and
being a keen sportsman, he found himself very fre-
quently invited to country-house parties. Here also
in 1867 he may have published anonymously his first
financial work, a small volume, entitled *La Banque
d'État et le Papier-monnaie*.[2] It is however the case
that Baron Brunnow sometimes added to his despatches critical reviews on British Budget and other
financial matters supplied by M. Saburov, to whose
able secretarial work his Ambassador continually
directed the attention of the Minister of Foreign
Affairs.

As things fell out, it was in London also that he
made his first acquaintance with Prince Bismarck in

[1] Brunnow, Baron Philip (1797–1875), of Baltic origin, passed
the best part of his diplomatic career in London as representative
of the Imperial Russian Government. Strongly Anglophil, he
worked for the promotion and maintenance of a good understanding between Russia and Great Britain, both previous to and after
the Crimean War. He was accredited to the Court of St James
from 1840 to 1854. At the close of the Crimean War he returned
to London as Ambassador, acting there from 1860 to 1874. He
signed on behalf of Russia the Treaty of 15 July, 1840 (Quadruple
Alliance), as also the Treaty of London of 18 May, 1852, and took
an active part in defending the interests of Denmark against
Prussia at an abortive Conference of the Powers convoked at
London in April, 1864. In 1871 he secured the acceptance by the
British Government of the Gortchakov declaration that Russia no
longer considered herself bound by the clause in the Treaty of
Paris (1856) under which her naval rights in the Black Sea had been
limited. Baron Brunnow was made a Count on 18 March, 1871.

[2] This statement is made on the authority of his son,
M. P. P. Saburov, but I have been unable to verify it.

1862. Bismarck, who had been Ambassador in Paris, was expecting to be appointed Minister of Foreign Affairs. Previous to returning to Berlin in his new capacity, he came over to London in 1862 to get to know the prominent British statesmen personally. Baron Brunnow, the Russian Ambassador, gave a dinner in his honour to which Gladstone was invited, as also Disraeli, leader of the Opposition. After dinner there was general conversation, but Bismarck set himself alongside of Disraeli and talked with him for the matter of half an hour. Later in the evening Disraeli came up to Saburov, and said, "What an extraordinary man Bismarck is! He meets me for the first time and he tells me all he is going to do. He will attack Denmark in order to get possession of Schlesvig-Holstein; he will put Austria out of the German Confederation; and then he will attack France—an extraordinary man".[1] "Evidently", continued M. Saburov, in narrating this incident to the writer, "Bismarck had the whole plan already in his head. We Russians were all on the best of terms with him at this time. He was a sincere friend of Russia. He had been Ambassador in St Petersburg. But things began to be different after his quarrel with Prince Gortchakov[2] in 1875."

[1] For a fuller account of this evening cf. W. F. Monypenny and G. E. Buckle's *Life of Benjamin Disraeli, Earl of Beaconsfield*, IV, 341–348.

[2] Gortchakov, Prince Alexander Mikhailovitch (1798–1883), who served as Foreign Minister and was later called to the high office of Chancellor in the Russian Empire, was undoubtedly the most powerful Minister in Europe around 1863. In the conflict between Austria and Prussia in 1866, Russia remained neutral, and permitted Prussia to reap the fruits of victory and establish

The following letter[1] under date of 5/17 July, 1862,
gives Brunnow's impressions of the visit at the time:

Monsieur de Bismarck has just made an appearance in
London on the pretext of visiting the Exhibition, but, in
reality, with the purpose of securing an interview with Lord
Palmerston and Lord Russell.

The friendliness of our relations as old colleagues at Frankfort, has induced him to open up to me on the object of his
journey and its result.

If I had to sum up my mind on the one thing and on the
other, I would say that the idea behind his journey was
unsound, and the purpose a failure. The reason for this is
very simple. Four days are not enough in which to get to
know the statesmen who are at the helm of affairs in England.
On principle they discuss only those questions which they
are under the necessity of settling; they are neither accustomed
nor have they the liking for aimless and unnecessary conversation.

The reserve which M. de Bismarck has met with in London
has astonished him all the more since he believes himself
designated to replace Count Bernstorff shortly at Berlin. He
thought that the English Ministers, aware of this eventual
succession, would attach more importance to entering into

her supremacy in Germany. Again, when the Franco-German
war of 1870–1871 broke out, Russia answered for the neutrality
of Austria. An attempt was made to form an anti-Prussian coalition, but it failed in consequence of the cordial understanding
between the German and Russian Emperors. Personally, Prince
Gortchakov viewed the unification of Germany with apprehension, and may be said to have saved France with the help of Great
Britain against the provocation of Bismarck, 1875. The subject of
the later estrangement of Bismarck and Gortchakov comes up
more than once in the Memoirs. Prince Gortchakov resigned in
1882, and was succeeded by de Giers (vide infra).

[1] Access to this and the immediately following letters, preserved
in the archives of the Russian Embassy in London, I owe to the
kind co-operation of Baron Alexander Felixovitch Meyendorff and
M. Sablin.

direct relations with him. Disappointed in this expectation, he felt a touch of annoyance at it, which he in no way tried to conceal from me. This dissatisfaction has prevented him from bringing to the appreciation of men and things in this country the degree of concentration and determination which I have noted in him everywhere else.

He is above all mistaken in attributing to Lord Russell an acquaintance with German affairs which he is far from possessing! He is equally deceived in placing this Minister much above Lord Palmerston! He formed this opinion on the basis of a single conversation which he had with the Premier on the day when the latter, after receiving the degree of Doctor of Laws at Oxford University, came back to town exceedingly tired, and certainly very little inclined to take the interests of Prussia to heart!

On both sides, the impression was unfavourable. M. de Bismarck and Lord Palmerston did not have time to do justice to each other.

Both have related to me the most outstanding points in their conversation.

M. de Bismarck tried to show that he was strong enough to direct parliamentary affairs in Prussia with the aid of a minority! Lord Palmerston replied that he very much doubted it.

In the second place, M. de Bismarck gave the hint that in a more or less distant future, the Prussian Government, in order to give a measure of satisfaction to the advanced opinion of the country, might find itself engaged in a conflict with Austria. Lord Palmerston replied, "I consider you have too much good sense to come to that".

Both of them retained a rather disagreeable memory of this interview.

Wishing to respond to the confidential attitude in which my old Frankfort colleague made me acquainted with these details, I told him that he would require to come back to England, and make a longer stay in order to correct the inaccurate impressions that he was taking away with him after too short a visit. He did not seem to appreciate the justice of that remark.

A second Memorandum of the same date as the preceding one, gives an account of the visit of the Saxon Minister of Foreign Affairs.

The visit of Baron Beust[1] followed closely that of M. de Bismarck. The Saxon Minister, more fortunate than the Prussian Minister, produced a good impression here. As he knew the ground already, he confined himself to those commonplace expressions of courtesy that commit you to nothing.

He tried nevertheless to discover the attitude of the English Ministers towards the scheme of reform which he proposed to introduce in the federal organisation of Germany.

He found Lord Russell indifferent to, and completely ignorant of, the matter. The British Cabinet attaches importance only to the maintenance of a good understanding between Prussia and Austria. The Union of these two Powers constitutes, in the eyes of Her Britannic Majesty's Government, the basis of the defensive system of the German Confederation. But the English Ministers do not in any way believe themselves called to take part in the settlement of the federal interests of Germany.

Lord Russell declared himself in this sense in telling me of his interview with Baron Beust.

"I am indebted to this Minister for some rather instructive information about the questions of domestic politics which are being discussed at this moment in the heart of the Confederation. In this debate, the struggle for influence engaged in between Prussia and Austria always takes the first place.

"I learn lastly that the Cabinet at Vienna has decided to

---

[1] Friedrich Ferdinand, Count von Beust (1809–1886), was Minister of Foreign Affairs in Saxony from 1849 to 1866, when he resigned office after the defeat of Austria. He subsequently had a brilliant career in Austria, and later as Ambassador in London and Paris. See his *Memoirs*.

make the attempt to get all the States comprising the Austrian Monarchy into the German Customs Union (*Zollverein*).

"This plan is the result of a double combination,—industrial and political.

"On the one hand the Viennese Cabinet is trying to give fresh scope to the natural prosperity of its States by opening to their products a larger market, free from all obstacles, in the whole extent of Germany.

"On the other hand also, in attempting to make Venice come into the Customs Union, the Viennese Cabinet is trying, without any doubt, to link her Italian possessions to the commercial interests of the Confederation, so as to consolidate further the military position which it occupies in face of Italy.

"Baron Beust does not admit that supposition at all. He asserts that the entry of Austria into the Zollverein would have a purely commercial interest, and that it would impose no political sacrifice on Germany.

"I am not convinced of the truth of this statement. I rather think that the Saxon Minister is disposed to favour the Austrian combination in that it would serve to increase the influence of the Viennese Cabinet over North Germany, and diminish in like measure the preponderance of Prussia.

"The latter inspires a fear in her neighbours, as to the cause of which Baron Beust did not leave me in ignorance. He thinks that Prussia aims at self-aggrandisement, sooner or later, to the prejudice of the sovereignty and independence of the bordering States. It is in order to resist this tendency that he leans towards Austria.

"He feels himself but feebly supported by the States of the second and third rank. He complains bitterly of their mistrust and jealousy. 'I would like to keep them from drowning, but they bite my hand.'"

On leaving London, the Saxon Minister goes to Paris, where his business is to terminate some arrangements connected with the conclusion of the Treaty of Commerce with France.

In 1870 M. Saburov was appointed Chargé d'Affaires at Carlsruhe, where he wrote his still unpublished *Mémoire sur l'Angleterre*, which helped to gain for him, in the summer of the same year, the post of Russian Minister in Athens, where he remained till 1879. His records of these years lie in the manuscript of his work *Ma mission en Grèce*.

A pleasant impression of his relations with his former chief and of his interest in his new work, may be gathered from the following letter to Baron Brunnow from Corfu, under date of 25 August/ 6 September, 1870.

Monsieur le Baron,

I have just received your kind and affectionate letter of 13/25 August, for which I beg you to accept all my thanks. It has for me the twofold value of being the voice of my old chief, who is good enough to take an interest in the début of his pupil, and it gives me, at the same time, the means of appreciating exactly the present intentions of England with regard to Greece.

With the help of your advice it will be easy for me not to fall into error on this point, through the often contradictory local opinions which I hear expressed around me, and through the behaviour and language of Erskine[1] himself, who, whilst

[1] Erskine, the Hon. Edward Morris, C.B. (1817–1883), son of Lord David Montague Erskine, British diplomat, who, after serving as Secretary at the British Embassies in St Petersburg and Constantinople, was appointed Minister Plenipotentiary at Athens, 7 May, 1864. Here, in 1870, he had to deal with a tragic event— the murder of some English tourists by a party of brigands. He was held responsible in some quarters for having failed to save the lives of those members of the party who had been taken prisoner (vide infra), and his conduct was severely blamed in Parliament and in some English newspapers, on the ground that he had not displayed sufficient energy and decision in the crisis. It is interesting to note that his Russian colleague took a more

doing his best to serve his Government with all the zeal of which he is capable, has his mind too much filled by the misfortune of not having saved his compatriots,[1] to be able to maintain the calmness necessary in his so difficult situation. That will not prevent me from giving a cordial character to my relations with him on every opportunity, in accordance with the nature of our present relations with England.

I expect to make great use of the argument with which you have just enriched my repertory, and which is summed up in these words: "Greece owes it to her own dignity to efface the memory of Marathon by a *spontaneous* action of reparation".

I will exert my efforts to get all the politicians with whom I shall be in relation at Athens to come to this point of view.

sympathetic view of Erskine's conduct. This was also the attitude of the Foreign Office, which found that he had done everything that was possible. Subsequently Mr Erskine was transferred to Stockholm (1872), and retired from the Service in 1881.

[1] Conditions in Greece were not very settled, and brigands had sometimes considerable political, military and social power. Likewise they had sympathisers, agents and accomplices in the Greek Parliament and the administrative bodies in Athens. A party of tourists, mostly English, escorted by four mounted gendarmes, was captured by brigands on 11 April, 1870, when returning from a visit to the Plain of Marathon. The party included two Secretaries of Legations (British and Italian), three other Englishmen, two ladies and a child. In the struggle two of the gendarmes were killed, and the ladies (Lady Muncaster and Mrs Lloyd) and child were sent back in charge of the other two gendarmes. The brigands then released another prisoner (Lord Muncaster), and through him commenced what turned out to be protracted negotiations with the British Minister and the Greek Government for a heavy ransom and full amnesty for themselves. While the negotiations were proceeding, they removed the prisoners to the village of Oropos. This territory was invested by Greek military detachments. The brigands, under the pressure of an attack which they considered to be a violation of a promise given to them, and in which some of them fell, murdered all their prisoners. The remaining criminals were eventually caught and executed. (Cf. Parliamentary Papers, May, 1870.)

For the true dignity of Greece is certainly enshrined in these two lines.

Unfortunately, Sir, the fatality which seems to weigh on this miserable matter since the first day, has created two circumstances here, which will make the execution of that programme difficult.

The first one is that the indefinite prolongation of the inquiry and the various incidents which accompany it have already warped public opinion in Greece. Wrongly or rightly, the Greeks are beginning to be bitter against England. Moreover, a wrong idea has crept into their minds which gains ground every day; they think that England wishes to make use of the Marathon catastrophe to strengthen her influence, to impose Ministries on them, in short to govern Greece.

I am far from ignoring the rôle that party rivalries can have had in this disposition of men's minds. Without any doubt there are people who call out that Greece is humiliated, simply in order to discredit the men in power. But the fact is none the less true: a certain irritation exists, and contributes greatly towards paralysing the generous impulse which during the first days drew from the whole of Greece —led by the King—a cry of indignation at the Marathon crime. Under these conditions, *spontaneity* in reparation becomes difficult for the Greek Government. In order not to lose its popularity, it is fatally brought to *bargaining* with England inch by inch, in place of fully and willingly offering her the necessary satisfactions.

So as to make it easy for Greece to follow this plan, it would be desirable for the English Government to leave her greater freedom to determine the conditions under which, for example, the pecuniary satisfaction will have to be effected. There is a rumour—and I have not been able yet to verify it—that Mr Erskine has already, in an official letter, demanded a pecuniary indemnity for Mrs Lloyd.[1] If this be true, I should much regret it. It would be infinitely preferable that this

[1] Widow of one of the murdered Englishmen to whom the Greek Government subsequently paid £10,000.

money should be paid willingly, without recourse to a Note. In Greece, a Note is a big affair. It is almost half a warship. When a similar event takes place, the Vice-Consul hastens to my house to tell me that it is being discussed with animation in the cafés and on the streets.

I think that if the pecuniary question could be settled without England being obliged to have recourse to an official Note, it would become easier for the Greek Government to give its conduct that element of spontaneity which it ought to have.

The second difficulty is unfortunately more serious, for it is connected with the weakness of the Ministry, whose position in the country is not well secured. Only a strong Government can persuade the country of the justice of the satisfactions which it must offer England spontaneously. M. Deligeorges' party is a mere fraction of the Chamber. Whenever he will take the initiative in the reforms to be carried out in the internal situation of Greece, he will find himself powerless to convince men who have at their command a number of votes five times greater than his. Imagine the Queen of England charging Mr Horsman[1] to pass the Irish Land Bill with Mr Gladstone's party on the Opposition benches!

I hope with all my heart that the Deligeorges Ministry, desirous to conduct the inquiry in an honourable and loyal spirit, will succeed in achieving this aim, which is its raison d'être. But if, before the Chamber, it does not succeed in holding its ground, they would be wrong to make use here of the name of England to oppose the accession to power of men whose influence and popularity are greater, and whose political adherents are more numerous.

To sum up: to make the task of Greece easy, the English Government ought to take into account the national susceptibilities, and not press its demands too much, so as to leave Greece time to offer them spontaneously. Each Note from Erskine weakens the position of the Ministers, and

[1] Cf. *The Life of W. E. Gladstone*, by John Morley, II, 444 n., 445.

supplies new weapons to the opposition parties. In this way, a "strong" Government will remain more than ever in the chimerical state of all the "grand ideas" of Greece.

In asking you, Sir, to keep me in your kind remembrance, I take this opportunity of renewing to you the homage of my profoundest devotion.

That his work in Athens was highly appreciated by his own Government may be gathered from the forwarding of a copy of a private letter from him on the Oropos affair, by Prince Gortchakov to Baron Brunnow with the following covering letter:

St Petersburg,
4 January, 1871.

To His Excellency, the Baron de Brunnow,
London.

My dear Baron,

I am sending you in confidence a copy of a letter from M. Saburov relative to the Oropos affair. Perhaps you will be in a position to derive useful assistance from some of the data which it contains.

Accept the assurance, my dear Baron, of my most devoted sentiments.

Gortchakov.

Private letter addressed to the Chancellor of the Empire by M. Saburov, dated from Athens, 26 December, 1870.

My reports of this date had just been sent off when I learned through Mr Erskine that the reply of the Hellenic Government to his Note had appeared to him not at all satisfactory, as had been reported to me. He thought it right to make a reply to it with a long Memorandum from Mr Cookson,[1] and thus enters into a controversy which I infinitely

[1] The British legal representative at the judicial proceedings which followed the capture of the brigands.

regret, for it can only embitter matters unless the good sense of Lord Granville puts an end to this troublesome turn of affairs, due entirely to the desire of Erskine and Cookson to safeguard their personal responsibility.

To make this incident clear, allow me, my Prince, to recapitulate it in a few words:

Erskine complains that two documents in the case were not communicated to him during the inquiry, and declared that this constituted an infringement of the agreement between him and the Minister of Justice.

The Hellenic Minister has denied the existence of this intention by the decisive argument that if the Royal Procurator, Papafranghi, had desired to conceal something from the English agents, he would not have published these two documents in his report as he did. Nevertheless, being desirous to satisfy the British Minister, he offers him the concession of re-opening an inquiry upon the individuals compromised by the two documents in question, and having an English lawyer present on the old footing.

Mr Erskine objects that it will be difficult for Mr Cookson to work along with the Royal Procurator, Papafranghi, after the latter has been suspected of having purposely concealed certain documents in the case.

The Hellenic Minister removes this difficulty by promising Mr Erskine to fill the place of Papafranghi by a new person, however painful that may be for an upright functionary enjoying general esteem, and whose honourable character has been certified to me by the King himself.

In spite of all these concessions, Mr Erskine does not seem to be satisfied. I do not know whether he formulates a positive demand in his reply, but from what he says, I have taken it that he would like the whole inquiry to be begun afresh, which would be an absurd demand.

I have refrained from raising a futile discussion with him. I contented myself with saying to him that I supposed he was going to submit this matter to Lord Granville, and that he would probably await his instructions.

In fact, I am convinced that Lord Granville's sense of
justice will lead him to see that there has been some exaggeration in the behaviour of his representative at Athens. My
one fear is that, judging the matter only through the prism
of Erskine's reports, the British Government may end in
sharing all the unjust suspicions of bad faith which the former
attributes to the Greek functionaries entrusted with the
Marathon affair. However, Lord Granville cannot ignore the
worth of all the satisfactions which have just been offered by
the Hellenic Ministry, as a proof of their sincere desire to
respect all the legitimate susceptibilities of England. As to
re-opening an inquiry already closed, Hellenic law is formally
opposed to such a course. All that can be done, and that the
Greek Ministers are prepared to concede, is to open a special
inquiry on the points indicated by the British Minister.[1]

Please accept, etc.

In the early summer of 1879 M. Saburov was
appointed Russian Ambassador at Constantinople,
but never entered on his duties there. As the relations between St Petersburg and Berlin began to be
somewhat strained, a succession of important conversations that he had with Prince Bismarck led
instead to his being sent in the end of September on
a special mission to Berlin. This mission—"Ma Mission à Berlin 1879–1884"—forms the subject of these
Memoirs. On 4 January, 1880, M. Saburov was
appointed Ambassador there, a post which he held
till 21 March, 1884. From General Schweinitz'[2]
Denkwürdigkeiten we learn that on the occasion of
Saburov's appointment to Berlin, de Giers gave the

[1] In Parliamentary Papers, C. 249 (1871), Item 13, being a
despatch from Mr Erskine, there are interesting references to
M. Saburov.
[2] See infra, p. 73, n. 1.

following characterisation of the new ambassador to Schweinitz, who at the time was German Ambassador at the Russian Court:

22 June, 1880. Giers does full justice to Saburov's Scharf-sinn[1] and to his gift as a stylist. In this respect he places him higher than Jomini, and thinks that he reaches the level of Brunnow whose first Secretary he had been, and whom he has taken as a model, not only as regards his style but even as regards some peculiarities of handwriting. But, added M. de Giers, "he has also certain things in common with Ignatiev. My maxim 'plus être que paraître' he has not made his own."

Saburov left the diplomatic service in 1884, and was made a member of the Senate.

There is one episode connected with the last phase of M. Saburov's public life which it is difficult to ignore. He was accused by de Giers[2] of having re-vealed to Katkov[3] the existence and terms of the

---

[1] Acuteness, ingenuousness.

[2] de Giers, Nicholas Karlovitch (1820–1895). A self-made Protestant of Nordic origin, de Giers entered the Russian Ministry of Foreign Affairs, and after holding various minor posts, became Minister to Persia in 1863. After serving in the same capacity in Switzerland and Sweden, he was appointed Director of the Eastern Department and Assistant-Minister for Foreign Affairs under Gortchakov in 1875. A man of sound judgment, he worked in the interests of peace against the popular movements following on the Herzegovinian insurrection to bring about a radical solution of the Near Eastern Question in the interests of Russia. Supported by Count Schuvalov, his views ultimately prevailed, and the Congress of Berlin followed. He was the practical head of the Ministry of Foreign Affairs during the period of Gortchakov's decline, and succeeded him on the retirement of the latter in April, 1882, holding the position till the death of Alexander III in 1894.

[3] Katkov, Michael Nikiforovitch (1818–1887), was a famous publicist, editor of the *Moscow Gazette*, who adopted a hostile attitude to the independence of Poland and every liberal movement

League of the Three Emperors, as also its renewal on 27 March, 1884, subsequently discussed by them and their Foreign Ministers and ratified at the re-union at Skierniewicé in Poland (15–17 September[1]). Naturally, this gravely offended the Emperor. M. Saburov at once denied the insinuation, saw the Minister of Justice, Manasséine, and wrote a report in his self-defence. The correspondence will be found in the volume entitled *L'Autocratie Russe. Mémoires politiques, Correspondance officielle et Documents in-édits relatifs à l'Histoire du Règne de l'Empereur Alex-andre III de Russie* (1881–1894), selected from the Papers of Constantin Pobiédonostsev.[2] The Minister of Justice writes to Pobiédonostsev about Saburov's great distress and admits that his explanations have the undoubted accent of sincerity.[3] Saburov's report (of date 19 May, 1887) is given in full.[4] It was shown by the Minister of Justice to the Emperor, on whom it produced a favourable impression. There is no doubt of the imprudence of having discussed secret documents with Katkov, who was a publicist in oppo-sition, but there is apparently no reason to believe

---

in Russia. Bismarck was one of his special antipathies, and Katkov was largely instrumental in impressing Alexander III with the necessity of supporting France against Bismarck's designs, and a German hegemony in Europe. He fearlessly attacked the pro-German influences at the Court and in the Russian Govern-ment.

[1] Cf. Elias de Cyon, *L'Histoire de l'Entente Franco-Russe*, Paris, 1895, pp. 56–65, 200 ff., many of whose statements, however, can only be accepted with great reserve.

[2] Paris, Payot, 1927.

[3] *Op. cit.* pp. 466–469.

[4] *Op. cit.* pp. 469–472.

that Saburov told Katkov anything that the latter had not already learned from other sources.[1]

With the last decade of the nineteenth century began a new phase in M. Saburov's activity, that of the financial and economic expert. His *Concerning the Currency Reform*, published in St Petersburg in 1896, was a brilliant criticism of Witte's financial reforms in Russia, which gained the latter's encomium as "the most courteous and serious critique" that had come to his notice. Largely as the result of this work, which was probably his most important contribution along that particular line, M. Saburov was nominated a Member of the Council of State in 1900, where in the Department of State Economics he devoted himself mainly to budget and finance matters. In the previous year he had brought out another work entitled *Materials for a History of Russian Finances* which covered the period 1866–1896. He also wrote several pamphlets, all of them published in St Petersburg and dealing principally with the Commercial Treaty

---

[1] Indeed, the actual name of Katkov's informant is given—Zinoviev, head of the Asiatic Department in the Ministry of Foreign Affairs, who is stated by Katkov to have remarked with regard to the Treaty, "D'ailleurs, tout cela n'est qu'un chiffon de papier que nous pourrons déchirer quand nous le voudrons" (p. 471).

Cf. also the following statement by de Cyon, who was a friend of Katkov: "Je ne connais pas M. Saburov et j'ignore les détails de l'accusation portée contre lui dans cette affaire. Ce qu'on lui reprochait principalement c'était d'avoir communiqué à Katkov les pièces diplomatiques publiées dans la *Gazette de Moscou* comme provenant de M. Tatistchev. Or ce grief aussi était mal fondé.... D'ailleurs la disgrâce Impériale n'atteignit M. Saburov que moralement; les sénateurs Russes étant inamovibles, on ne put le révoquer" (*op. cit.* pp. 331, 332, and pp. 234–247).

of 15/28 July, 1904, between Russia and Germany, showing its serious disadvantages for Russia.[1] There can be little question that the expiry in 1914, with no prospect of renewal, of this one-sided treaty, which was practically forced on a weakened Russia at the end of the Russo-Japanese War, was one of the silent factors in determining the German antagonism to Russia. A lecture on Prince Gortchakov, given at a "Pushkin Evening" in the Alexander Lyceum in St Petersburg in 1905, which was subsequently published in the *Lyceum Magazine*, also falls into this period. M. Saburov's last production, previous to the events of 1917, was an anonymous article entitled "Bismarck and Bülow" which was published in the Petrograd newspaper, *Ryetch*. It was an attempt to show that the supposed "developments" of Bismarck's ideas by Bülow had no relation to Bismarck's ideas whatever.

It should be added that diplomacy and finance did not exhaust the interests of this many-sided man. About 1890 he became interested in pomiculture. The orchards on his country estate had in the end over 15,000 apple trees, whose annual inspection was a source of pleasure to him. He had a natural gift for architecture, which expressed itself in models of Greek temples, the Pyramids and original designs, carried out sometimes in prepared cardboard. He also made a beautiful collection of antique Greek

[1] This treaty, which was concluded under the title of an additional treaty to that of 29 January/10 February, 1894, imposed heavy customs duties against Russia on the export of her agricultural products across the German frontier. It had a duration of ten years.

statuettes and vases from Tanagra, which he sold
about 1884 to the National Museum in Berlin and
the Hermitage in St Petersburg.[1] The piano, which
he had studied under Adolf Henselt, and chess, were
amongst his favourite diversions. In character he
impressed all those who knew him by his kindhearted-
ness, and constant willingness to help.

In outlook M. Saburov was Liberal in tendency,
as was his brother, the Minister for Education. Already in 1915 events had confirmed him in opinions
that he had held for long. Thus he had always felt
that it was a mistake to try and Russianise the Finns.
It seemed to him, and to many others, as if Russia
had been taking revenge on her own people after the
Russo-Japanese War. "The whole project was false.
It only made enemies in our own country. In future
policy", he continued, "we must also be more liberal
to the Jews: we went too far. It is mainly in political
circles that feeling is strongest against them. The
abolition of vodka was something that the Emperor
alone could do: no Minister or party could have
afforded to throw away the millions of revenue that
came in from it. Prohibition makes the finance of
Russia difficult to-day."

He was of opinion that the war with Japan, "which
was a very foolish step, through its weakening of
Russia", led to an improvement of relations with
Great Britain. It had also another result. It showed

[1] A sentence in a letter from Count Herbert Bismarck to his
father connects the sale with the necessity on M. Saburov's part
of providing funds to meet the heavy expenses incurred in maintaining his establishment during his tenure of office as ambassador
in Berlin (D.G.P. III, 327).

the War Minister the deficiencies of the Russian army. These deficiencies would have been even more marked to-day[1] if the Russo-Japanese War had not taken place, and Russia would not have put up the fight she has done. As a result of it, the artillery in particular was thoroughly re-organised: young officers who were proved to be incapable were ruthlessly superseded. That war also showed the incapacity of General Kuropatkin[2] who was considered in Court and other circles as a sort of successor of Skobelev.[3]

[1] The date of conversation is some time in the early summer of 1915. Many will never cease to believe that the chivalrous advance of the Russian army into East Prussia in August, 1914, in answer to a desperate appeal, before their plans were matured or their preparations complete, was a big element in the saving of Paris.

[2] Kuropatkin, General Alexis Nikolaievitch (1848–1925), former chief of staff to Skobelev, and contrasting with him in many ways. Methodical, undecided, conscientious, a very able military and scientific writer and theorist; although personally very brave, he yet shrank from heavy responsibilities, and was handicapped by his extreme caution. In 1890 he was made Military Governor of Transcaspia, and later became Minister of War. He was the unfortunate Commander-in-Chief of the Russian army in the Russo-Japanese War (1904–1907).

[3] Skobelev, General Michael Dmitrievitch (1843–1882), one of the most romantic figures in Russian nineteenth-century history. As courageous as he was eloquent, he became violently Germanophobe and Pan-Slavist, particularly after the Congress of Berlin. He was the great hero of the Russo-Turkish War, 1877–1878, known to the Turks as the White Pasha, appearing on the field of battle in a white uniform, indifferent to all danger. At Plevna he took by assault the key to the positions of Osman Pasha, but was not supported by the other Russian generals, and the battle was lost. In Central Asia he took the fortress of Geok Tepe, near Khiva (1881) by assault, after hand-to-hand fighting against a stout Turkoman defence. There was a touch of romance about all his military exploits, whether successes or failures.

If the Japanese War had not taken place, he would have been the Russian Commander-in-Chief.

In view of the particular character of the principal achievement in which M. Saburov had a share, as evidenced in the Memoirs, it is not to be wondered at that he should feel distress in finding Russia at war with that other country for good relationships with which he had striven so long and so earnestly. Yet he accepted the fact and its implications in absolute loyalty. In discussing the possibility of the under-standing between Russia and Great Britain as ex-emplified in the opening years of the Great War becoming more or less permanent, he said: "We cannot speak about permanent alliances. England has never made permanent alliances. But there is no reason why this understanding should not be lasting. All Russia's ambitions will be satisfied with the Straits opened and in her hands. The idea of an advance upon India is preposterous. If we get the same results as after the defeat of Napoleon we shall do well. The alliance of Austria, Prussia, etc., lasted after that for forty years. If the present alliance lasts forty years that will be a great result, and a fine guarantee for the future. Germany has prepared for this war for forty years. I of course had always advo-cated alliance for Russia with Germany. England was the natural enemy: as for Republican France, we could never be sure of her behaviour: she only wished alliance to get back Alsace-Lorraine. Alex-ander II's policy was a policy of alliance with Ger-many. We could then be safe: we could retain our ends and interests in the East, as against our one adversary England. The alliance with Germany ensured the neutrality of Austria: France would not move for fear of an attack by Germany. On the death of Alexander II, he was succeeded by Alexander III, who, however, would not have anything to do with Germany. Indeed the foundations of the understanding with France were laid by him. I left diplomacy because the outlook of Alexander III was not that of his father. To-day I am a very sincere advocate of alliance with England and France; but there is, of course, nothing else for us to do. The situation has completely changed. As the result of this war, however, I think that the large countries chiefly concerned will all be ruined. Russia, for example, will shortly issue a foreign loan for fifty millions. My anxiety is that we should get the wherewithal to carry on the war without greatly increasing our paper money. If we cannot get a foreign loan and restrain the emission of paper money, every hope will vanish of introducing financial order into our country after the war. We also hope that if the Straits are opened in the next two or three months, our exports will recommence, and the financial tension be lessened".

The last occasions on which I saw my friend were in the late spring of 1917, after the first weeks of the Revolution. Lenin had arrived in Petrograd, and for the first time I had seen the word "anarchia" in a daily paper, referring to a peasant disturbance in the country. I saw M. Saburov one afternoon in May and found him very seriously disturbed by the situation generally, and even more by what he intuitively felt to be impending. To the octogenarian it seemed as if the fashion of his world was in process of passing away; his ageing mind had difficulty in grasping the significance of events. Over a simple dinner consisting of a black-cock, some black bread and a bottle of white wine, he unburdened himself upon the events of the day. It seemed to him as if he had "fallen on a new planet". The "lower classes" had got the upper hand. The late Government ought to have given them a moral education, and not have left them in a state of barbarism. "The peasants think, now that they have liberty, that they can take everything—houses, furnishings, land; they have no idea of what is right and wrong. They have taken possession of my woods, and appropriated my cut timber. The Provisional Government have made a proclamation to the people saying that they must wait,—the agrarian question will be settled by the Constituent Assembly, which, they can rest assured, will take their interests into account. But they are powerless to restrain the peasants, and stop this sort of thing. They have abolished the old police force, and have a plan for a new one, but nothing actually exists with which to keep the country in order. Already it is impossible for my eldest son[1] and daughter-in-law (*née* Sheremetiev) to return to their estate in the Government of Moscow, because the peasants have appropriated everything. I fear", he added, "that the new policy of the Government may be to continue the war, but 'without annexations and contributions'. This has produced a bad effect upon the soldiers at the front, who ask 'Then why do we fight at all?'"

[1] Later murdered by peasants.

I asked him if he would outline the situation as it appeared to him. He began by citing examples of remarks recently made by the Emperor, as also of an unwonted indifference on his part, that tended to confirm an opinion held in some quarters to the effect that the hapless monarch was being secretly drugged, in order that the possibility of opposition on his part to plans attributed to other Court elements might be removed. "The Revolution came about so easily because the troops in Petrograd were not regular troops, but merely peasants from the Reserve—men with the ideas of country people—who did not wish to fire upon their fellow-men. If there had been regular troops, the Revolution would have been crushed. Every regiment that was moved up simply followed the example of the first regiment. The Provisional Government feel that they have no force behind them. The troops have recognised them, but the other Assembly (i.e. the Soldiers' and Workers') has more power. Some people wish the Germans would attack us, because they think it would stop this revolutionary talk, and in presence of an invasion the people would return to work in the factories. At present they only work in certain districts, or on occasion. The streets are full of people, and there is no end of fêting on account of the Revolution.

"The Liberty Loan is meeting with some success. The Minister of Finance (Tereschenko) must have immediate resources. I am studying at present the question of inconvertible paper money, and the agrarian problem. You recollect what happened during the French Revolution. Latterly a great war was carried on with Austria and Prussia under much the same conditions as in Russia to-day, and there was no other means of paying the war expenses except by issuing paper money which latterly lost its value. The French Government in the Directoire came out of this difficulty. They had on their hands plenty of land—the confiscated lands (and other property) of the Church, the Crown and the émigrés. On the other hand, there were the peasants who were poor and wanted land. The French Government linked the two questions together, and in order to supply the peasants with the means to buy this land, they issued new paper money with the value of francs,[1] and for this new paper money they exchanged a part of the old paper money which had become almost worthless, and purchasers who wanted land paid in this new money. The result was that the francs which had lost their value were gradually brought back by this new paper which went into circulation, and in time the franc was reinstated in value. So for us there is also surely some means of getting out of this crisis, although it will be a not less difficult matter for us than it was for France.

"In my opinion there are three possible ways of dealing with the land question. I hope that Professor Milyukov's plan will be followed, under which proprietors will be obliged to sell part of their lands to the peasants at its real value. The Government would fix the number of acres which a proprietor must retain,

---

[1] Actually livres: the franc was not introduced in place of the livre till 1795. For an account of these assignats cf. *Cambridge Modern History*, VIII, 695 ff.

as also the number which he must sell. A proposal of this sort will be submitted to the Constituent Assembly. The extreme elements want confiscation of the land. Lenin wants nationalisation, under which the whole of the land would belong to the Government, and the Government would let it to individuals. I still hope, however, that in the Constituent Assembly a majority would stand for payment to proprietors.

"In the days of the earliest princes there were councils—the Boyarskaya Duma, for example—assemblies that met not to decide, but to give advice to the over-lord. Before and after the election of the first Tsar of the Romanov dynasty in 1613, there were such consultative bodies on an even larger scale (*zemskii sobori*). The Duma may be considered a development of them. It is not functioning to-day, however, as the Tsar dissolved it. Some members got together under the leadership of Rodzianko and formed this present Government. The Council of the Empire has not been dissolved, but it is in a state of suspended animation. The Constituent Assembly will form a new Government, and insist on the Duma functioning again. It will also have to decide whether there shall be one or two Chambers. At the moment the tide is running strongly in favour of a Republic, but the people are not quite ripe for this. If one of our generals succeeded in crushing the German army, he might become so popular that he could be a Dictator, like Napoleon I. But how Russia with her immense number of provinces could remain a single republic, is difficult to see. So many regions are de-

sirous of autonomy that a dictatorship may be necessary. We must expect, however, that the republican
régime will last some time now."

I asked him what possibilities he saw of a lasting
peace. "If Germany consents to submit to the conditions of the Allies for the assurance of peace, it could
take place. All the Governments at war must undertake to submit any dispute or difference to the Hague,
and not have recourse to war, with the understanding
that if any country does not thus submit, all the others
will make a coalition against it. That would be sufficient to maintain peace for many years. Disarma-
ment is a difficult matter practically. With the present system of reserves, it is difficult to disarm Germany and Russia. After three years of service the
soldiers go back into the reserves, but they are always
soldiers. The reserves are in actual existence and
continually being made. I do not see a solution of
this difficulty."

After the Revolution in March, 1917, M. Saburov,
as a Senator, was appointed by the Provisional
Government to a Commission associated with the
Senate. With the accession of the Bolsheviks to
power in November he was dismissed, as indeed
were all the Senators. A few months later, on
28 March/10 April, 1918, M. Saburov died at Petrograd after a short illness, having just entered on his
84th year. The fashion of his world *had* passed away,
and with it had gone all interest in life.

II

HISTORICAL

An article entitled "Russie, France, Allemagne
(1870–1880)", which was published by M. Saburov
in *La Revue de Paris* of 15 March, 1912, forms an
admirable introduction to the later Memoirs. It is,
therefore, reproduced here in translation.

Forty years ago the equilibrium of Europe was profoundly disturbed. The result of the Franco-German
War was to modify the relations and affinities between
the different Powers, and to reconstitute the equilibrium between them on new bases. This, however,
required a certain amount of time. The complete
story of that reconstruction would indeed be long;
I shall confine myself here to setting forth the ideas
under whose dominating influence a modification of
the relations between Russia and Germany after the
war of 1870 set in.

From the commencement of that war there was a
confused feeling that the transformation of Prussia
into a German Empire would alter these former relations; Cabinet policy seemed to have had its day;
that of nationalities tended to replace it with its point
of view more radical, and its susceptibilities keener,
than those of Princes. Up to that time two sovereign
houses made their policy conform to the ties of
parentage which united them. Behind these august

figures, events suddenly set in opposition two rival races, separated by the feeling of danger, inasmuch as the aggrandisement of the one might mean the diminution of the other. The consciousness of this danger set their instincts of preservation at work, as also their national ambitions. They asked themselves if this work would end one day in an apportionment of dominion between the Slav and Germanic races, or else in a collision which would shake the world.

Such were the ideas, vague as yet, which germinated in minds on both sides of the frontier. Their influence on the governmental action constitutes the dramatic interest of the last ten years of the reign of the late Emperor Alexander II.

It appears from a recent publication[1] that the attitude of this Sovereign has been little understood in France. The author of this article, M. Émile Ollivier, a former minister of the Emperor Napoleon III, expresses himself in these words:

> The King (of Prussia) addressed a confidential letter to the Tsar in which he appealed to his friendship to protect him against the intervention of Austria. The Tsar, a narrow-minded man with no foresight, violent and good-natured at the same time, without personality in his ideas, full of respect for the memory of his father, always put sentiment before political considerations, and was intractable when he obeyed an impulse of his heart. He showed himself such on this occasion. He promised without hesitation and most effusively.

M. Ollivier seems to have forgotten the events which preceded the war of 1870, and which imposed

[1] "La Guerre de 1870," by Émile Ollivier, *Revue des Deux Mondes*, 1 February, 1911. (Note in original.)

on the Russian Emperor the line of conduct which he
followed.

Alexander II had received the heavy heritage of the
Crimean War. The Treaty of 1 March, 1856, had
taken away from us a province, and the power to
reconstitute our naval forces in the Black Sea; and
by the convention of 15 April of the same year, France,
Austria and England had bound themselves to make
war on us in the event of an infringement of that
treaty. That was the permanent coalition against
Russia.

A single Power remained faithful to us,—Prussia.
So it was no longer the moment to continue with
Germany the dualistic policy of the Emperor Nicholas
and to defend Austria against the ambitions of Prussia.
On the contrary; the latter in fighting her own battles
in the plains of Bohemia in 1866 worked unconsciously
for our political recovery; the victory of Königgrätz
was, after the war with Italy, the second blow struck
at the validity of the treaty of coalition of 15 April,
1856.

Then came the war of 1870 which everyone foresaw. Napoleon III, on the outlook for an ally, turned
to Austria. The eventual alliance was broached at the
interview of the two Sovereigns at Salzburg in the
autumn of 1869. That alliance determined our line
of conduct. It was becoming evident, indeed, that if
Prussia succumbed, we should fall again into the
situation of isolation and impotence which the Crimean
War created for us with an Austrian Germany in
addition. This is the conviction that inspired the

policy of Alexander II at the commencement of the war of 1870. To keep Austria neutral in the struggle which was forthcoming was a necessity for Russia at this moment; one can say without exaggeration that in the state of matters at that time, the Prussian victories were likewise ours. The denunciation of the Treaty of Paris in 1870 is the very proof of this.

But now, from the first Prussian victories which already let us foresee the prospect of a powerful German Empire at our gates, the *Moscow Gazette* in a series of articles made itself the echo of the "patriotic anxieties" of one portion of the public. To the young generation, the period of the Crimean War was only history. They could neither share in the ideas nor the rancours of those who had seen the fall of Sebastopol. On the contrary, the things of the moment moved them. It seemed to them that the near establishment of a German Empire would upset the European equilibrium, and that Russia, in view of her own security, ought to save France from total defeat; if not, she would remain isolated in the presence of the great Germany who had just shown the measure of her military superiority in vanquishing, one after the other, the two great continental Powers.

To the men who had seen the policy of the preceding epoch in practice, it seemed, on the contrary that it was more than ever necessary to foster the Prussian alliance. That Prussia, enlarged and strengthened, had at last become a useful ally,—the ally we had needed in difficult times, and who now could guarantee us against the coalitions that barred the Eastern road to us.

After the Peace of Frankfort, the Emperor Alexander remained faithful to this order of ideas, and the world was informed of the fact through the exchange of the famous telegrams between the two Sovereigns.

"Russia", people said at that time, "has allowed herself to be taken advantage of by Prussia." This saying, by dint of repetition, became a historical truth for the Moscow patriots. Now, never was accusation more unjust. If there was exploitation, it was mutual.[1] Indeed, it was only from that time that the Emperor Alexander felt himself politically at ease in Europe, and that he restored Russia to her old place in the world.

In 1873, the Emperor of Germany, full of years and glory, came to St Petersburg, accompanied by Prince Bismarck and Field-Marshal Count Moltke. The men who had forged the new German Empire came to pay their respects, and, so to say, repeat to the Sovereign of Russia the historic words of the Versailles telegram: "After God, it is to you that we owe the victory". Certainly, the satisfaction felt at that time by the Emperor Alexander was worth the million expended —so they said—on this occasion to make the reception worthy of the meeting of the two masters of the world. For they were that at this moment. It was for us the same situation as at Tilsit without the reverses of Austerlitz and of Friedland. The Emperor Alexander had achieved this without drawing his

[1] M. Saburov explained that the German defeat of France made such a coalition against Russia as she had faced during the Crimean War impossible, while the earlier German victory over Austria had "simplified Russia's position".

sword by identifying his interests with those of
Prussia. What is astonishing in the fact that the idea
of a permanent alliance should come in this moment
of triumph to the minds of the two Sovereigns?

This alliance would probably have brought about
important results at the time of the Eastern crisis
which broke out soon after, if the Emperor Alexander,
an autocrat by right, and in fact, had been likewise
such in disposition. But, whilst he moved so reso-
lutely towards the Prussian alliance, the anti-German
current grew and penetrated to the heart of the
Government itself through the wide gateway of the
Ministry of Foreign Affairs. The Chancellor, Prince
Gortchakov, had, from the beginning, viewed the
unification of Germany with apprehension. At the
commencement of the war, he had disapproved—
without being able to prevent it—of the promise,
spontaneously given by the Emperor Alexander, to
prevent Austria from taking sides by placing two
hundred thousand men on her frontier. Later, during
the siege of Paris, distrustful of the promises of Prince
Bismarck, who at that moment was ready to promise
everything, he advised the Emperor by no means to
wait till the definite victory of Prussia before annulling
the clauses in the Treaty of Paris relative to the Black
Sea. He did it in a peremptory manner which made
a conflict possible, thus forcing Prussia into obligatory
connivance with Russia in case England and Austria
might wish to defend by force the inviolability of the
Treaty of Paris. At this critical moment, the danger
of a general war was keenly felt in the Prussian camp,

and Prince Bismarck, interested above all in maintaining the isolation of France, saw himself constrained to work for Russia by pressing England to give a pacific solution to the question of the Black Sea. He succeeded in this, and Prince Gortchakov's calculations were justified by events.

But in spite of the increase of favour which this master-stroke so justly gained for Prince Gortchakov, a tacit disagreement existed between the Emperor and him. The Emperor Alexander, logical to the end, saw in the greater Prussia a means of strengthening himself. He recalled that at the beginning of his reign it was the weakness of Prussia which had emboldened Austria to join the Western coalition. He did not at all admit that Prussia could ever become an enemy. Accordingly he was anxious for the alliance with the German Empire; it was the necessary consummation of the policy of his whole reign.[1] As for Prince Gortchakov, who was not as sure of the feelings of Prussia, having been unable to hinder her rapid growth, he wished, like the Emperor, to derive profit from it, but through other channels. He foresaw that the desire for revenge would live in the French nation, and he dreamed of a mediating position for Russia which would make her the arbiter of European affairs. He liked to compare her to a rich

[1] In explanation M. Saburov stated that the Emperor Alexander II saw that Austria was becoming a close ally of Prussia, which meant that the latter was becoming too powerful. The defeat in the Crimean War had placed Russia in a quite isolated position, the only way out of which was by an alliance with Prussia. This, the point of view of Alexander II, was undoubtedly the right one for Russia.

heiress who let herself be wooed, but kept her liberty
and did not give her hand to any man.

Which of these two points of view was the true one
at this moment of our history? The disappointing
results of the last Eastern war furnish the answer to
that question. I will add that the Prince was seventy-
five years old. At that age the future is short; one
does not like to foresee new events. On the other
hand, we may be permitted to suppose that the Emperor Alexander, who still had to obtain reparation
for the surrender of Bessarabia, foresaw the possibility of an Eastern crisis in which the friendship of
Germany could be of great assistance to him.

Therefore, the Emperor on the one hand followed
his own policy, and on the other, his Chancellor neutralised it.

These two contradictory actions were necessarily
bound to produce corresponding hesitation in the
feelings of the German Government towards Russia.

This is the moment to find out who made the
initial mistake. Was it Russia or Prussia who first
broke the bond of close solidarity which events had
long since established between them?

Amongst the Russian public, people have not ceased
to throw the responsibility for it on Prince Bismarck.
This reproach seems to me to have little foundation.
Assuredly, that statesman, by bringing about the
unification of Germany, had his eyes open to the
dangers which would threaten her in the future. It was
no interest of his to add the hostility of Russia to the
ill-will of France. It was not in his power to change

the geography which imposes on Germany three vulnerable frontiers. Austria, it is true, was no longer to be feared. The generosity of her conqueror had left her territorially intact and was smoothing the way to a future entente with that Power. It was not so easy to come to terms on the other two frontiers. France had been defeated, but she was only weakened momentarily; her military strength had recovered with a rapidity that disconcerted the Germans, and Prince Bismarck, while favouring the republican régime in France, made a reckoning which events have not justified. In fact, after twenty years of sterile diplomacy, the German Chancellor succeeded neither in conciliating France nor in dooming her to anarchy.

On the eastern side, the German frontier can only be protected by an alliance with Russia. Prince Bismarck understood that better than anyone. So he had no interest in provoking, by a change of front, the anti-German reaction which showed itself in Russia after the events of 1870. That reaction had its source in the events themselves; it was destined, inevitable; it was the spontaneous expression of a national feeling, indifferent to the calculations of politics; and it is there that we must look for the starting-point of the new phase on which the relations of the two countries entered from the year 1870.

Nevertheless, I repeat, it would be difficult to say how matters would have turned if the will of the Emperor Alexander II had been of the same metal as that of his predecessor or his successor, and if he had kept his Chancellor in the position of simple executor of his mind. Nothing is more dangerous for a Sovereign than to keep a Minister whose ideas differ from his own; he runs the risk of becoming unconsciously the tool of that Minister, who has the advantage over him of directing the details of affairs.

That is precisely what happened in 1875. At that date, the French Government, alarmed by the reports of its Ambassador at Berlin on the subject of a conversation with M. von Radowitz,[1] sought the intervention of the Russian Cabinet to protect it against the bellicose inclinations of Germany. This step received an eager welcome from Prince Gortchakov. It constituted for him the sought-for opportunity of playing the rôle of peace-making arbiter between France and Germany. He persuaded the Emperor, who was going to Ems, to stop at Berlin to talk over matters with the Emperor William. Being himself of the party, he succeeded in securing the co-operation of the English Cabinet for more official dealings with Prince Bismarck, conjointly with the English Ambassador.

Here is the account of what took place at that conference: I have it from the very lips of the three people who took part in it.

The following is Prince Gortchakov's version: "France addressed herself to us to protect her against the warlike designs of the German military party. The Emperor discussed the subject with the Emperor

---

[1] Radowitz, Joseph Maria von (b. 1839), entered the German diplomatic service in 1860. He acted as Chargé d'Affaires in Constantinople 1872: thereafter was recalled to take charge of the Eastern Department in the Ministry of Foreign Affairs. In 1882 he was appointed German Minister in Constantinople, and sent as Ambassador to Madrid in 1892.

William who completely reassured him on this matter, by saying that so long as he lived, Germany would make no more war. As for myself, I had a friendly but firm talk with Bismarck. He complained that people doubted his desire to maintain peace, whilst he was spending restless nights working towards the end of assuring it. I replied to him : ' It is these sleepless nights that disturb us. Remember that you carry the burden of your glory; when you suffer from insomnia, Europe cannot sleep; when you have a headache, Europe has a high temperature '. I must do him the justice of saying that he accepted the compliment and the lesson like a sensible man. He repudiated all hostile designs against France; he had only wished to give her a friendly warning. We parted on the best of terms ".

Here is Lord Odo Russell's[1] account: "One day I received a telegram from the Foreign Office stating that Paris was very disturbed over a conversation of Radowitz with Gontaut-Biron.[2] I went to Prince Bismarck to ask him to put me in a position to re-

[1] Ampthill, Odo William Leopold Russell, first Baron (1829–1884), British diplomatist, began his career in 1849 as attaché at Vienna. He then served in the Foreign Office from 1850 to 1852 under Lords Palmerston and Granville. Thereafter he passed successively to Paris, Vienna, Paris again and Constantinople. He was appointed Secretary of Legation at Florence in 1857, and remained in service in Italy till 1870. In November of that year he was sent on a special mission to the headquarters of the German Army at Versailles. The good personal relationships developed with Bismarck led to his appointment as Ambassador at Berlin in 1871, which post he held till his death. He attended the Congress of Berlin as third British Plenipotentiary with Lords Beaconsfield and Salisbury.

[2] Gontaut-Biron, Duc de, was French Ambassador at Berlin.

assure my Government. The Prince charged me to write to London saying that they were wronging his intelligence in supposing that he wished to risk the existence of the German Empire on the hazards of war. It was not against France, but against the militarists of the two countries that he bore a grudge. If one let them do as they liked, the flame of war would soon be kindled. It was in order to resume the charge of these burning questions that he had determined to bring them within the arena of diplomatic explanations. The explanation had taken place; that was all that he wished; war would not follow. I wrote all these details to Lord Derby.[1] Some days later, the Emperor Alexander arrived at Berlin with his Chancellor. At the same time, to my great surprise, I received an order to take part in the interview that Prince Gortchakov proposed to have with the German Chancellor. I had to obey, although convinced of the uselessness of a step which would probably irritate Prince Bismarck. Accordingly, I decided to play the rôle of the dumb character in the play. I arrived on purpose a quarter of an hour after Prince Gortchakov, who greeted me with the words, 'Come, dear Ambassador, you are not *de trop* in our conversation'. I took a seat and confined myself to listening and counting the blows in this tourney of words between the two Chancellors. I confess that all my admiration was for Prince Gortchakov: he showed himself superior in coolness, courtesy, finesse, and,

[1] This despatch is on record at the Foreign Office, but there is apparently nothing with regard to what follows. Cf., however, Sir W. Grant Duff, *Notes from a Diary* 1886–88, I, 129.

I must say, in breadth of view. Prince Bismarck felt
ill at ease, like someone chafing at the bit. It was the
first time that I had seen him short of replies. Next day
I had a visit from the Secretary of State, von Bülow.
After some unimportant remarks, he assumed his
most official air, and made to me the following communication: 'His Highness the Chancellor, charges
me, Mr Ambassador, to express to Your Excellency,
his regrets that your repute with your Government
is not as good as His Highness had hoped'. To
this unexpected outburst, I replied, 'Be so kind as
to say to the Chancellor on my behalf, that I also
had an exaggerated idea of the repute which His
Highness enjoyed with the Russian Government'".

Such is Lord Odo Russell's version.

As for Prince Bismarck, he only once, long after,
made an allusion to this incident to me in the following terms: "It is often more difficult for me to come
to an understanding with my own Government than
with foreign Governments. We have a Staff which is
perpetually at war with our three neighbours, not
even excepting Austria. It is their profession, but it
is not mine. In 1875 our tacticians went too far, and
I had to intervene. They thought that France was
recovering too quickly from her defeat. Happily, the
Emperor does not wish any more war during his reign.
All the same, I did not wish to leave him in confidential communication with his Staff. That is why
I provoked an explanation with the French Government. I knew at least where I would stop; but the
military never know".

He added with warmth: "Unfortunately, Prince

Gortchakov did not wish to understand this, and preferred to score a diplomatic success at my expense".[1]

To complete this information, I will conclude with a curious statement by M. Blowitz, *The Times* correspondent in Paris, whose acquaintance I made by chance on one of my journeys, many years later: "Some time before the arrival of the Emperor Alexander at Berlin," said M. de Blowitz to me, "the Duke Decazes, Minister of Foreign Affairs, summoned me in order to say: 'You can do us a great service; grave news reaches us from Berlin: they are going to try to pick a quarrel with us over our armaments. The Emperor of Russia, to whom we have appealed, is inclined to avail himself of his journey to Ems to stop at Berlin and speak to the Emperor William, his uncle. But in order to be able to broach

---

[1] In D.G.P. i, 209–300, there are convincing data with regard to Bismarck's aggressive attitude towards France in 1875. The Emperor William I appears as peaceably disposed, and the German Ambassador and military attaché in Paris alike report in their private despatches to Bismarck that France had no intention of attacking Germany. Thus, when Bismarck wrote to Prince Hohenlohe (the Ambassador in Paris) on 26 February, 1875, that France was buying 10,000 horses in Germany with a view to war against Germany (p. 245) Hohenlohe answered firmly that there was no ground for this belief. He forwarded later the report of the military attaché, Major von Bülow, of date 11 April, 1875, who stated categorically that the truth of the matter was that there was no war party in France, nor individuals who had any influence in that direction, either in the army or amongst the people (*weder in der Armee, noch im Volke*, pp. 250–253). Bismarck's statements about the menacing attitude of France are thus seen to have been mere figments of his imagination. The danger to the peace of Europe at that time lay neither in France nor in Russia, but in Prince Bismarck's purposeful mind—a danger that was fortunately averted by pressure in particular from Russia.

such a subject without the appearance of interfering in the affairs of the German Government, it is necessary that public opinion be put on the alert; all Europe must learn that she is perhaps on the eve of a war. We cannot do this through our newspapers; we would be accused of having arranged an intrigue; but *The Times*, an English paper and neutral, can do it. We will supply you with all the facts that you desire'. I wrote to the Editor of *The Times* to ask for his consent. He replied to me that he could not publish a correspondence accusing a friendly Government of planning a brigand's attack on France, unless the Foreign Office furnished him with official data confirming the danger of a war. I communicated this reply to the Duke Decazes, who after a meeting of the Cabinet, sent for me and let me read the despatches of Count Gontaut-Biron, giving an account of his conversation with M. Radowitz. The Duke added that a copy of these despatches had just been sent to London to be communicated to the English Government. He again made a pressing appeal to my love for the country of my adoption. This time I did not hesitate further, and having gone home, I wrote out my report and sent it to the Editor of *The Times*, tendering my resignation in the event of the correspondence not being published. Two days later the article appeared, and was reproduced in all the continental newspapers, producing a panic on all the exchanges of Europe. The rosette of the Legion of Honour which you see in my buttonhole dates from that occasion".

These details, if correct, need no comment.[1]

[1] Cf. de Blowitz, *Memoirs*, chap. v.

Thus Prince Gortchakov had achieved his ends. Without openly opposing the policy of alliance followed by the Emperor, he had inaugurated his own. Russia had just dictated peace to Germany as in the most glorious days of the Emperor Nicholas. To make the fact more visible to every eye, a circular dated from Berlin announced to the Russian representatives abroad that the maintenance of peace was assured. All the enemies of Germany rejoiced. In Russia, the patriots of Moscow held up their heads. As in 1863, at the time of the Polish affair, they honoured Prince Gortchakov, acclaiming him as the true representative of the national policy.

The consequences of this incident were of first-rate importance. Prince Bismarck felt his prestige compromised. With the exaggeration caused by the vexation of a statesman who up till then had not known a check, he saw great Germany humiliated in his person, as feeble Prussia had been at Olmütz twenty-five years before. So Germany, in spite of her prodigious triumphs, had not freed herself from the Russian tutelage! And unless he conquered Russia in a third deadly combat, at the risk of compromising the results gained, the German Chancellor would hardly be able to redress the balance in his favour: all the aggrandisement of Prussia had its counterpoise in the irresistible force which was pushing France towards us.

It was at this moment without doubt that there sprang up in the mind of the German Chancellor the idea of strengthening the centre of Europe by a close union with Austria.

Three years he waited, keeping his rancour deeply hid. In seeing him favour and support all the wishes of the Russian Government through the diverse phases of the Eastern crisis up to, and including, the Congress, one would have said that he had long ago forgotten the incident of 1875. But he was just biding time and place, and would remember it at the fitting opportunity. He wished to wait till the ground at Vienna was sufficiently prepared for the bringing forth of the combination of which he dreamed. Therefore he saw, doubtless with satisfaction, the revival of the Eastern question which was going to provide him with a vast field for his political manœuvres.[1]

I shall not write here in detail the history of the mistakes made in the course of the laborious negotiations which preceded and followed the war of 1877. It will be sufficient for me to say that Prince Bismarck always retained the advantage over Russia of knowing what he wanted.

Let me pause only over the principal fact which, in that history, will dominate these events,—that of our sudden failure at the gates of Constantinople.

The original plan of campaign had been to go no further than the Balkans, and to create a limited Bulgaria. The Emperor and Prince Gortchakov shrank from the consequences of a thorough campaign, and

---

[1] In vol. VII of Ernest Lavisse's *Histoire de France contemporaine* entitled "Le Déclin de l'Empire" Prof. Seignobos has a chapter entitled "L'Alerte de 1875 et la Rentrée de la France dans le Concert européen" (pp. 416–420), in which he refers to Saburov's article, and gives a considerable measure of support to his point of view.

preferred to hold to our traditional policy, that of
eating the artichoke leaf by leaf. It was also a means
of conciliating the contradictory opinions of the partisans and opponents of that war, and of not being
compelled to set going all the military forces of the
country. But above all, it had the advantage of avoiding a European intervention. The Powers were more
or less in agreement on this plan, and resigned themselves to seeing Turkey pay for the horrors committed
in Bulgaria by the loss of a province. The interests of
England were not at stake so long as Constantinople
remained outside our operations. Austria, on her side,
could not lay claim to territorial compensations as
long as Turkey was not beaten. In short, this mode-
rate programme, not being of a nature to require any
kind of an alliance, suited, above all, Prince Gortchakov, who was anxious to retain his freedom with regard
to Germany, and did not desire her co-operation.

Unfortunately, this programme was not long maintained. Soon after the crossing of the Danube, the
Staff of the Grand-Duke Nicholas demanded complete liberty in its operations as an indispensable
condition for the success of the campaign. This
demand, so just from the military point of view, could
not be refused; but it no longer fell in with the
political plan, and that is what the authors of this
plan ought to have foreseen. As early as the month
of June, General Gourko crossed the Balkans for the
first time. After the fall of Plevna, the whole army
swept through them like an avalanche, and, meeting
no further resistance, arrived straight at the environs
of Constantinople.

The great problem presented itself. No one was prepared for it—neither Europe, nor Russia. They had agreed upon the restricted programme; but they had not foreseen the new eventualities to which the rapidity of events had given rise. There had been, it is true, a negotiation with Austria, who, in view of a possible collapse of Turkey, had secured for herself the promise of the two frontier provinces. But the situation did not arise since Turkey was allowed to exist; they dismembered her only in part; they respected the capital. It was necessary then to negotiate with Austria on some new basis, or else try to come to an understanding with Germany in order to neutralise the efforts of the Viennese Cabinet.

With England they had hastily exchanged a promise to touch neither Constantinople nor Gallipoli. On this condition the English fleet was not to force the Straits. But this arrangement was abandoned before the effervescence of public opinion in England; and Lord Derby, who had made it, had to retire from the Cabinet.

In this situation, full of uncertainties, it was necessary to secure a pledge. This is what England did by making her fleet enter the Sea of Marmora and artfully taking away the island of Cyprus from the Sultan in distress. That is what Austria did in stipulating with England and Germany for the surrender of the two provinces which she was no longer certain of getting from us. Russia's pledge was within reach: it was Constantinople; but she hesitated to seize it, and this unique moment was irrevocably lost.

And yet the Emperor had had the intuition of what

should be done; the order to occupy Constantinople had been given. It was published in the Official Gazette the very day when they learned that England, breaking her promise, had made her squadron enter the Dardanelles. The public has never known exactly the reasons why this order was not carried out.[1]

A sort of fatality pursued the Emperor Alexander in his best inspirations. It was because, during his reign, so rich in events, the natural kindness of the man prejudiced the energy of the sovereign. That is why, at this memorable epoch, the fruits of victory escaped us everywhere.

Prince Bismarck did not expect so much from it. He had simply foreseen that this war, by putting the Slav passions in motion, would end by frightening

[1] In discussing this situation in 1917, after the first phase of the Russian Revolution, M. Saburov stated that the old Grand-Duke Nicholas was tired of the war, and not sufficiently alert; he did not occupy Constantinople in accordance with the instructions telegraphed to him, and the Emperor never forgave him. General Loris Melikof told M. Saburov that on the occasion when he went to the Emperor to make his report on the trans-Caucasian part of the campaign, after the war, the Grand-Duke Nicholas had immediately preceded him in audience. From the outer room he overheard the Emperor storming at the Commander-in-Chief for his failure to take Constantinople. The Grand-Duke tried to defend himself by saying that the telegram had arrived too late. Shortly after, he came out of the imperial presence pale and agitated. When Loris Melikof entered the royal chamber he found the Emperor in a slight faint, brought on by the vehemence of his attack on the Grand-Duke. "Is not our fortune strange,—I will even say stupid," M. Saburov added, "with regard to Constantinople? Once we stood outside its gates and did not enter: later Germany consented to our having it: and now when England and France are agreeable, and we could probably have secured it, we refuse to entertain the idea!"

Austria, and would prepare her for the use he intended to make of her. Events had worked for him better than he had expected. Russia, without compass and without ally, was rushing towards the unknown; and there only remained for the German Chancellor the care of choosing the opportune moment for disclosing his hand.

Shortly after the signing of the Treaty of Berlin, the European public read with surprise in the columns of *The Times*[1] the account of an interview of Prince Bismarck with the correspondent of that newspaper sent to Berlin at the time of the Congress. The German Chancellor did not hesitate to make public his old complaints against the Russian Chancellor. "I am", he said, "a frank friend of my friends, and a frank enemy of my enemies. Prince Gortchakov must be aware of this by this time. It is to the affair of 1875 that he ought to attribute his political defeat at the Congress."

From this moment the quarrel became public. The two Chancellors no longer communicated with one another. The leaves of absence of Prince Gortchakov to take care of his failing health became more and more extended; and all the burden of the political conduct of affairs fell on the Emperor Alexander himself, who, faithful to his old feelings towards Prussia, could hardly understand the complicated game of the German Chancellor, in whose conduct he only saw ingratitude.

This misunderstanding ended by an outburst in the autumn of 1879, accompanied by incidents which

[1] Of date 7 September, 1878.

I do not consider myself authorised to divulge, but which well-nigh brought about a serious quarrel between the two Governments. It is enough for me to say that Prince Bismarck had gained his end. It was not war he wished; he wished it less than any one. But the pretext was found to incline the Emperor William to enter into that alliance with Austria which opened a new chapter in contemporary history.

CHAPTER I

KISSINGEN

IN the summer of 1879 I left Greece, having been appointed Ambassador at Constantinople in succession to Prince Lobanov[1]. Before proceeding to Russia, I availed myself of my leisure to take the cure at Kissingen. Prince Bismarck arrived there soon after, with his wife and his son Herbert. I dined with him twice, and we had some talk of which the following is a résumé.

10/22 July, 1879.

The Prince: "I have always been the friend of Russia by conviction. It is good to have as friend behind you a nation of one hundred millions. And yet when Count Schuvalov[2] came to me some months ago to propose a second Congress, I frankly replied that I would not take part in it. I said to him, 'At a new meeting I should have to vote for you or against you. It has not been my habit to vote against you;

---

[1] Lobanov-Rostovsky, Prince Alexis Borissovitch (1824–1896), Plenipotentiary Minister in Constantinople 1859–1863, whither he returned as Ambassador 1878–1879. He then filled the same office in London 1879–1882, and in Vienna from October, 1882 till 1895. In the latter year he was appointed Minister of Foreign Affairs, but died the following year.

[2] Schuvalov, Count Paul Andreievitch (1830–1908), was Russian Ambassador in Berlin from 1885–1894. His brother Peter (1827–1889) succeeded Baron Brunnow as Russian Ambassador in London in 1874, and took an active part in 1875 in connection with the settlement of the Franco-German crisis.

and as to voting for you, I have learned to my cost that it is a thankless task to serve Russia'".

When I protested warmly against this last statement, the Prince continued: "Judge for yourself. I have often acted as Russian agent rather than as German Chancellor. I carried through the question of Batum alone after a sharp struggle with Lord Beaconsfield. I only succeeded after threatening to dissolve the Congress. I did the same over the question of the mouths of the Danube on which Andrassy[1] did not wish to yield. I proved to him that Austrian interests would not suffer at all by it. I defy any one to mention a single Russian proposal which I opposed during these three critical years. But Prince Gortchakov treats his allies like subalterns. When they believe they have done well and merited some acknowledgment, he thinks that they do not come upstairs quickly enough in answer to his ring.

"When I was ready to serve your interests at Vienna and at London, I was deprived of the means. I was asked to support your proposals when as a matter of fact, they had already been rejected. Now, that is quite different from supporting a proposal that has not yet been declined.

"At the beginning of the Eastern crisis I had declared myself ready to vouch for the loyalty of Austria,

---

[1] Andrassy, Count Julius (1823–1890). Hungarian statesman. Appointed 17 February, 1867, first constitutional Hungarian Premier. Chancellor from 6 November, 1871, succeeding Beust. Author of the famous "Andrassy Note". Principal Austrian Plenipotentiary at the Berlin Congress, 1878. Resigned 7 October, 1879, after signing the Austro-Hungarian-German Treaty on the same day. Cf. his Life by Eduard von Wertheimer.

provided that you came to agreement with her on some solution or other. I was even willing to promise to compel her if she did not keep to her engagements. Why did Russia not take advantage of these offers? It is true that there was an interview at Reichstadt. But the arrangements which were come to there, and of which I learned, not through Prince Gortchakov, but through Andrassy, were in no way definitive. There was not a single binding engagement of which it would have been possible for me to guarantee the execution. Everything was contingent. It was rather an arrangement between two Powers profoundly distrustful of one another, and desirous of retaining their liberty of action. This is so true that when the moment came to avail themselves of it, they were not able to agree, and each accused the other of bad faith.

"At the time of the Treaty of San Stefano[1] you had one of two policies to follow. You could have maintained this Treaty by force of arms. In that case you ought to have warned us. We should have helped you to keep Austria from interfering and isolate England. It was also necessary, after Plevna, to strengthen your army by fifty thousand men, not to stop before Gallipoli, but enter Constantinople while assuring Europe on oath that you would evacuate the city after the war. England, rather than risk herself in a struggle with a doubtful issue, would probably have modified her tone.

[1] Signed 3 March, 1878, on the conclusion of the Russo-Turkish War. Some of its stipulations, e.g. that with regard to the Greater Bulgaria, were subsequently modified by the Congress of Berlin (June, July, 1878) in the interests of Turkey.

"But after the entry of the English fleet into the Sea of Marmora, the favourable moment had passed, and Russia did wisely in deciding upon the second policy, that of the Congress. For at that stage England would certainly have declared war upon you, dragging in Austria and perhaps France.

"Only, having accepted the decisions of the Congress, you should have made them known to the nation, by comparing them not with the Treaty of San Stefano, but with your previous Treaties with Turkey. At what other period, indeed, has Russia secured such brilliant results? You even deprived Turkey of all her fortresses; in fact you spread yourself as far as the Balkans, whence you will threaten Constantinople whenever you wish. I do not speak of other advantages secured: the excellent frontier obtained in Asia, the independence of Serbia and of Montenegro, these two obstacles set up on the road to Austria, etc. All this constitutes a series of successes worthy of your victories. Your people should have been made to realise this, and not to forget that the victory had been won, and that Europe at the Congress had acknowledged it as due to you.

"That is what I had wished for Russia. Before the war I said to Oubril[1] that what the Russian nation needed were new victories to celebrate. It could not remain indefinitely under the shadow of the defeat in the Crimea. Russia and Prussia must have victorious

[1] Oubril, Count Paul Petrovitch (b. 1820), was Russian Minister in Berlin from 1863 to 1879. Being in the full confidence of Prince Gortchakov, he was distrusted by Prince Bismarck who expressed a wish for his transference. He was appointed Ambassador in Vienna (1880–1882), and was later made a member of the Council of State.

armies in order to cement a century-old alliance; for we must go back to the Seven Years' War before finding the two countries at grips with one another. And even then that was only 'a war of cotillons', as Frederick II said: an alliance of three women framed as the result of a gossiping intrigue of Madame de Pompadour. Russia had no political interest in it....

"I believe that there is no other instance in history of two neighbouring States having interests at once so complicated and solidary. It is a providential sign. They speak from time to time of the Baltic provinces, as a means of disuniting us. I get angry whenever I hear Russians calling them German provinces. Call them Lettish provinces or some other name, if you do not wish to recognise them as characteristically Russian provinces. In any case they are not German lands as we understand that term. If I had to deal with the question of nationalities, it is not there that my attention would be turned. The nobility alone is of a so-called Teutonic origin, and so far as it is concerned, the Emperor of Russia has no more faithful subjects. For that nobility has an interest in belonging to a country where it will never be at a loss to find important and lucrative posts.

"It is our misfortune that knowledge of the Russian language is spreading too much in Germany. To-day they read your newspapers. Our journalists take offence and answer back. Your journalists, flattered by the effect they produce abroad, retort by going one better; and so a polemic is established which perverts opinion on either side of the frontier, and is not without effect upon the Governments themselves...".

Extract from a second conversation.

14/26 July, 1879.

Prince Bismarck: "They consider me an ungrateful individual in Russia. They are wrong. Three years ago I was prepared to put the German army at your service if you had been willing to come to a thorough understanding on all our mutual interests. Without that condition it was not possible for me to drag my country into a war and burn our boats with regard to the other Powers. Our stake is the retention of Alsace-Lorraine. If you had given us a guarantee on that matter, I was ready to follow you through thick and thin (*durch dick und dünn*). Otherwise, can we be certain that, under another reign, Russia will not change her policy? My overtures elicited no response, or at least Prince Gortchakov turned a deaf ear to them. I continued accordingly in my rôle of friend, and I think I gave a proof of it to the Congress; but I could no longer be an ally through thick and thin".

Not having been in the secret of the negotiations to which the prince had just made allusion, it was difficult for me to continue the conversation on this point. I confined myself to expressing the opinion that Germany was sufficiently powerful to defend her conquests alone. "Besides," I added, "is it always necessary to draw the sword to render a service to a friend? Did not the Emperor Alexander save Prussia from a coalition in 1870 without mobilising a single soldier? The system of neutralising Austria, if it could always be faithfully followed by both sides, would be more valuable than an offensive and defensive alliance, for it is without the burdensome aspects, and does not compel each of the contracting parties to keep its forces constantly at the disposal of the other. That was all right last century when warfare was conducted with small armies."

The Prince listened to me attentively. "Yes", he replied, "a mutual guarantee against coalitions is perhaps preferable, nowadays, to a territorial guarantee."

But he added that he did not think that Petersburg was disposed at the moment to enter into a serious entente with Germany. Here he kept coming back to his complaints on the subject of his relations with Prince Gortchakov. He believed that he had done him an ill turn with the Emperor, etc.

My Impressions.

Prince Bismarck, while making a display of his long-standing sympathies for Russia, seemed a prey to some secret irritation of which I could not adequately account for the causes. There was in it, indeed, something slightly more definite than a mere cooling of relations with Prince Gortchakov.

On my way through Berlin I saw Radowitz, my colleague at Athens, who was acting as provisional director of the Ministry of Foreign Affairs. His confidences showed me that I was not mistaken. With the aid of information that I picked up there, I have been able to draw up a sort of inquiry into our relations with Germany since the time of the Congress.

We were dissatisfied with the Treaty of Berlin, and consequently with Bismarck, of whom we had expected more.

He, in his turn, believing that he had done his best to serve us, felt offended. Hence a rising tide of irritation on either side, the consequences of which were already making themselves painfully felt by us in connection with Eastern affairs.

In fact, in the different questions which came up in the Executive Commissions, the German delegates received orders to vote with the majority. We can no longer rely upon their vote as formerly. That is a fixed resolution on which it will be difficult for us to get the German Government to change its mind in the present state of our relationship. We rightly feel increased irritation at this, and therefore, to go from one thing to another, our relations with Germany are moving towards a more serious crisis than is realised.

It is, in fact, the moment to take care that the attitude adopted by us in 1870 in favour of Germany does not prove a mistake. At that time we had contributed greatly to the power of Prussia. We had done this to put our old ally in a position to render us similar services. A Prussia was not sufficient to save us from a European coalition; a Germany, rival of France, could do so.

Now this is precisely the point on which Prince Bismarck particularly insists in order to affirm that Germany has faithfully discharged her debt to us. At the beginning of the war he had categorically declared at Vienna that he would not tolerate any Austrian movement on our flank as long as the campaign lasted. After the Treaty of San Stefano the situation had changed, but even then he would still have lent us his co-operation for the purpose of in-

demnifying Austria and isolating England if we had
let him know it was our intention to maintain this
Treaty by force of arms.

That is the defence of his conduct. It is for the
Imperial Cabinet to judge of it.

I will confine myself to stating that if the present
situation is prolonged, we run the risk of seeing our
attitude interpreted at Berlin in a sense which would,
perhaps, go beyond our intentions. We are no longer
anxious for a Triple Entente; but at Berlin they are
already not far from believing that we have also had
enough of the traditional Dual Entente, and are
searching for new combinations.

If we let this conviction become rooted in the mind
of our neighbours, it is more than probable that Bismarck, with that characteristic impetuosity of his,
will not be long in seeking new alliances.

Alliances.

To-day it is not a matter of contracting alliances
for an impending and definite object. We are not on
the eve, but on the morrow of a war,—a war which has
set in motion new political combinations, not realised
as yet, but on the way to realisation if our diplomacy
does not take care.... There is especially in operation
a movement of evident rapprochement amongst the
great Cabinets, outside our own. The task of to-day
would consist then in checking this process of cry-
stallisation, a thing which would be impossible for us
to do if we isolated ourselves. It is a matter of knowing what is the point where our diplomacy must strike
if it is to break up the group of European intimacies.

In other words, to which Power ought we to draw nearer in order to re-establish an equilibrium in which we would have our share of influence and action? Is it France? Is it Germany?

Any intimate rapprochement with France could only be based on the supposition of a permanent antagonism between that Power and Germany. Our friendship is only necessary to France in what concerns her hope of "Revenge". But it would be hazardous to rely on the continuance of that antagonism. It is a situation where we run the risk of finding ourselves between two stools. For Bismarck, so full of resource, could some day revive the famous scheme of Benedetti for indemnifying France, or exchange Lorraine for some non-French province, if he saw in that a means of avoiding a war out of which he was not sure of emerging a victor. A rapprochement between us and France can only encourage him in these ideas. In that case we shall only have worked to overturn, to our detriment, the whole trend of contemporary history without having gained a new ally, for France, detached by Germany, would no longer have need of us.

Even if we give an impression of drawing nearer France with the sole purpose of bringing the German Chancellor round to us, we would run the risk, in that game, of arriving at a contrary result. We would only make him more inclined to listen to the proposals which perhaps reach him from London and from Vienna, with a view to finding a means of reconciliation with France by some political combination. For our patriotic instinct ought to tell us that such is the final aim of our adversaries on the Danube as on the Thames. It would be carrying off the best card that we have ever had in our hand!

The above indicates sufficiently in what direction our efforts must be directed. Often, in politics, the old ideas are the best. Close friendship with Prussia is one of these ideas, and whatever the misunderstandings of recent times, they have but little weight in the balance of the advantages which this close understanding assures us.

Here is a summary enumeration of them:

(1) As long as Bismarck is sure of us, he will certainly not dream of letting go of Lorraine. It therefore rests solely with us to perpetuate indefinitely the political estrangement of the two countries, thus rendering every coalition against us difficult, if not impossible.

(2) For a year we have seen the intimacy between Berlin and Vienna becoming more marked. That is a direct result of the uneasiness from which our present relations with Germany suffer. To-day, for Bismarck, that intimacy is still only a makeshift which we can bring to an end. And we must not accustom him to seek at Vienna the support which he has found up to the present at Petersburg.

(3) For nearly a century the friendship of Prussia has done us the incalculable service of covering our most important frontier. We can reckon in milliards what the defence of that frontier against a hostile Prussia would have cost us during that century. A friendly Prussia, on the contrary, places us in the privileged position of being the only Power in Europe

which need fear no attack, and which can reduce its budget without risk, as our August Master did after the Crimean War.

Present Relations between Russia and Germany.

There was a time when the idea of an Entente between the two Empires, with a view to mutual preservation against the danger of coalitions, seemed practicable. The Emperor furnished in 1870 the first example of an application of that idea which, put into loyal practice on both sides, was destined to assure an uncontested preponderance in world affairs to the neighbouring Empires.

Unfortunately a regrettable misunderstanding now makes the development of that political conception difficult in our future relations with Germany.

Must we admit that this misunderstanding can stifle in the germ the fruitful idea in which our Sovereign has taken the initiative? Will this idea be relegated in history as a unique example of political prevision, instead of illuminating the march of future generations?

That is the problem of to-day. The considerations which follow will perhaps prove the advisability of approaching the solution of this problem without too much delay.

Already Europe is put on its guard by the prospect unexpected—I was going to say, unhoped for—by her, of a change in the relations between Petersburg and Berlin. The Cabinets interested in poisoning these relations are already at work, as is proved by the following fact: in the Executive Commissions instituted in virtue of the Treaty of Berlin, these

Cabinets reserve their votes and declare that they
wish first to consult the opinion of the German
Government in its capacity of President of the Congress of Berlin. These tactics can be easily understood.
These very Cabinets would have taken good care not
to do so if our relations with Germany were those of
other days. But they know that this is not the case;
they speculate on the uneasiness which is felt there
in order to put Germany's vote in direct contact with
ours, at a moment when, at Berlin, they are little
inclined to do us a service.

Would that not be the chance to catch these Cabinets
in their own trap; to dispel, by a frank explanation,
the misunderstanding which weighs on our relations
with the German Chancellor; to bring him back on
to a path, where, as I believe, he will be only too glad
to return, and to get the upper hand, in concert with
him, in all the questions that are still unresolved?

We are approaching a critical moment where Germany has the choice of two ways before her. Either
I am badly mistaken or I am right in believing that
Prince Bismarck, in order to close his historic career
with success, is considering to-day the best means of
re-uniting the elements of stability which his work
still lacks, since his confidence in the friendship of
Russia was shaken.

Alliance with Austria; reconciliation with France
by means of a territorial re-arrangement; such are
the ideas which, perhaps, haunt his uneasy spirit at
this moment. None of these ideas would suit us, for
they would change the present conditions of equilibrium in Europe to our detriment.

CHAPTER II

INTERVIEW AT ALEXANDROVO, LIVADIA

August–September, 1879.

AUGUST 5. Having reached Petersburg, I gave the preceding Memorandum to M. de Giers, who, after reading it, said: "You have come too late. The Emperor has just sent a letter to the Emperor William which will, I fear, set the match to the powder. Under the influence of the reports from Constantinople, the Emperor, in his letter, complains bitterly of Bismarck, whom he accuses of disturbing the relations between the two Governments by his hostile attitude. The Emperor has written this letter *ab irato* without consulting anybody". Giers added that he would, however, try and bring my Memorandum to the notice of the Emperor, although he does not hope for much in the Sovereign's present state of irritation.

August 12–14. Visit my brother at Dorpat.

August 15. On my return to Petersburg I learn that the Emperor had invited me to dinner at Tsarkoe the previous evening. I go straight to M. de Giers who gives me the news of the day. The Emperor leaves this very evening for Warsaw, en route for Livadia. Miliutine[1] and Giers are to accompany him.

---

[1] Miliutine, General Count Dmitry Alexeievitch (1816–1912), a man of strongly pronounced liberal convictions, was Minister of War under Alexander II, of whose great reforms he was one of the chief promoters. He received the title of Count on 30 August, 1878. His brother Nicholas was a well-known social reformer.

Oubril telegraphs that the Emperor's letter has produced the worst possible effect at Berlin. Bismarck is taking a cure at Gastein. Field-Marshal Count Manteuffel[1] has been sent to Warsaw to demand explanations. The Emperor has read my Memorandum and covered it with approving annotations. Giers has invited me to go with him in the Imperial train which is to meet the Emperor at Tsarkoe. On arrival at Tsarkoe, I get out of the train. The Grand-Dukes and members of the Court were waiting at the station. The Emperor on his arrival recognises me in the crowd, and takes me aside into the adjoining room. Conversation for half an hour. Irritation against Germany entirely disappeared. All my conclusions approved.

August 16–20. Stay at Dorpat.

August 21. Leave for Berlin.

August 23. At Berlin I learn the news of the meeting of the Emperors at Alexandrovo. Confidences from Radowitz. Opinion of Manteuffel with regard to Miliutine—"he is before everything a Russian; he has no preconceived ideas; he will go with Germany if he becomes convinced that it is in the interests of Russia to do so, and against Germany if he is persuaded of the contrary."

August 28. Arrive at Reichenhall.

---

[1] Manteuffel, Field-Marshal Edwin Hans Karl (1809–1885). Appointed Chief of the Military Staff in 1857. Resigned in 1865 to take over the Governorship and Military Command in Schleswig-Holstein. He was typically Prussian in bearing and administrative relationships. His distinguished military career culminated in his being made General Field-Marshal in 1873, while six years later he was appointed viceroy in Alsace-Lorraine.

August 29. Summoned by telegram to Livadia.

September 4. Reached Livadia via Vienna and Odessa. Giers explains that the Emperor has decided to clear up the situation. A fortnight has slipped away since the interview at Alexandrovo: Bismarck seems unaware of it and is lying low at Gastein. A telegram from Vienna announces his approaching arrival in the Austrian capital with the intention of entering upon important pourparlers with the Cabinet there. The Emperor wishes to send me to Berlin to discuss things with Bismarck. Giers relates to me in retrospect some details of what took place at Warsaw and at Alexandrovo.

At Warsaw, the Marshal Manteuffel began his explanations with a stiffness thoroughly Prussian. Giers stopped him at once, and proved to him that the Emperor, far from seeking any quarrel, was on the contrary animated by the best feelings. He gave Manteuffel the copy of my Memorandum with the notes in the Emperor's own handwriting to read. The idea naturally arose of arranging an interview between the two Sovereigns, and in consequence of Manteuffel's detailed reports, transmitted by telegram to Berlin, an interview at Alexandrovo had been decided on in twenty-four hours. Miliutine and Giers accompanied the Emperor. The explanations were cordial and completely satisfactory. There had been an exchange of decorations and Miliutine received the Black Eagle.

The day after my arrival at Livadia the Emperor convoked a Council under his Presidency to discuss the bases of the instructions which were to be given to me, and I was charged with drawing them up. The sederunt consisted of Count Miliutine, Count Adlerberg,[1] de Giers and Prince Lobanof who had just arrived from Constantinople. I was also present. The following are the Instructions approved by the Emperor:

Extract from Instructions given at Livadia.

8 September, 1879.

Whatever be the desire of all the Cabinets to consider the Treaty of Berlin as the basis of political equilibrium in the East, it would be a bold thing to affirm that that piece of work has in it conditions of great permanence. Moreover, elementary prudence makes it imperative for us to study immediately the character of the difficulties that can arise in the East in the more or less near future.

These difficulties fall into two categories:

(1) Those that can arise at any moment. One can put here, in the first place, the possible occupation of Roumelia and the line of the Balkans by the Turkish troops.

(2) The more remote eventuality of an internal crisis in Turkey.

In order to settle the difficulties that may arise from this double source, we need an ally. Russia cannot expose herself, as in 1854, to the danger of a European coalition. In short, in place of the system of an iso-

---

[1] Adlerberg, Count Alexander Vladimirovitch (1819–1882), son of the former Minister of the Imperial Household, and successor of his father in that post after 1872. He enjoyed the full confidence and friendship of the Emperor Alexander II.

lated influence, exercisable at Constantinople, it would be desirable to substitute a close Entente with whichever of the Powers may be most disposed to accept it, and best placed to give us the assistance we require in the East.

That Power is Germany. She alone can help us to form, amongst the Cabinets, a majority on the question of the eventual occupation of Roumelia by the Turks.

As to the more remote eventuality of a new Eastern crisis, it will also be easier for us, be it to negotiate with our adversaries or to conquer them, if we are successful in finding the necessary support in a close Entente with Germany.

Before deciding on this step, it is important to get a clear idea of what we shall wish and be able to secure, if the question of the East should impose itself once again on the attention of Europe.

The Treaty of Berlin has evidently been dictated with some hostility to Russia. Whereas our army evacuated the theatre of events, this Treaty planted Austria in a central strategic position with the evident intention of giving over to her the chief direction of future events in European Turkey.

The same rôle has been assumed by England in Asiatic Turkey in virtue of the Treaty of Cyprus,[1] and in the Straits in virtue of her naval preponderance.

Trouble in Albania or in Macedonia would be sufficient to-day to give Austria the pretext to pro-

---

[1] 4 June, 1878, under which Great Britain agreed to support Turkey against Russia by force of arms in certain eventualities, and was in return assigned the island of Cyprus to be occupied and administered by her.

vide herself for the second time with a European mandate in order to extend her occupation beyond Novibazar.[1]

As for England, she is already thinking of taking in hand the whole system of military defence in Asiatic Turkey. There she selects her consuls from amongst the military, and considers all these regions as coming into the sphere of her influence. All these facts would indicate her intention of occupying the Straits at a given moment, and of holding them by sea and by land.

But there are two things which we cannot allow:

(1) An extension of Austria beyond the regions allotted under the Treaty of Berlin, and including positively Serbia and Montenegro.

(2) A permanent occupation of the Straits by England. So, in European Turkey, we may be brought into inevitable conflict with Austria. That is where the rôle of Germany will become decisive. The service which we could demand of her in that circumstance would be to see to the localisation of the conflict.

As to the eventuality of a war with England, whether in Asia or for possession of the Straits, Germany could not help us directly, but she can render us indirectly the important service of depriving England of a Continental ally by keeping Austria neutral.

[1] The Sanjak (a subdivision of a vilayet or Turkish province) of Novibazar lay like a projecting tongue in the north-west of European Turkey, between Serbia and Montenegro. It was of great strategic importance, as the direct route between Bosnia and Salonika passed through it, and it virtually commanded all the roads between Bosnia, Roumelia and Serbia. Hence the possession of it was a necessity for Austrian expansion to the south-east.

It is then only by the action of Germany that it would be possible for us to divide our adversaries and beat them separately, if the chances of war remained favourable to us.

In view of her situation with regard to France, Germany has also the greatest interest in guarding against a possible coalition. This solidarity between the Eastern and Western questions, already dimly foreseen after the events of 1870, becomes more noticeable every day in the general situation, and will end by obtruding itself upon the statesmen who direct the affairs of the two neighbouring countries.

Already Prince Bismarck had had a presentiment of the importance of it when, at the beginning of the Eastern crisis, he had formed the idea of an offensive and defensive alliance between us and Germany.

Has that idea come to maturity? We may doubt this. The misunderstandings resulting from the Congress of Berlin are still of too recent a date to pass without transition to a general Entente.

Therefore it would be desirable to let a certain interval elapse between the recent meeting of the Emperors and the thorough-going negotiations that might begin afterwards.

The course of action then for the moment would be limited to making sure, by a direct explanation, of the real personal feelings of the German Chancellor, to reassuring him with regard to ours, and thus we would complete the work begun by the interview at Alexandrovo, by associating in one and the same thought the Emperor William and his powerful Minister.

In the conversations to which this explanation will give rise, it is necessary to anticipate the eventuality where Prince Bismarck would himself take a more serious initiative. If this came about, the views developed in the present Memorandum will serve as a guide in the conduct of the negotiations at Berlin.

September 10. Departure from Livadia. En route I glanced at the German newspapers. They were full of details about Bismarck's visit to Vienna and of rumours of an alliance which he had negotiated there with Austria.

First Explanations at Berlin.

September, 1879.

On my arrival at Berlin, our Ambassador, impressed by the rumours of a new Austro-German alliance, drew a very dark picture of the situation for me, and even went so far as to tell me that it was now beyond remedy.

Without losing heart, I determined to profit by the confidences of M. d'Oubril so as to procure a further chance in the accomplishment of my mission. To prepare the ground, I paid a visit to von Radowitz, and told him that if there was any truth in the rumours which reached me from all quarters on the subject of the conclusion of an alliance hostile to us, I would prefer to break off my mission rather than compromise the dignity of the Emperor by risking being received as an intruding third party. I laid particular stress upon the fact that my commission was connected with circumstances previous to Prince Bismarck's visit to Vienna, and that it would be a mistake on the

part of any one to look for any relation whatever between the mission with which I was charged and the
recent pourparlers between the Cabinets at Vienna
and Berlin.

These observations, transmitted to the right party,
seemed to have produced the desired effect, and contributed to assure me a reception, which, I am bound
to say, exceeded my expectations.

The Prince, informed of my arrival, received me
the same day, and although overwhelmed with work
and audiences, kept me three consecutive hours. He
began by thanking me for having helped to dissipate
certain prejudices of which he had become the object
in Russia.

I interrupted him in order to say that all I had done
was to report his words faithfully.

"There were two ways of understanding you," I
added: "I could have seen in your language a desire
to seek some pretexts for liberating yourself from
your old sympathies, in order to take up new friend-
ships. Well, I did not understand you that way. I
thought that your recriminations sprang from regret
at seeing our long-standing relationships becoming
impaired, and that this regret pre-supposed a desire
to re-establish them. That is the way I interpreted
your words: I bear the responsibility of it before the
Emperor and all those in Russia who would like to
find in you again the friend of former days. Tell me
if I have made a mistake; for that is at bottom the
purpose of my mission."

The Chancellor, visibly impressed with the frankness of this appeal, answered me cordially: "Yes, you

were a thousand times right. Say so to the Emperor, and accept again my thanks for having done me this service by him ".

He then began to group in one picture all the indications which had combined, in the course of the summer, to call up before his alarmed mind the spectre of a coalition against Germany!

At the Congress of Berlin, he had believed that he had rendered us services. He desired that the Russian people should know this, not from any amour-propre, but from a more serious political purpose. He wished to encourage in Russia a current of opinion favourable to Germany, to accustom the two nations to lean one upon the other, and thus facilitate for the two Governments the task of carrying out big matters together.

Instead of this, what had he seen? The Russian newspapers, with the *Golos* at their head, which Prince Gortchakov and the Emperor himself had recommended as a sound newspaper, had begun a series of personal attacks on him. The new disposition of Russian troops along the frontier—a matter without importance at ordinary times, but which assumes a gravity of the first importance when suspicion enters into the minds of Governments; the new battalions formed after the war; the resignation of Count Andrassy of which he did not satisfactorily understand the motives; a confidential communication from Paris on the subject of a proposal for an alliance which seemed to have been made there by us; a rumour of a similar nature sent on from Rome; all these indications following one another, were so many disturbing presumptions. Now, in politics, one cannot be guided by presumptions alone. It is just as if one were in a wood filled with suspicious characters, where one feels oneself instinctively on the defensive. He also recalled his offer of alliance which had been declined at a moment when an active alliance seemed so necessary to Russia. Could it be that they had another in mind? Finally, there came the letter from the Emperor, preceded by a significant conversation with Schweinitz.[1] "I know very well", he added, "that it was a letter from nephew to uncle. But it is a nephew whose every gesture represents a force of two million bayonets!"

Here I interrupted the Prince to say that I did not wish to contend further with all these phantoms. The very fact that the Emperor wished to terminate the interview at Alexandrovo by a direct explanation was in my eyes an unanswerable reply to all these apprehensions.

The Prince replied that he had no desire to recriminate, but that he was anxious to give me a complete account of the course of his ideas at the time when doubts had prevailed over him. "I wish", he said, "to continue this narration, for I am anxious to give the Emperor a proof of sincerity in letting him know what has taken place at Vienna.

"Andrassy had sent in his resignation. I could not understand the true reason for it. Austria, at that

[1] Schweinitz, Hans Lothal von (1822–1901), German General and diplomat, began his military career in 1840. Appointed military attaché in Vienna 1861, to which city he returned as Ambassador ten years later. Transferred in similar capacity to St Petersburg in 1876. He was made a general in 1884, and retired in 1892.

moment, could adopt one of two policies. Either she could play a game à la Kaunitz, ally herself secretly with Russia under the influence of the military party, and fall upon us, or she could dream of making Russia give ground in the Orient, by allying herself first with England, then with France, so creating a situation like that of 1854. This second eventuality did not suit me any better than the first. We would have been compelled to remain neutral or unite with Russia in order to play a trick on the coalition. We would have been two against three, which is not advantageous. As for neutrality, I, at any rate, do not like to be neutral. One generally comes out of that situation with two enemies on one's hands.

"I decided then to go to Vienna to interview the Emperor Francis Joseph directly. I asked him if he intended to modify his relations with Russia one way or the other. He replied in the negative. I had to have guarantees, and secured them in the following manner. By nature, Austria is essentially apprehensive and apt to take umbrage: that is what always makes her so disposed to throw herself into the arms of the West. I wished to dig a ditch between her and the Western Powers. With that object I had to re-assure her. They asked me what I would do in the event of a war between Russia and Austria. I answered in the words of my last speech in the Reichstag. I said that much depended on the question who should be the aggressor, but that in any case Germany was interested to see that neither of the two combatants should be mortally wounded (*sich verblutet*). As Austria is the weaker of the two and as it is she who would risk most, this language re-assured her. I secured, on my part, that Austria renounces the forming of Western alliances in order to defend her interests in the East. She can, if she so desires, discuss with you such and such a question for the next ten years; but henceforth she gives up all other means than those of diplomatic action.

"I thus succeeded in carrying out what I call the first act of my political system—that of placing a barrier between Austria and the Western Powers. In spite of this summer's clouds, which I consider as passing ones, I do not despair of realising the second act—that of the reconstitution of the League of the Three Emperors (*Dreikaiserbund*), the only system offering, in my opinion, the maximum of stability for the peace of Europe."

From the commencement of the interview I was waiting for this moment. I had a presentiment that it would come, and I determined to profit by it immediately. Interrupting the Prince, I said, "Prove to us that this Entente will be profitable to us, that we shall find in it the pledge of peace in the East, and I do not think that the Emperor would then be opposed to a Triple Entente on a practical basis."

I then explained to him the Roumelian question. I made him understand the dangers of the entry of Turkish troops into that province. The Turks are preparing for this. The English, secretly, urge them to it. If Christian blood came to be spilt again, the same scenes would take place in Russia as at the time of the Bulgarian massacres. The same generous sentiment would possess the masses; the tide of Pan-

Slavism—that bugbear of Austria and of Germany—would once again become popular, and the Emperor be placed between an inadmissible humiliation and a new war; the disagreements with Austria would reappear at every point. There lies a common interest between us, to which I directed his attention.

The Prince seemed impressed with the gravity of this question such as I had just explained it to him. He acknowledged that the occupation of Roumelia by the Turkish troops would present real dangers, and that it was desirable to avoid this.

I reminded him that in virtue of the Treaty of Berlin, Turkey could only send troops into Roumelia on the request of the Governor-General. Now the Turks know that Aleko-Pasha will never formulate such a request, and the partisans of occupation are working to turn him out of office.

After a short discussion we agreed on the following mode of procedure:

The Russian Government would take up this question with the German Cabinet through an official communication. Prince Bismarck would then take upon himself to bring Austria to our point of view, and as a preventive measure, the three Cabinets would exert their influence at Constantinople to keep Aleko-Pasha in the post of Governor-General of Eastern Roumelia.

I told the Prince that I would hasten to give an account of this result to my Government, who would without doubt see in it the first proof of the usefulness which the new dominant position of Germany at Vienna is able to offer us.

I was anxious to pass this remark in order to make the Prince feel that, for the future, he was going to be guarantee, so to speak, for the good conduct of Austria with regard to us. From this point of view it will be advantageous for us to treat at Berlin, in preference to direct pourparlers with Austria. The latter has herself desired this rôle of dependence. Let her take the consequences.

CHAPTER III

THE AUSTRO-GERMAN ALLIANCE

AFTER many years of persevering labour, Prince
Bismarck has at last moulded Austria to his
liking. He himself outlined for me, in a few
strokes, the history of this task.

In his opinion the existence of Austria is a necessity
for Germany, for the reason that one does not know
what to do with these 20,000 square leagues. There
is, it is true, no Austrian nation, but there is an
Austrian patriotism which one will never be able to
replace at Vienna by a German patriotism.

The necessity of an Austria being demonstrated,
there flows from this another inevitable consequence:
Germany, in view of her own security, cannot allow
Austria to have any other alliance than with herself!

In order to secure this end it was first necessary to
defeat Austria and expel her from the Germanic Confederation. It was then necessary to strengthen the
Hungarian element in order to finish off the deger-
manising of that monarchy, and get it to stand completely aside from German affairs. Andrassy filled
that rôle, first at Pesth, then at Vienna. His presence
in affairs was a guarantee that the unwritten alliance
would continue to exist de facto. His retirement has
necessitated fresh guarantees.

With this intention a Memorandum was signed at
Vienna by Prince Bismarck and Count Andrassy. It
is not yet a Treaty, because it lacks ratification by the

Sovereigns. Neither is the signature of Haymerlé,[1] the new Foreign Minister, found on it. But there is no doubt that this Memorandum will be turned later into formal stipulations.

The leading idea of this document, which the Prince read to me, is the following: Austria agrees not to enter into political engagements with other Powers outside and unknown to Germany. Accordingly, no Western alliance, no separate alliance with Russia.

The wording of the Memorandum indicates in a very marked way the intention to leave the door open in the eventuality of Russia being disposed to take her place within this Entente.

After finishing the reading of this document, the Prince continued in the following strain:

"The Dreikaiserbund, an idea which I have pursued all my life, was thought of long before my time. It is the Emperor Nicholas who was the originator of it. You will never devise a political system offering more guarantees than this for the maintenance of all the conservative elements of modern societies."

The Prince then developed this conception as he

---

[1] Haymerlé, Heinrich Karl, Freiherr von (1828–10 October, 1881), Austrian statesman. Appointed Secretary of Legation at Athens in 1857, he served in Dresden, Frankfort and Copenhagen. In 1868 recalled to Vienna, where he worked directly under Beust in the Ministry of Foreign Affairs. He was appointed Minister at Athens in 1869 and at the Hague in 1872. He returned to the Ministry of Foreign Affairs under Andrassy, but was sent as Ambassador to Rome in 1877. He was third Austrian plenipotentiary at the Congress of Berlin in 1878, and succeeded Andrassy as Minister of Foreign Affairs on 8 October, 1879, making it his principal endeavour to maintain the policy of his predecessor.

understands it for our time. His ideas were assuredly not unanswerable, but I preferred to listen to him in silence in order not to compromise, by idle discussion, the results which we are anxious above all to secure.

Thus, he began by saying that the Emperor Nicholas had always insisted on the necessity of a close alliance between Austria and Prussia so as to form a dam against the revolutionary tides of the West. Amidst the old Germanic Confederation this alliance had become impossible. But since the events of 1866, one can conceive of a new Confederation replacing the old one, on broader bases, and exempt from the rivalries which had brought about the failure in purpose of the old combination. The Russia of the Emperor Alexander would have to congratulate itself as much as that of the Emperor Nicholas, for a Triple Alliance can henceforth become a reality.

In our last conversation on 17/29 September, referring to the disclosures which the Prince had made to me at Kissingen, I came to speak to him about the proposal for an alliance which he had had forwarded to us in 1877 by General Schweinitz.

I told him that this part of my report had particularly attracted the attention of the Emperor. I did not conceal from him that, in consequence of circumstances as yet insufficiently cleared up, the Emperor had never been aware of the proposal. I added that in my eyes, a return to the old relationships of cordiality would make an alliance of that sort practicable, if ever the rulers of the two countries found it necessary to co-ordinate the interests of Russia in the East with those of Germany in Europe.

After a moment's silence the Prince said to me: "My desire for an alliance remains the same; but I ought to let you know at once that there has been a change in the situation. In 1877 I was ready to enter into an offensive and defensive alliance with you. To-day I can no longer do so; if an alliance were to be effected, I should only consider it in the form of a *defensive* alliance".

I replied that I myself understood the matter in the same way. Germany had to defend herself against a possible attack from France. Russia might have to defend herself one day against an attempt on the part of England to take possession of the entrance to the Black Sea. God grant that the status quo last as long as possible. But if Turkey comes to disappear as the result of an upheaval that everybody has been expecting for a century, and England profits thereby to seize the Straits, shall we not be in a position of legitimate self-defence in seeking to anticipate her and prevent her posting her sentinels at the gates of our Empire?

The Prince replied without hesitation: "From the way in which you have stated the question, I must admit that that would be a case for a legitimate defensive, for an Empire like Russia cannot let herself be cooped up by England in the Black Sea".

I then recalled to the Prince the exchange of ideas which had taken place at Kissingen, and I asked if he was still of the opinion that we could arrive at an Entente with a view to a mutual guarantee against the danger of a coalition. The two events to provide against would be these: a Franco-German war for

Alsace-Lorraine, and an Anglo-Russian war for possession of the Straits.

Before replying, the Prince meditated for some moments, visibly interested at the turn which the conversation had taken. Finally he said to me, "In the event of war between Russia and England, we should then have to keep Austria neutral. Well, our task would be greatly facilitated if you did not take umbrage at a pledge which we shall perhaps be under the necessity of giving to reassure her as to her territorial integrity. I will go further: why should not Russia give her that guarantee along with us, if, as I hope, the Triple Entente becomes realisable?"

I expounded the reasons for which such an arrangement seemed impracticable.

In the first place, the integrity of Austria, while desirable, is not as indispensable to our security as it seems to be to Germany. Now, parties only agree to saddle themselves with a guarantee when there is some vital interest at stake. In the second place, against whom shall we give this guarantee to Austria? Against Italy? Austria will always be stronger than Italy. Against ourselves? In that case the practical value of the guarantee vanishes. Against Germany? We certainly should not agree to risk war with Germany in order to maintain the territorial integrity of Austria!

The Prince, while reserving his opinion on the subject of the Triple Entente as preferable to a Dual Entente, entered, none the less, into a detailed discussion on the very object of the projected accord, such as I had just defined it.

We finally reached agreement on the following points:

Russia would have as objectives:

(1) To oppose the occupation of the Straits by England.

(2) To oppose all territorial change in Turkey without her preliminary assent.

The objectives of Germany would be the following:

(1) To leave France without an ally if she wished to attack Germany.

(2) To maintain the territorial status quo in Austria.

These different points were formulated in three articles, roughly outlined before rising.

Article I. In the event of war between England and Russia, Germany will remain neutral, and undertakes to prevent, by force if need be, any other Power from joining with England.

Article II. In the event of war between France and Germany, Russia will remain neutral, and undertakes to prevent, by force if need be, any other Power from joining with France.

Article III. Russia will respect the territorial integrity of Austria. The latter, on her part, will not extend her sphere of action in the East beyond the boundaries laid down under the Treaty of Berlin, without preliminary agreement with Russia.

When we had reached this result, the Prince said to me: "In a matter of this importance I must submit everything for the approval of my Sovereign. I cannot trust my memory when it is a question of a precise statement. Be good enough to note down these three points on a sheet of paper"—and he handed me one of his pencils across the table.

I admit that I was taken unawares. Did he wish a sample of my handwriting for some purpose of which I was ignorant? He had not yet seen the Emperor William who was at Baden, and who in consequence had not yet had time to ratify the arrangements come to at Vienna. This scrap of paper in my handwriting was perhaps necessary to him in order to overcome the hesitation of the Emperor, and obtain his consent to some stipulation that was being kept from us. The incident in connection with Benedetti[1] came also suddenly to my mind. Perhaps this was the very pencil that the Prince had offered to the unfortunate French diplomat in order to compromise him with his own handwriting.

Assuming an embarrassed air, I answered the Prince that I was not yet authorised to enter into *written* agreements, and not having the status of Ambassador, I could hardly take that responsibility upon myself.

I saw by the Chancellor's smile that he had under-

---

[1] The reference is to the draft of a Treaty drawn up between Bismarck and the French agent in 1866, which represented the French claims for compensation consequent on the assistance of France in arranging the preliminaries of the armistice signed at Nikolsberg between Prussia and Austria. Among the terms was the promise of German assistance in the event of the annexation of Belgium by France. The idea was probably suggested by Bismarck, but although the Treaty was never concluded, Bismarck kept the draft, in Benedetti's handwriting, and published it in *The Times* in 1870, a few days after the outbreak of war between France and Germany. See Benedetti's *Ma Mission en Prusse* (Paris, 1871).

stood, and that we were both thinking of Benedetti, without mentioning his name. Taking back his pencil, "Well," he said, with affability, "dictate the three points to me: I will act as your secretary".

After this little episode I thought it right to warn him that I was in no way charged to undertake formal negotiations, and that I regarded our exchange of ideas as a continuation of our conversations at Kissingen, with the view of assuring myself, at all events, that an Entente between the two Governments was possible.

There remained for me to learn the opinion of the Prince as to the time at which such an arrangement could be reached.

He is decidedly of the opinion that it would be imprudent to put it off. According to him we must strike while the iron is hot. He is not answerable for the Crown Prince, who, under the influence of his wife, would probably not agree to sign a Treaty directed against England. The Emperor William himself feels an almost invincible repugnance to signing treaties of alliance. In 1866 there was a moment when he, Bismarck, had lost all hope of making the King sign the Treaty with Italy.

But to-day he hopes to persuade him, and he will begin by sounding him on the first occasion.

In the meantime, the Prince insisted on absolute secrecy, and expressed the desire to see me at Varzin during the month of December, in order to discuss the matter again after having seen His Majesty.

At parting, the Prince begged me to give his respects to the Emperor, and to assure His Majesty that he would always find in him the old devotion to his person, that he was always the same, before, as during, the Congress, and that if, after the Congress, people had thought he had changed, it was not he who had changed, but they who had changed their point of view. He is profoundly grateful to the Emperor for the favourable reception which had been given to his explanations at Kissingen.

Grounds for my belief in the existence of a second Memorandum signed at Vienna by Prince Bismarck and Count Andrassy.

When Prince Bismarck read me the Memorandum referred to above, I was separated from him by all the breadth of his writing-desk which has twice the dimensions of an ordinary writing-table. He held the document in his hands in such a way that it was impossible for me, in spite of good eyesight, to see the page which he was reading. It was only when he was obliged to turn the first page that I was able to notice for an instant the figure II inscribed at the head of the document. I saw it sufficiently distinctly to be certain that I had not been deceived.[1]

Apart from that direct proof I find another in the very contents of the Memorandum which was read to me. It only contains in effect engagements entered into by Austria—an engagement not to contract a Western Alliance, an engagement not to depart from the ways of diplomacy in her differences with Russia, etc. Austria will not have bound herself in this way without having secured something in exchange. If

---

[1] See Note at the end of this chapter.

she has promised not to attack, Germany must have promised her that no one would attack her either. The stipulations of the Memorandum with which I have been made acquainted seem to have in view the removal of the possibility of a conflict between Austria and Russia, and so to render useless the guarantee which, I suppose, has been given to Austria. In short, the intentions which have prompted this Memorandum are so favourable to us that we could have signed it ourselves, and Bismarck will not have gone to Vienna merely to sign such a soothing document.

But even if the existence of a Memorandum No. I were proved by the preceding reflections, I am far from seeing in it an indication of bad faith or of duplicity. Having pledged himself to secrecy with regard to the Court of Vienna, he has not kept it well, as is habitually the case in similar circumstances. If he has not shown me everything, he has told me all; and he has done so, without doubt, not through indiscretion of speech, but intentionally. In his account of his stay at Vienna he said to me twice that it was "necessary to reassure Austria". To the Emperor Francis Joseph's query as to whether Germany would support Austria in the event of war with Russia, he replied: "Much will depend on the question as to who is the aggressor".

Finally the Prince said to me: " I would have wished you not to take umbrage at a guarantee which we might perhaps be under the obligation to give Austria with regard to her territorial status quo".

I admit that it is difficult to be more explicit. In acknowledging all this, without showing me the document itself, the Prince went much further perhaps in his confidences than he thought compatible with the loyalty which he owes to his new ally. So I see in this rather a proof that he does not wish to deceive us, and that he sincerely desires an Entente with us, if we are anxious for it ourselves.

I left Berlin to go to Jugenheim, having received instructions to communicate the results of my mission to the Empress. I had also to deliver a message from the Emperor to Prince Gortchakov, who was at Baden-Baden. Thence I returned to Livadia where I spent a week. On 8 October I left for Petersburg.

Soon after, I received a letter from M. de Giers intimating the Emperor's intention to appoint me Ambassador at Berlin in place of Oubril, who would be transferred to Vienna. At the same time, de Giers sent me the rough draft of a Treaty worked out at Livadia on the basis of my three Articles, but greatly enlarged, and bringing into my future negotiations the question of the Straits in a form which seemed to me unacceptable to Germany.

On the return of the Emperor to Petersburg, I presented the following Memoir on that subject:

The Question of the Straits.

From the point of view of the interests of Russia, there is only one satisfactory solution of this question, the one formulated in the historic saying of the Emperor Nicholas, "We must have the key of our house".

This key alone will be able to give us complete

security on our southern frontiers. A single fortification at the mouth of the Bosphorus will take for us
the place of a fleet, of an army and of a whole line of
fortresses necessary to-day to maintain our coasts on
the Black Sea in a state of defence.

This radical solution is impracticable to-day. It
does not admit of possible negotiation with England.
Force alone will be able to bring it about some day.

But the importance of it is so great that it ought to
remain the principal objective of our policy, from
whatever quarter the Eastern Question again makes
its appearance.

In addition, the nature of the problem is such that
no ally will be able to lend us effective assistance, for
no Power possesses strong enough naval forces to
contend against the British navy.

All that diplomacy will be able to do will be to
deprive England of the ability to contract continental
alliances so as to create a diversion in the rear of our
army.

Such ought to be the sole aim of our future negotiations with Germany. It would be unwise to com-
plicate them by demanding from her services which
she would not be in a position to render us, even if
she had the goodwill to do so.

Indeed, the military co-operation of Germany
would be completely illusory in a conflict with England. She could only offer us land forces, of which
we would hardly have any need. As for her ships,
they could only shut themselves up in their ports, or
else be destroyed on an element where England rules
in uncontested mastery.

Therefore, rather than appeal for ineffective help for which we would need to pay by perhaps costly obligations, it will be preferable to confine ourselves to asking from Germany only the useful service which she could render us—that of holding the rest of Europe in check, when the hour of the supreme struggle for possession of the Straits has struck for us.

I will go further. Germany, as a neutral Power, can be of greater service to us than if she became a belligerent siding with us. In the first place, the blockade of our Baltic ports will not be so easily achieved as when Prussia was of no account there. To-day, Germany, having become a naval Power, possesses interests in the Baltic which England will have to take into consideration. It will no longer be sufficient for the latter to declare all our ports blockaded; an *effective* blockade, such as is required by the Declaration of the Congress of Paris, will necessitate the presence of a greater number of warships, which will make a diversion useful for our military position on the Bosphorus.

Besides, as long as Germany remains neutral, her Baltic ports will be open for the marketing of our produce by way of transit, and the state of war will not involve complete stagnation in our commercial activity.

All these considerations serve to show the difficulties, perhaps insurmountable, which would be encountered if we wanted to include the question of the Straits in the programme of our negotiations at Berlin.

In spite of my objections, the matter of the Straits remained included in the number of questions which I had to take up at Berlin. I accordingly only circumscribed it in a way not to fail in the principal object of my mission—that of re-establishing intimate relations with Germany, and thus depriving the Austro-German Entente of the justification for its existence.

The Emperor ordered the modification of my instructions in this sense, and Baron Jomini[1] was

[1] Jomini, Baron Alexander (1814–1888), son of a Swiss who was in the French service till 1814, when, having had a disagreement with Napoleon, he entered the Russian military service. The father had already earned a reputation as a military writer and tactician on account of which he had been ennobled by Napoleon. Baron Alexander Jomini passed his whole diplomatic life in the Ministry of Foreign Affairs in St Petersburg, where he was the right-hand and stout supporter of Prince Gortchakov and his policy. He was the author of the famous "Notes Polonaises", inspired and signed by Prince Gortchakov. He also wrote a book entitled *Étude diplomatique sur la guerre de Crimée*, par un ancien diplomate (St Petersburg, 1878). M. Onou relates that a few months before his death Jomini went to see Count Pourtales, then German Chargé d'Affaires (12 July, 1888), and warned him that if Austria did not change her provocative policy in the Balkans, a war would follow which would be fatal to her. He expressed his regret that Germany seemed inclined to support Austrian policy, which filled him with serious apprehensions about the future. Bismarck is stated to have written sixteen marginal notes on the report of this conversation, but to have remained unconvinced by it.

M. Onou who, as a relative, passed his whole youth in the house of Baron Jomini, recollects hearing Baron Jomini express his opinion about M. Saburov, considering him a clever but in some respects weak man, and condemning his personal regard for Bismarck. "Quand ce pauvre Saburov vient en contact avec ce tigre de Bismarck", Baron Jomini is reported as saying, "qui lui fait naturellement patte de velours, Saburov perd la tête. Cet homme intelligent tombe sous le charme de son ancien collègue Prussien et avale toutes les énormités que veut lui faire croire ce tigre de Bismarck".

charged to come to an arrangement with me on that subject.

In the interval I wrote to Radowitz asking him to inform Prince Bismarck that my nomination to Berlin made my visit to Varzin unnecessary.

Note from M. de Giers.

23 December, 1879.

Thanks for communicating the letter from Radowitz which is indeed of good augury, and which will doubtless encourage you to touch upon the question of the Straits in your negotiations. The more I think about it, the more I become hopeful that you will succeed in carrying it through.

I left for Berlin in the beginning of January, 1880.

NOTE.

A reference to the text of the documents constituting the Austro-Hungarian-German Alliance of 1879 as given in Prof. A. F. Pribram's standard work, *Die politischen Geheimverträge Österreich-Ungarns*,[1] shows that they took the form of (I) a Protocol between the Austro-Hungarian and German Governments describing the preliminary steps towards an Alliance, dated at Vienna, 24 September, 1879; (II) a Joint Memorandum signed by the Austro-Hungarian and the German Plenipotentiaries outlining the purposes of the Alliance, dated at Vienna,

[1] Cf. English edition by Prof. A. C. Coolidge, Harvard University, *The Secret Treaties of Austria-Hungary 1879–1914*, I, 18–35.

24 September, 1879; and (III) The Treaty of Alliance between Austria-Hungary and Germany of date 7 October, 1879.

Now, in *Die grosse Politik der europäischen Kabinette 1871–1914*, III, 126, there is quoted a letter of date 4 November, 1879, from the Emperor William I to the Tsar Alexander II, in which the former states how on the basis of their long-standing friendship he feels it his duty to send him a copy of a Memorandum embodying the results of conversations between Prince Bismarck and Count Andrassy. To judge from the explanations given in the letter, this must have corresponded to the document that Bismarck read to Saburov, while it is certain from the character of the later part of the letter, and even more so from the Tsar's reply in acknowledgment (*op. cit.* III, 132), that the Memorandum could not have contained the Articles of the Treaty directed especially against Russia.

Further, in Bismarck's Autobiography he deliberately makes the following statement with reference to this Treaty: "The Emperor's chivalrous temper demanded that the Czar of Russia should be confidentially informed that in the event of his attacking either of the two neighbour-powers he would find himself opposed by both, in order that Czar Alexander might not make the mistake of supposing that he could attack Austria alone. I deemed this solicitude groundless inasmuch as the cabinet of St Petersburg must by our answer to the questions sent us from Livadia have already learned that we were not going to let Austria fall, and so our Treaty with

Austria had not created a new situation, but only legalised that which existed ".[1] It is not easy, however, to believe that Alexander II would have sent a trusted Ambassador on a special mission of this nature if he had known the exact details of the engagement entered into by Germany and Austria against him. Saburov certainly knew nothing of the terms of the Alliance, whatever he may have suspected. Some confirmation of these conclusions may be gathered from Eduard von Wertheimer's *Life of Count Julius Andrassy*.[2] Andrassy is quoted as saying that he

[1] *Bismarck, the Man and the Statesman*, trans. A. J. Butler, II, 268–269. The reference in the original *Gedanken und Erinnerungen* is II, 248. He refers twice to the "ritterliche Gefühle" of William I, but is naturally silent about his own sharp practice.

[2] Cf. *op. cit.* III, 291–310. The following are some of the more significant passages. Reference is made (p. 291) to the unwillingness of the Emperor William I to sanction the Austro-German Treaty of 1879 unless he could inform the Tsar Alexander II about the matter. The narrative continues: "Ein solcher Vorgang schien ihm ein nötiges Zeichen seines freundschaftlichen Entgegenkommens für die Erklärungen, die eben Saburov in Berlin abgegeben hatte. Dieser russische Diplomat, der...zu den wärmsten Fürsprechern eines guten Verhältnisses Russlands zu Deutschland gehörte, war gerade...in besonderer Mission in Berlin eingetroffen. Im Auftrage Alexanders II. hatte er an Fürst Bismarck die Frage zu richten, ob dessen Gesinnungen für Russland noch immer die gleichen seien wie 1877, worauf der Kanzler entgegnete: Sollte er noch weiterhin Ratgeber Kaiser Wilhelms bleiben, so würde er seinen Einfluss in dem gleichen Sinne ausüben wie vor dem Congresse und während desselben, nie aber könnte er Bestrebungen unterstützen, durch die Oesterreich-Ungarn gefährdet würde.

"Nun erwiederte der Russe, er finde diese Haltung des Kanzlers ganz natürlich, um so mehr, als die russische Politik in Zukunft auf der Basis des Berliner Vertrages stets eine defensive bleiben werde....Bismarck war überhaupt nicht sicher, ob der russische Staatsmann aus eigenem Antriebe oder ermächtigt von

would rather renounce altogether the conclusion of the new agreement than intimate the terms to the Russian Court. The following was his suggestion of the procedure that should be adopted in order that

Alexander II. die Erklärungen über die defensive Richtung der russischen Politik erteilte—lehnte Saburov es doch ab, die von ihm gemachten Äusserungen zu Papier zu bringen und mit seiner Unterschrift zu versehen. Der Kanzler fühlte sich zum Zweifel an der Aufrichtigkeit Saburovs noch durch dessen weitere Eröffnungen angeregt (p. 293). In 3, 6 Stunden lang währenden Unterredungen hatte der Russe das Thema von Deutschlands Neutralität in künftigen Kriegen mit England, von Bündnissen, Teilung der Turkei und Eroberung Konstantinopels erörtert—lauter Dinge, die Bismarck mit Recht auf weitgehende russische Pläne schliessen liessen.

"Kaiser Wilhelm, hochgefreut über die, wie er meinte, durch den Mund Saburovs gegebenen Friedensversicherungen Alexanders, wollte wissen, welche Antwort Bismarck hierauf erteilte. ...Weniger erfreut von dieser Anfrage war Bismarck. Er sah darin nur das Bestreben, die Entscheidung hinauszuschieben. Jede Verschleppung jedoch dünkte ihn gefährlich....Sie, die Russen— rief er aus—werden gewiss bestrebt sein, Oesterreich-Ungarn Deutschland wegzufischen oder doch dieses zu irritieren. Bismarcks Geduld schien nun endlich zu Ende zu gehen.... Während Bismarck nochmals auf Vermeidung jeder Verschleppung drängte...kam aus Baden-Baden von Otto von Bülow die Nachricht, dass das 'Spiel' sofort gewonnen wäre, wenn dem Kaiser das Zugeständnis eines geeigneten Briefes an Alexander II. gemacht würde....

"Bereits am 2 October hatte der Kanzler den deutschen Botschafter in Wien beauftragt, Andrassy zu sondieren, ob er auf eine Beschränkung der Geheimhaltung eingehen würde, womit Bismarck dem Verlangen seines Herrschers entgegenkommen wollte (p. 294)....Vor Allem war Andrassy dagegen, dass in dem eventuellen Briefe Kaiser Wilhelms an Alexander von einem 'Vertrage' gesprochen werde. Die blosse Erwähnung davon müsste unbedingt die Folge haben, dass man in Petersburg die Mitteilung des ganzen Textes verlangen werde. Er machte daher einen 'Gegen-' oder, wie er sich verbessernd sagte, 'Parallelvorschlag' der im folgenden bestand...."

Russia should have no pretext for asking to see the exact terms of the Treaty. "The Kaiser Wilhelm, after the Treaty has been signed and approved, should communicate fully to the Tsar not the Treaty but the Memorandum drawn up and signed by the two Ministers of Germany and Austria-Hungary." In this Memorandum, he argued, the idea of an agreement was implicit. In a footnote Wertheimer quotes a statement from Marczali, who published the Memorandum in an article in the *Deutsche Revue* (1906), to the effect "that not this but a shorter Memorandum was sent to Petersburg", adding that so far as he is aware, Marczali's statement is inexact.[1] It is abundantly clear, however, that the vital significance of the Dual Alliance had not been disclosed to the Tsar.

Accordingly, it seems probable from Saburov's account of what took place, that Bismarck read aloud to him only the somewhat innocuous II as above, and that what Saburov suspected the existence of was not so much I as III, which was signed thirteen days later than I and II, and doubtless constituted a separate document. Saburov's eyesight had not deceived him.

[1] The footnote (*op. cit.* III, p. 294, n. 3) concludes: "Soviel mir bekannt, giebt es kein anderes als das von Marczali veröffentliche Memorandum. Diesem selbst wohnt aber nur eine das russische Kabinett informierende Bedeutung inne, dem man ja nicht die volle Wahrheit über das Bündniss sagen wollte"

CHAPTER IV

THE MILITARY QUESTION

A T the close of the war with Turkey our cavalry regiments had come to take up their former quarters again on the Austro-Prussian frontier. This disposition, made necessary as the result of improvements brought about in the rapid means of mobilisation on the part of our neighbours, had given long-standing offence to the Prussian Staff. Newspaper articles, more or less unofficial, had already stated this grievance on different occasions. Our Embassy at Berlin noted them as intended to stir up public sentiment, either in order to prepare it for an increase in military expenditure, or contrive a pretext for a quarrel with us, as Prussia had done with Austria in 1866.

From the beginning, I had to struggle against this difficulty. On my arrival at Berlin, Radowitz came to see me, and advised me of Bismarck's desire to have a "quite friendly and intimate" talk with me about it.

At the first word I stopped him, feeling the necessity of avoiding that dangerous ground. I said to him that if the Prince were doing me the honour of considering me as a useful intermediary between our two Governments, he must take into consideration my position and my reputation, and not demand more than these could provide. In the *political* sphere, I can indeed be of some service since the Emperor is

S M   7 pleased, on occasions, to pay gracious attention to my opinions. But as soon as questions belonging to the department of our military administration are introduced—questions which can never fail to arouse legitimate susceptibilities—the usefulness of my rôle ceases directly, for I shall find myself immediately between the hammer and the anvil. I have not concealed from Radowitz my surprise at seeing grievances which we do not understand cropping up incessantly. Satisfactory explanations about this matter have been made at Alexandrovo, and later between Prince Bismarck and myself in the month of September. We have had reason to think that the incident was settled. Not at all. The same subject comes up again in a letter from the Emperor William in the month of November. The reply from the Emperor Alexander appears to have allayed all anxieties: a telegram from the Emperor William bears witness to this. We think that the matter is finished. Some weeks later, despatches appear in the newspapers, and bring the business up once again. These telegrams are followed by contradictions in our official newspapers. We believe we have shown that there is neither concentration of troops nor military preparation of any sort on our part. And now, on my arrival, I am warned that I shall have to discuss the matter once again. What does this insistence mean?

Radowitz, whilst assuring me that I shall have no occasion to take the matter so very seriously, remarked that after the interview at Alexandrovo and my explanation to the Prince in the month of September, there had been a hope that we would do something to demonstrate our determination to resume the old intimacy and calm public opinion.

I then recalled to him the very words of Prince Bismarck on this subject. The Prince had particularly said to me: "These questions only become serious matters for me when suspicion enters into the relations between Governments. My security does not lie at all in any barracks near the frontier, but in the cabinet of the Emperor Alexander". Having left Berlin convinced that all suspicion was gone, and that the Prince no longer attached any importance to this or that transference of our troops, I had the right to communicate this impression to the Emperor and his War Minister. Moreover, to agree to change the disposition of our troops now would be confessing to a thing that does not exist: it would be admitting that we had knowingly threatened Germany during the last six years.

To this, Radowitz had no reply.

21 January, 1880.

My conversation with Radowitz brought about the result I had in view. Two days later I had my first interview with Prince Bismarck. He spoke with me about all sorts of things, but not a single word on the matter of the disposition of our troops. But I was not content with that. To leave a question in uncertainty is perhaps the worst way of settling it. I considered the occasion favourable to take the lead and provoke an explanation, so that later it might be impossible for him to return to this matter, and that we might not always have this sort of sword of Damocles hanging over our heads.

I said that I did not understand intimate relations, such as we seemed to desire, without absolute frankness. Also I did not hesitate to confess to him that I had difficulty in understanding why there had recently been fresh indications of a tendency to resuscitate the question of the disposition of our troops on the frontier.

Here is, almost word for word, the Prince's reply. "It is true that you have much cavalry on the frontier, and that our Staff are passing sleepless nights because of this. The first time that Moltke spoke to me about it was, I think, in 1875. I told him that in the history of our previous wars, our Staff often complained that the Russian army was too far from our frontiers and did not come up quickly enough. During the war in the East, the cavalry was withdrawn. We hoped that it would not come back again. But it has come back, and the Staff has again become uneasy. Moltke spoke about it to the King, and said to him that if a similar disposition had taken place on the Austrian or French frontier, it would have been necessary to mobilise a part of the army immediately. For the moment the matter was left at that."

After a moment's silence, which I took good care not to break, so as to establish undeniably that the Prince addressed no request to me, he passed to another topic.

They know now here that they would meet with a categorical refusal from us if they were to raise a question of that sort. I made this clearly felt, and no demand has been formulated. In this way the question of *dignity* is safeguarded.

In spite of this I am convinced that this matter will always remain a latent grievance, especially in military circles. The opinion that they hold upon questions of troop disposition is not the same as ours. Rightly or wrongly, they draw a distinction between a permanent system of defence, such as fortified towns, strategic railways, etc., and the system of Kriegsbereitschaft (preparedness for war) adopted by us. According to them, the one is a sword in the scabbard, the other a sword without the scabbard, and it is that which hurts the susceptibilities of the Prussian army.

It would be bold to affirm that there will never again be clouds in our relations with Germany. Now, it is in these disturbed periods that the German Staff will be able, one day, to gain their point, and, for love of the art of strategy, re-establish the symmetry by opposing six divisions of cavalry to ours, so neutralising our present advantages. Now, I ask myself, what shall we gain by it, and what will be the result of these concentrations of cavalry on both sides of the frontier?

It was only two months later that we got rid of this nightmare, thanks to the firmness of Count Miliutine, Minister of War, and to the conciliatory spirit of General Schweinitz, the German Ambassador at Petersburg, as will be seen from what follows.

In February I returned to Petersburg. During my absence from Berlin, a quite warlike article appeared in the *Norddeutsche Allgemeine Zeitung*, the official organ of the German Cabinet. A panic followed on the Exchange in Berlin and Petersburg. The article credited the Russian Government with a scheme to construct a new series of fortresses on our western frontier, with a view to making ready for a premeditated attack on Germany.

It is true that the following day the same newspaper published a second article disavowing the first. In any other country these contradictions would have been an indication of a certain disorder in governmental spheres; but in Prussia, under the vigorous régime of her Chancellor, such a supposition was inadmissible. One was obliged to think that Bismarck did not yet wish to bury the military question, and that it was necessary for his plans, whether to calm Austrian uneasiness on the score of the recent rapprochement to us, or in the hope of shaking the position of our War Minister whom he considered to be a dangerous man for Germany. This last supposition was confirmed by a rumour announcing a forthcoming mission with which General Schweinitz would be entrusted at Petersburg, on the subject of the disposition of our cavalry on the Prussian frontier.

On the other hand, I had the opportunity of making sure that our military experts were themselves divided upon this matter. In the opinion of Count Todleben,[1]

---

[1] Todleben, General Count Edward (1818–1884), famous military engineer, improvised the defence of Sevastopol in 1854 during the Crimean War, erecting fortifications under the fire of the Allies. His mastery in defensive fortification was equalled by his skill in siege operations. He conducted the siege of Plevna in 1877 after the earlier reverses of the Russian arms in trying to take the place by assault. He received the title of Count in 1879. Many Russian fortresses were built or reconstructed under his supervision. His character commanded esteem, and he occupied various administrative posts in the civil service.

this screen of cavalry, established at too great a distance from the rest of our troops, would be immediately forced to retreat in order not to be cut off. Nevertheless he realised the impossibility of any change whatever under foreign pressure.

Before my departure, I asked General Miliutine to furnish me with the necessary arguments in the event of a fresh explanation with the German Government. He sent me a detailed Memorandum on this thorny question.

At my first interview with Bismarck in the month of March, I confessed to him that for six weeks I had been grateful to him for not having taken the initiative in an explanation on a subject about which, I knew, he thought a good deal. That made it possible for me to point out the danger to Petersburg without being considered simply as the speaking-trumpet of Berlin. The question had been re-examined with particular attention, and I had no doubt that if the Emperor had seen the slightest serious cause for anxiety in our system of disposition of troops, His Majesty would not have hesitated to remedy it. Here I developed some of the arguments supplied in the Memorandum of Count Miliutine. Finally I asked the Prince if it really was so important a matter in his estimation.

"As a military matter", he replied, "I attach no importance to it. The danger to us is not great. The advantage which you would derive from it at the opening of a campaign is small. You will be able, in the first week, to invade a part of East Prussia, and to destroy such railway bridges as your cavalry will be able to reach in a twelve hours' march, such other bridges as it can strike in twenty-four hours' marching, etc. All these details are pointed out by our General Staff. But after our concentration this cavalry will probably need to fall back.[1]

"For me the question does not lie there. I consider it important rather as a symptom of the psychological attitude of which this particular regrouping of troops has been the result. Whatever one may say, cavalry regiments on the frontier have the appearance of a threat. The very men who conceived this disposition sounded our adversaries last summer at Paris on the subject of an alliance." (Here followed my explanations with reference to the Obrutchev incident which will be found later on.)

The Prince continued thereafter: "Your cavalry, I grant you, is no real danger to us; but those who put it there assuredly did not mean to give us a token of confidence. You come to say to us, 'Let us be friends and allies', and behind you stands your War Minister with a pistol levelled at us. I believe your words, which represent your Sovereign's mind; but the unpleasant sight of the pistol makes me hesitate".

In uttering these last words, the Prince, who never misses an opportunity to mingle humour with seriousness, seized a revolver which he always has on his table, and, while speaking, aimed it at me. I pointed out to him in the same tone that the chances between us were not equal, since his pistol was loaded, while that of General Miliutine was not!

After the two of us had laughed heartily, the Prince

[1] The comparison with the actual course of events in 1914 is striking.

went on: "You are mistaken if you think that I dream of securing the withdrawal of your cavalry. As the result of a negotiation, that withdrawal would no longer have any value in our eyes. *We* do not ask, *we* do not desire, that withdrawal. We would have liked that the Emperor had wished it himself. I have never given Schweinitz any instruction other than to avail himself of the Emperor's personal goodwill to ascertain whether His Majesty gets a clear idea of the moral bearing of this step, taken, I know, several years ago, but which none the less is, in our eyes, a tacit avowal that you admit the possibility of a conflict with us. Under the Emperor Nicholas you did not admit this possibility; so we were not uneasy, although you had then more troops in Poland than you have to-day, as General Miliutine says.

"But this is what has happened. Schweinitz first of all consulted a personage with whom he is in close relations, one of the most devoted servants of the Emperor, and whose opinions, invariably favourable to a good understanding with Germany, have always inspired us with complete confidence.[1] This personage said to him that he would encounter great difficulties, above all concerning the national amour-propre which could be roused when seeing your cavalry regiments withdrawn under the moral pressure of Germany. That certainly was not my object. Besides, this hint was sufficient for me. There would be no greater misfortune for us than to bring to light a disagreement between our way of looking at things and that of the Emperor, whose personal inclinations are

[1] The General Todleben. (Note in the original.)

our most serious guarantee for peace. I sent Schweinitz orders to refrain from all argument, and never
to return to that subject. As I said to you, the military
aspect of the question is of so little importance that
in order to satisfy the strategy of our General Staff,
it will be sufficient to send a brigade of infantry to
protect the places which it considers to be most
exposed in East Prussia. We shall send no cavalry,
for we look on cavalry as a means of attack. And
provided that this measure does not alarm you, it will
be sufficient, so far as we are concerned, to put an
end to the agitations which this question was beginning to arouse in Germany".

The whole of this conversation was of an entirely
private character. Instigated by myself, it was an
intimate talk carried out in an atmosphere of trust,
but in no way the official communication of a fore-
gone conclusion.

The Incident of General Obrutchev.

This incident in itself has lost all political importance, for Prince Bismarck is convinced that the
Emperor never dreamed of having the French Government sounded on the matter of an alliance. But
nevertheless, he thinks that sometimes things happen
in Russia which never come to the knowledge of the
Emperor.

Here are the fresh details given to me by the Prince
at our previous conversation.

He heard the news first from Prince Hohenlohe,[1]

---

[1] Hohenlohe-Schillingsfürst, Prince (1819–1901), German
statesman. After a distinguished career at home, in which as head

to whom M. Waddington[1] appeared to have said in
confidence that General Obrutchev,[2] our Chief of
Staff, had sounded him on the matter of an alliance;
to which Waddington replied to him that this would
not be acceptable to France who wants peace, and
who, moreover, was not militarily prepared.

The same version was transmitted to him after-
wards through "the official channel of the French
Government". That could then only be through
Count Saint-Vallier, my colleague at Berlin.

Then came a circumstantial report from the German military agent in Paris. Bismarck was at Varzin,
and the Emperor William intercepted this report,
being afraid that his Chancellor would make a serious
matter of it. Bismarck was the last to hear of it. In
this report was quoted the testimony of an Italian
general who was present at the French manœuvres.

of the Bavarian Government, he played a part second only to that
of Bismarck in bringing about an effective union of the South
German States with the North German Confederation, he was
appointed Ambassador in Paris, 1873, where he remained for
seven years. He attended the Congress of Berlin as third German
representative. He acted as temporary head of the Foreign Office
in Berlin on the death of von Bülow in 1880, and succeeded
Caprivi as Chancellor in 1894. He resigned on 17 October, 1900.

[1] Waddington, W. H. (1826–1894), French diplomat, travelled
extensively in Asia Minor. Was elected to the National Assembly
in 1871 and made Minister of Public Instruction in 1873, and again
from 1876 to 1877. In the latter year he became Minister for
Foreign Affairs in the Government of Jules Simon, and was principal French Plenipotentiary at the Congress of Berlin, 1878. In
February, 1879, he became Premier but resigned in December.
He was appointed French Ambassador in London in 1883, and
held the post for a decade.

[2] From 1878 Adjutant-general, and from 1881 Chief of the
Russian Military Staff.

They reported, further, that General Obrutchev had been in correspondence with the French military men who were best known to be favourable to an alliance with Russia, in particular General Galliffet[1] and Colonel Gaillard.

Finally, the recent reports of the German Embassy in Paris mention the fact that several political personages blame the Waddington Cabinet for having declined the confidential overtures made by the Russian Government the previous summer.

That is the whole legend. It is so strongly rooted that all possible denials will, at most, only succeed in convincing the interested parties that our Emperor knew nothing at all about it. This result, moreover, has been obtained. Bismarck, seeking to reconcile his information, which he considers positive, with my not less categorical denials, remains under the impression that General Obrutchev had perhaps wished to report to Petersburg some useful data on the state of French opinion.

According to him, the danger is nevertheless great for Germany, for if the French Government showed itself disposed towards this alliance, and the General had been able to communicate this to Petersburg at the moment of greatest tension in our relations, who knows what turn events would have taken then?

I have been unable to refrain from defending with a certain animation the veracity of one of our most distinguished generals, whose integrity is above all

[1] Galliffet, General the Marquis de (1830–1909). After a distinguished military career, he became Minister of War in M. Waldeck-Rousseau's Cabinet (June, 1899–May, 1900).

suspicion. Nevertheless, however legitimate the desire of General Obrutchev to confound the inventors of the gossip by a question addressed directly to M. Waddington, it would have no practical result. The latter will always find a way of softening the expressions which he used to the point of rendering the version absolutely harmless, whilst the evil has already been done. It will be difficult to pin him to his words.

I hope that we have now heard the last of this unpleasant incident.

Bismarck told me that he had conveyed to Schweinitz at the time the details with which he had just made me acquainted.

CHAPTER V

THE GREAT AFFAIR

January, 1880.

THE first week after my arrival at Berlin was taken up in necessary audiences with the Emperor, Empress and the members of the Imperial family. Prince Bismarck, who arrived some days after me, from Varzin, received me for the first time on 19 January. We adjourned conversation on serious matters till the following day. This conference was followed by two others, on 24 and 26 January. The following is the detailed account:

Conference of 20 January, 1880.

I asked the Prince if he had consulted the Emperor on the projected agreement that we had outlined in the previous September.

He had not done so. To begin with, he had not seen the King again since that time, and having learned of my approaching arrival in Berlin, he had wished to await anything new that I would have to tell him on this subject.

In the second place, he had reflected on the advantages and the inconveniences of an arrangement between two parties. A mutual engagement to preserve one's self from coalitions, necessarily supposes a promise on the part of Germany to attack Austria in certain eventualities. But that is a very dangerous secret to have in one's possession! The slightest indiscretion will produce an incalculable impression in Vienna, and will bring about the revival of their mistrust and fear. Austria will instinctively begin anew to seek western alliances, and the results so laboriously secured by Germany will be lost.

"Believe me," he said, "it is not in your interest to try and embroil Austria and Germany. You too often lose sight of the importance of being one of *three* on the European chess-board. That is the invariable objective of all the Cabinets, and mine above all. Nobody wishes to be in a minority. All politics reduces itself to this formula: to try to be one of three, so long as the world is governed by the unstable equilibrium of five Great Powers. That also is the true preservative against coalitions. There was a time when Prince Gortchakov entertained the illusion of a close Entente with England. I wished then to enter it as a third, and Austria would not have been necessary to me if that combination had been achieved. But I soon realised that it was a chimera. There is still too much antagonism between you in the East; you will need a great 'Koniggrätz' one day in order to settle this great Asiatic dispute. Further, since that time, my favourite idea has been the Triple Entente with Austria. The first attempt miscarried, and I had to begin this work again by making the Entente between two of the parties stronger, in order to return afterwards to the Triple Entente with you, if you are sincerely disposed towards it."

After listening attentively, I said to the Prince that if he recollected clearly our conversations in the month of September, there was nothing in our ideas that was hostile to Austria. To such a degree was this true that she would herself have been able to subscribe to all that was said at that time. I had not come to-day, either, to propose any aggressive combination to him. It is a question of a purely defensive agreement. Our starting-point is the very terms of the Memorandum signed at Vienna by the two Chancellors of Germany and of Austria! This Memorandum expresses the intention to facilitate the pacific solution of all the difficulties passed down to us by the Congress of Berlin. Now, amongst these there is one of the first importance. It is the question of the Straits.

The Prince interrupted me: "If there is no question of infringing existing Treaties, let us speak about it".

I said to him that we only insisted on an equitable interpretation of the Treaties. I gave him the history of it. I explained to him, how, in 1841, we surrendered our exclusive advantages, stipulated in the Treaty of Unkiar-Skelessi,[1] in order to acquiesce in the principle that the question of the Straits was *a European interest*; how, later, England shook the principle of the closing, first by insisting, in 1871, on the admission of a grave exception to that rule, and then in challenging, by her declaration at the Congress of

[1] Unkiar-Skelessi, Treaty of (8 June, 1833). In return for assisting the Sultan of Turkey against the rebel Mehemet Ali, Nicholas I received very advantageous recognition and concessions. Under this Treaty Turkey undertook to close the Straits against the navy of any Power with which Russia might be at war, with full protection guaranteed by Russia. The Black Sea, Constantinople, and the Dardanelles thus came directly under Russian control for the time being.

Berlin, the mutually obligatory character of that stipulation; finally by trying to put her new doctrine in practice by the threatening attitude ultimately adopted by her Ambassador at Constantinople. This last incident showed more than anything how easy it would be for an English squadron to force the entrance to the Straits, so putting in question the security of our position in the Black Sea. In conclusion, I put the following question to the Prince:

"Granted the existing Treaties, do you think that in the event of war between England and Russia, Turkey, as a neutral Power, would have the right to allow an English fleet to enter the Black Sea?"

After having reflected for a moment, "Certainly not," said he to me; "I will even go further. Without prejudging the opinion of our experts, I will say that even if these Treaties were not in existence, Turkey would have no right to do so. According to international law, territorial waters extend to cannon range. But in the Straits there is not even place for a cannon range. They are accordingly territorial waters, and Turkey, in allowing an English fleet to enter, would in this way be lending a part of her domains to the operations of one of the belligerents, which would be a violation of neutrality, according to all the principles adopted. But why did you not clear up that question at the Congress of Berlin?"

It was difficult for me to reply, for I had put the same question to myself more than once. However, I found a plausible answer: "Apparently the political atmosphere of the Congress was too unfavourable to us to risk a discussion".

"You are mistaken," he replied. "I remember perfectly hearing several plenipotentiaries express ideas favourable to your thesis, and even wonder at seeing you defending the interests of your protégés so warmly, whilst forgetting your own."

I brought the Prince back to the question. I said to him that the aggressive attitude of England was making it a duty for us to be on our guard, and envisage, as a possible eventuality, a conflict with her, without Turkey being this time concerned in it. A question may arise about Batum or Central Asia or Persia. But in these instances the Treaties relative to the closing of the Straits take on great importance for us. We must know if Turkey, if Europe, will allow the violation of these Treaties! We must know if England, after having made us renounce the exclusive advantages of the Convention of Unkiar-Skelessi, in the name of *European* interests, will challenge this same European interest on the day when her *particular* interest will inspire her with the desire to enter the Black Sea! The feebleness of Turkey gives us no longer any protection. That is why we are ready to come to an understanding with those who, for purposes of defence, would in their turn have need of us.

I availed myself of this argumentation, for as it was a matter of introducing a new question without giving the impression of demanding something over and above what I had formulated at the time of my previous mission, it was best to put this question at once in the foreground in such a way as to impress my interlocutor strongly. I think I succeeded in this; at least the Prince acknowledged as a general proposition that our cause was legitimate. But he came back afresh to the inconveniences of an arrangement between two, much preferring a Triple Entente, whenever that Entente should become possible. I did not gainsay him on this point in order to see whether by this detour we might not find a way of arriving at our object, and bring the Chancellor out of that constraint which I had visibly remarked in all his bearing.

Evidently afraid of having gone too far, he said to me: "Moreover, I very much doubt whether a Triple Entente would succeed with Haymerlé on these bases. I liked Andrassy better. Haymerlé is a skittish horse. Every time you make a proposal to him he asks himself, 'Where is the trap?' Lately I advised him to reply to the provocations of the Italian irredentists by vigorous measures. He did nothing, and I am convinced that he suspects me of having wished to bring about a war between Austria and Italy".

Seeing that the Prince was resolved to evade a serious conversation, I determined to get to the bottom of the matter and make one last attempt.

What struck me above everything was the contrast between his present behaviour and the frankness of his ways in the month of September, when I arrived from Livadia. At that time Prince Gortchakov was on leave, and in public people spoke of his retiring. A month ago he had returned and resumed the direction of the Ministry. This thought was as a flash of light to me.

"After all," I resumed with indifference, "I am quite content to see an adjournment of serious discussions, for I also have my doubts about final success.

At Vienna there is a skittish Minister, at Petersburg we have a Chancellor whose great age no longer permits him to display his former activity in the direction of such delicate negotiations in all their details."

I had not finished my sentence when I saw a complete transformation at work in the Prince's physiognomy. From that moment he became cordial and communicative.

"Wir werden ein Jahr zusammen leben", he said to me. "We have had the same idea. Well, I did not wish to be the first to express it, so that no one could accuse me afresh of wishing to overthrow your Chancellor. That God may grant him life and health, is a wish I share with all his admirers. But if a proposal is made to me in which I have to play high, I must consider above all how to handle the matter well, so that no injury may result from it for my country. But, whether rightly or wrongly, I do not think that Prince Gortchakov is a sincere friend of Germany. I do not want to go back to the affair of 1875 when he wished to humiliate us. I cannot speak to you either, without reserve, about the military conventions, because I do not know whether you are in the secret."

I answered in the affirmative.

"Well," he resumed, "these conventions were to be used as prelude to a Treaty of Alliance between the three Courts. My Sovereign relied on this. The Emperor of Austria and Andrassy were quite willing, and had occasion to hope that the Emperor Alexander would consent to it. It is Prince Gortchakov who was responsible for the failure. Andrassy assured me that he knew this for certain. Think what a position you

would have had during the war in the East if you had
had a Treaty of Alliance in due form with Austria
and us! It is from that period that the distrust of
Prince Gortchakov in Vienna also dates. You had
a very strong Russian party there. The Archduke
Albert,[1] who had always urged the Emperor Francis-
Joseph to a Russian alliance in preference to one with
Prussia, came last year and told the Emperor that he
had changed his mind since he had learned of the
way in which the Russian Government conducted its
negotiations with Austria."

Here I remarked to the Prince: "Audi et alteram
partem".

He continued: "Do not feel offended at what I tell
you. We are talking now as friend with friend. So
I do expect that all that I have told you in confidence
will remain between ourselves. Well, rightly or
wrongly, they believe in Vienna that Prince Gortchakov wished to finesse, to beguile Austria with arrangements full of loopholes, and to carry off the prize by
the fait accompli of the Treaty of San Stefano. With
all these precedents, and distrustful as I have become,
judge for yourself whether I shall be able to sleep
quietly after having placed a compromising secret in
the hands of Prince Gortchakov. But, on the other
hand, I am anxious that the Emperor should have no
doubt of my desire to establish firm bonds between
our two countries. You will always find me so dis-

---

[1] Albert, Frederick Rudolf, Archduke of Austria (1817–1895),
followed a military career. As Field-Marshal he commanded the
army at Custozza (1866). He took a leading part in the reorganisation of the Austrian army, and wrote on military matters.

posed, and as a proof, I am quite ready to discuss
with you forthwith the bases of an accord, since I
know that you have the confidence of the Emperor.
The ground will thus be prepared for the day when
we shall be able to resume negotiations officially.
I persist in giving the preference to a triple agreement. I do not see why Austria should refuse it, but if
she refuses, we shall have the right to ask ourselves
whether her friendship is as sincere as I thought. In
any case, there will always be time to come back to
a Dual Entente with you".

As it was getting late, we put off the continuation
of this interesting conversation to another day. I left
the Chancellor with an apology for having wearied
him so long.

"On the contrary," he replied, "our talks become
intensely interesting."

Conference of 24 January, 1880.

In devoting himself to an analysis of the points on
which an entente might be established, Prince Bismarck returned anew to the advantages of a *triple*
arrangement. The objectives of Russia are the following: She desires to protect herself against coalitions.
She wishes also to strengthen the principle of the
closing of the Straits. Now both objects will be more
surely attained as one of three rather than one of two.
So far as *coalitions* are concerned, Germany alone will
be able to do as follows: She will be able to undertake
in writing to prevent France from taking sides. But
she will not be able to make an engagement in similar
form against Austria, not that she would tolerate an

attack on Russia by Austria, but because a stipulation *in writing* against Austria would make that country once again distrustful of Germany and throw her again into the arms of the Western Powers. Should it so happen, it is more than probable that Germany would have sufficient influence at Vienna to hold Austria back, just as we save from suicide an individual whose existence is necessary to us. Thus Russia will have the moral certainty of being sheltered from coalitions in mutually securing herself with Germany against France, without whom no coalition is possible. Italy is of no account as a Great Power. There are countries extinct like certain heavenly bodies, which do not return to life a second time. To-day Italy is nearly a republic, and her unity will not hold out against it.

So, for a treaty between two, Germany will only be able to bind herself against France. That will be sufficient to provide the moral certainty that a coalition will no longer be possible, but the mathematical certainty will only be secured by attracting Austria into this system. Forming a permanent coalition ourselves, we shall have no fear of one against us.

It is the same with the closing of the Straits. What will Germany be able to do by herself to prevent the violation of them? She can protest, write notes, but her army will not be able to swim to London, nor pass over the body of Austria to go to fight in the Straits. The question changes in aspect if one can interest Austria in it. She is in a better position to threaten Turkey, and compel her, in concert with Russia, to fulfil her obligations of neutrality. By means of a Triple Treaty, a real and effective guarantee will be secured.

I remarked to the Prince that as the negotiation of a Triple Treaty had not been contemplated in my instructions, I would need to submit these ideas in the first instance to the Emperor. The difficulty consists, in my opinion, in the lack of enthusiasm felt both at St Petersburg and Vienna for entering into too close relationships. This is due to certain historical memories. A certain sympathetic atmosphere is lacking in both of us.

Prince Bismarck understands this objection. In his opinion Russia is justified in not forgetting the perfidious and ungrateful Austria of 1854 so soon. It is she who was the first to destroy the system of the Emperor Nicholas, to which Europe was indebted for thirty years of peace. But everything has changed at Vienna since that period. Perfidy is no longer there; fear alone has remained.

"The Emperor Francis-Joseph himself", he added, "said to me with profound sadness, 'They accuse me of being eager for new conquests. How could I dream of that with the bad luck that has pursued me all my life? I have been beaten by the French, beaten by the Prussians; even by the Italians, for the battle of Custozza was really lost, and if the Italians retired, it was in obedience to an order telegraphed from Paris. I have long since given up war. I have no luck'."

I said to the Prince that even if the Emperor were to accept the new combination, it could only be brought to a happy conclusion by the Prince himself taking it in hand.

"That is the way I understand it," he replied, "and moreover there is some reasonable chance of success. Austria, because of her commerce on the Danube, has an interest in preventing hostilities in the Black Sea. And then she gains so much in being reassured with regard to you, and if the choice is between a treaty of alliance and the prospect of bloody conflicts, it is the first duty of Governments to close their ears to the antipathies of public opinion, and to save their peoples from their own impulses."

Finally we agreed to put something down in writing before my departure, in order to state our ideas precisely and avoid misunderstandings.

Conference of 26 January, 1880.

I showed Prince Bismarck a sketch[1] giving a résumé of the conclusions of our last conversation. He studied it attentively and appeared very much satisfied with it. He said to me: "Before proceeding to observations of detail, let us agree as to the procedure. To begin with, this is not as yet an official negotiation. I shall not speak about it yet to the King. Formerly he kept secrets well, but at eighty-three this is not the case. On your side, I ask you to represent to the Emperor the importance that I attach to absolute secrecy. There are some very indiscreet persons in Petersburg. In order to persuade Austria, it is necessary that she does not distrust me, and that I should be the first to speak to her about the matter".

He then passed to an analysis of the document.

---

[1] The text of this sketch with M. Saburov's covering letter is given in D.G.P. III, 146, 147. Vide infra, pp. 273–275.

He agrees entirely with the first part which indicates the objects to be attained. He would like, however, to add to it what he considers an indispensable precaution against the possibility of disagreement within the Alliance, by inserting the following words: "If a dispute or grievance should arise between two of the signatory Powers, this dispute would be referred to the mediation of the third, and settled by a triple agreement".

Passing to the articles, he would not have set in the forefront the one relating to the Straits. That would be a more tactful way of dealing with Austria.

With regard to the Straits, the position would be stronger if it were founded on an incontestable principle of International Law rather than on an interpretation of existing Treaties. It would be necessary to modify the wording of that article in this sense.

In the witty definition of the Chancellor, the object of this Treaty will be to protect the "flabby parts" of the three Empires.

Towards the end of the conversation he returned to the necessity for conducting these negotiations with extreme prudence. "Nobody", he said, "will have occasion to rejoice over an intimate rapprochement between us; neither England, who only dreams of isolating you, nor France naturally, nor even Austria up to a certain point. Austria would like to have a monopoly of alliance with Germany, but she would also like to preserve her own freedom of action. Even at the present time she probably does not tell us all that she thinks. That certainly cannot suit us, and I shall not be sorry to put her sincerity once more to the test by this proposal of an accord between three. But an untimely indiscretion can spoil everything. All the hostile elements in Europe will exert themselves to wreck this project."

I returned to Petersburg on 2 February to submit my report to the Emperor by word of mouth. My statement was the subject of several secret deliberations with His Majesty between Count Miliutine, M. de Giers and myself, unknown to Prince Gortchakov. My project underwent several modifications. I was also authorised to agree to the admission of Austria to the projected Entente.

On my arrival at St Petersburg, I set forth my personal point of view in the following Memorandum:

Conclusions.

Our interests in the East are of a double character: some clash with England, the others with Austria.

The security of our military and political position in the Black Sea comes under the first category.

The emancipation and political organisation of the kindred races in the Balkan Peninsula come under the second.

The latter was the object of our efforts in the last campaign. Immense progress has been made in this direction. We can now settle down with pride and wait a while.

The task would be too heavy indeed if Russia, pursuing two aims at one and the same time, came into collision with a reunited England and Austria.

The moment seems favourable to separate these two adversaries. The present situation in Europe even makes it a duty for us. We know that hostility to Austria will involve us in a probable conflict with Germany. Accordingly the most elementary prudence counsels us to halt on the road which had the last war as its consequence, and devote our attention to the other aspect of the Eastern question,—the one which touches the interests and security of the Empire more directly. In other words, let us be less Slav, and more Russian.

The present inclinations of the German Cabinet favour this in a remarkable manner. Prince Bismarck anticipates these ideas. It suits him infinitely better to see Russia orientate her policy in a direction which leaves the interests of Austria alone. He voluntarily agrees to make things easy for us, in consenting to protect, with his new ally, the vulnerable point where England can strike us. Agreements concluded on these bases would complete our plan of defence, and make an attack from this side very difficult, if not impossible, for England.

So it would be desirable, in my humble judgment, to agree to the counter-project of Prince Bismarck, and in place of an arrangement between two parties, to give the preference to the conclusion of a treaty between three, whilst assigning to the German Chancellor the responsibility of making Austria participate in it.

We must choose one of two alternatives; either Austria will accept, and then our interests in the Straits, as Prince Bismarck has rightly explained, will have secured a more efficacious safeguard than that from an Entente between us and Germany.

Or Austria will refuse. There will likely result from that a coolness in her relations with Germany; the seed of mistrust will have been sown, and Germany, by a natural reaction of things, will once more remove the principal centre of her political affinities from Vienna to St Petersburg.

In either case, we shall have gained.

May I be allowed to finish these lines with a general consideration.

All the impressions that I have received at Berlin only confirm my conviction on the matter of the necessity of persevering in the way of an understanding with Germany, in conformity with the decision taken by the Emperor. This conviction is based on the following reflection:

The real source of the distrust which has made its appearance in Germany with respect to us lies in the fact of her geographical position between two great military States, of which one is animated by a desire for revenge, whilst the intentions of the other remain unknown.

Observing anxiously the march of our affairs, the Germans think they see, in the manifestations of the daily press and even in our Government circles, currents of opinion surging round the throne in a struggle for supremacy. It is of the highest importance for them to know which of these currents will finally prevail in a lasting manner in the guidance of our foreign policy.

Therefore—and I do not hesitate to say it—the most conclusive argument which I have employed when talking with Prince Bismarck has been drawn from the uneasiness inspired in him by the possibility of a rapprochement between France and ourselves, and from the prospect of bringing to an end this nightmare which haunts him, at the price of the loyal co-operation that Germany would afford us for the safeguarding of our national interests.

I have reason to believe that the Prince has grasped the whole import of this idea, and that he sincerely sticks to it, for he sees in it a serious pledge for the security of Germany herself!

The situation would entirely change in aspect to-day if we were to go back upon our steps. The mistrust, of which we already had a foretaste last summer, would arise again on both sides with redoubled intensity. It will become embittered by questions of military susceptibilities which, in their turn, will not be slow to translate themselves into defensive measures and concentrations of troops on both sides of the frontier.

Politically, Germany is at this moment in such a situation that she could become, should it so happen, the centre of a formidable coalition directed against us. The elements in this coalition are clearly indicated. It will be formed before

France, torn by factions, has had time to clear up her ideas and shake off the English alliance, to which she is fettered.

In this respect it would be impossible to deceive one's self. The first act of that coalition will be the creation of an intermediary State formed out of the fragments of the ancient Poland which they would succeed in snatching from us. For, whatever be the past political declarations of Prince Bismarck on the subject of the Poles, they were only real when they formed part of a system of alliance with us. They would change entirely in the event of conflict. The re-establishment of a Poland, armed with age-long hatred, would then become for Germany a barrier necessary for her future security.

Such is the general effect of my impressions. I dare to submit them to the Imperial Government with the frankness which the Emperor has deigned to allow me.

CHAPTER VI

CHANGE OF MINISTRY IN ENGLAND

March–August, 1880.

HAVING returned to Berlin in the first days of March, I intimated to Prince Bismarck the definite assent of my Government to the conclusion of a Triple Entente with Austria, and asked him what method he was going to adopt in handling the matter.

During my absence, he had done two things. He had spoken to the Emperor William, but without going into particulars. He limited himself to saying that he considered it desirable to reconstitute the Triple Entente on solid bases, and that the instructions with which I was provided were conceived in the same spirit. The Emperor William gave his consent the more readily that he had offered much opposition the previous year before consenting to the separate Entente with Austria, negotiated at Vienna.

Then the Prince charged Reuss[1] to sound Baron Haymerlé, but without taking any step, even confidentially. Haymerlé received these overtures with very little alacrity. He still shares, to a high degree,

[1] Reuss, Prince Henry VII, German statesman and cavalry general, b. 1825. Appointed German Ambassador at St Petersburg 1871. Married 6 February, 1876, Princess Marie, daughter of the Grand-Duke Karl Alexander of Saxe-Weimar. In 1877 he was appointed Ambassador in Constantinople, and sent to Vienna in July, 1878, in the same capacity. He left the diplomatic service in 1894.

the old Austrian prejudices against us. Everywhere, in the East, he sees tendencies towards a Panslavist policy. In Serbia, in Bulgaria, even in Rumania, he perceives no change in the attitude of our agents. In Serbia he incessantly comes up against their opposition, whether the matter in question be a railway or a treaty of commerce. In Bulgaria, the Russian Government recalls M. Davydof, the only friend whom Prince Alexander[1] has in the country, and the Prince is left to the mercy of officials or improvised politicians who push him into adventures, and receive their instructions from other sources than that of the Ministry of Foreign Affairs. The conspiracies of the Moscow Panslavists and of certain military men who went in former times to seek their fortune in Serbia, thus recommence there under another form. In short, in Prince Bismarck's expression, Haymerlé "did not hand out the change" to the overtures of Prince Reuss.

I said to the Prince that all this was very discouraging, and that at St Petersburg keen disappointment would be felt at it, after the so favourable impressions that I had brought back from Berlin a month before....

Berlin, 29 March, 1880.

The event of the day is the unexpected result of the elections in England.

It would be difficult to exaggerate the great im-

---

[1] Alexander of Battenberg (1857–1893), first Prince of Bulgaria. The union of Eastern Roumelia with Bulgaria followed on the revolution of Philippopolis (18 Sept. 1885). After an exciting reign, he resigned his throne, and left Bulgaria on 8 September, 1886.

portance of this event from the point of view of our situation with regard to Germany and Austria.

The aggressive policy of the Tory Cabinet, and the pressing need which we experienced of securing ourselves against the possible effects of its hostility, all created for us a position of inferiority in the task which we were pursuing. To-day the rôles are changed. It is in Germany and Austria that the advent of a Whig Ministry inspires apprehensions. The name of Gladstone serves as a bugbear to them. Bismarck sees him already stirring up revolution in all the corners of Europe, and inaugurating for a second time the policy of Canning in encouraging the republican party in Italy, and the unbounded ambitions of the Greeks with respect to Constantinople.

Observing attentively the effects which the English elections were bound to bring out in Berlin, I knew better than to make haste in resuming my conversations with the Prince, preferring to wait till he took the initiative.

Yesterday he asked me to go to him.

In this interview he spontaneously broached the great affair. Here is how he began. "I was in haste", he said, "to let you know the impressions which the English elections have made upon me. There is no doubt that the republican spirit is astir in every part of Europe. In Italy, since the death of Victor-Emmanuel, there remains to their King only his title. France goes from bad to worse; that people imagine every day a régime more republican than that of the day before. And now, all the republican parties have their eyes turned towards England in the hope of

finding the encouragement there that the name of
Gladstone promises them. I have said all this to the
King, and I added that there was a good side to the
matter; and that is that I shall now have the means
of setting Haymerlé's Austria in motion, and of re-
moving the obstacle which stood in the way of the
fulfilment of our programme. For Austria herself is
not so safe as she supposes. It would be the height
of imprudence for her to ignore the coming struggle
between the monarchical and the republican principles. And if the three Emperors are slow to unite
in view of this common danger, it is the most exposed
of the three that will be the first to suffer from it."

Seeing that the Prince, with his political tact, had
completely grasped the importance of the new situation, and that his desire to realise our project had gained
in intensity, I did not hesitate to make him understand
all the interest which he had to speed matters up.
I told him that it was above all necessary to make
Vienna feel the necessity of seizing the opportunity
before it had gone; for I could not be responsible for
the criticisms which the advent of the new English
Ministry might arouse in St Petersburg in the long
run. It may be that Gladstone is the enemy of Austria, but he is not our enemy! And if the conclusion
of the Triple Entente happened to encounter obstacles,
it would perhaps be too late to return to it when we
shall have found a "modus vivendi" with England
which is agreeable to us. So I strongly advised the
Prince to make haste if we wanted to avail ourselves
of Russia's present attitude.

"That is what I have already done", he replied to

me. "Reuss was here on leave, and I have just hurried up his return to Vienna. He set off again the day before yesterday."

For my own part, in my friendly correspondence with M. de Giers, I expressed the fear that the prospect of an entente with England would plunge us in new illusions. Whatever the improvement in our relations with England, we shall always have near us a powerful Germany; we shall always have the difficulty of struggling against the two currents which manifest themselves only too clearly in the public opinion of the New Russia and the New Prussia, against that mutual antipathy arising from the too rapid growth of our neighbours. That is a situation which will always carry the risk of leading to catastrophes if the Governments remain in tow to the popular impulse, instead of restraining and guiding it. Formerly we had no need of written treaties with Prussia; the alliance was in the situation; signatures were needless. To-day it is different. That is why I should have liked us to preserve the serious character of the work undertaken at Berlin; not to consider these pourparlers as solely intended to beguile our neighbours while we get over the critical period of our present isolation. I should understand this sort of calculation, if Bismarck were as old as our Chancellor; but he has still a good ten years of activity, and he will have time to do us plenty of harm. The critical period will then be longer than is supposed. As long as he is there, our best security is to continue to be sincerely willing for an entente with him. So, imbued as I am with the gravity of the moment, I await with the most lively impatience the instructions which will be given to me....

Berlin, 9 April, 1880.

Prince Bismarck communicated to me the following news which reached him from Vienna.

Haymerlé has been very speedily reassured with reference to the new English Cabinet. Lord Granville hastened to transmit to Vienna assurances intended to efface the impression caused by Gladstone's speeches. In return, the impressions produced in high circles by the victory of the Whigs continue in all their force. Prince Reuss gives an account of a conversation which he had with the Archduke Albert. The latter, after severing his connection with the Russian party last year, has entirely returned to-day to his old convictions.

Prince Bismarck has sent word to Haymerlé that he was much surprised to see him so quickly reassured. He forgets that Russia, no longer having England as an adversary, will be freer in her movements in the East, and may quite well take no account of Austrian interests, if the latter does nothing to reassure her regarding her own interests. Russia, in reality, has very legitimate anxiety. She fears the violation of the Straits by England. The attitude of Mr Layard,[1] the British Ambassador at Constanti-

---

[1] Layard, Right Hon. Sir Austen Henry, G.C.B., entered the diplomatic service in 1847. His career oscillated between Parliament and diplomacy. He acted as Under-Secretary of State for Foreign Affairs in 1852 and 1861, and was appointed Minister

nople, showed last summer that the Treaties no longer
afford that security in the Black Sea which Russia
had a right to expect from them. In their clearly
understood interest, Germany and Austria ought to
re-assure Russia on this matter, for the Powers which
do not feel re-assured with regard to their own
interests generally become dangerous neighbours.

Haymerlé showed himself very timid in broaching
the question of the Straits. He made the objection
that it constituted an English interest of very great
importance; that it would be a case of following a
course entirely opposed to that of England, and of
foregoing for ever an alliance with that Power.

The Prince had the reply sent to Haymerlé that
this reasoning was ill-timed. In the time of Lord
Beaconsfield there was a choice between an English
alliance and a Russian alliance; the one could be
sacrificed to the other. To-day, that is no longer the
case. The English Liberals have no alliance to offer.
The only alliance open is that with Russia. Besides,
in the question of the Straits, Russia, far from being
aggressive, seeks, on the contrary, merely to defend
herself. The only side on which she could be aggressive
with regard to England is in Central Asia, in Persia,
in Asia Minor. But there she asks for support neither
from Austria nor from Germany; these two Powers
then remain outside a sphere of action which might
compromise their relations with England!

Plenipotentiary at Madrid, 23 October, 1869, and special Ambassador *ad interim* at Constantinople 31 March, 1877. He was then
nominated Ambassador to the Sultan of Turkey, 31 December,
1877, which appointment he held for three years.

Such has been up to this point, in substance, the dialogue which has arisen between Vienna and Berlin. Whatever may be its final issue, it has already produced one important result. Our action is working its way in, like a wedge, between these two Powers. Bismarck, roused for the fight, gets visibly angry under Haymerlé's opposition. "Haymerlé", he said to me, "is in a fair way to become a second Buol;[1] and you know what I thought of him."

In order to overcome this resistance, I suggested to the Prince the expediency of impressing Haymerlé with the fact that Germany and Russia were already agreed upon certain principles, and of communicating them to him in wording which would have the form either of a Memorandum or any other form that the Prince might choose. Having accepted this idea, he made only one objection which appeared to me very sound.

"Up to this moment", he said, "I have not spoken at Vienna in your name; Haymerlé does not know that we are acting together. I have only sounded him; I have expressed my desire to see the re-establishment of the Triple Entente; I have stated on what conditions I believe it to be possible. If I had done more and undertaken a regular negotiation, they would have thought in Vienna that Russia wishes to attain to it only by way of Berlin, and there would perhaps have resulted from that a new coolness be-

[1] Buol-Schauenstein, Karl Ferdinand, Count von (1797–1865), Austrian diplomatist and statesman, was Ambassador at London in 1851. The following year he became Austrian Prime Minister, and held the office till 1860. For references to him by Bismarck, etc., cf. *Reflections and Reminiscences*, 1, 93, also p. 115.

tween Austria and you. In order to go a step farther, that would be the moment for you to break silence, to add a word so as to show Austria that there is a question of the Straits which I have not invented by myself. There is nothing to hinder M. de Giers, in his conversations with Kálnoky,[1] from making no mystery of the point of view of the Russian Government on the subject of the stipulations relative to the Straits, and of the surprise caused in Russia last autumn by the proceedings of Mr Layard. That would constitute for Haymerlé a first indirect indication that already we employ the same language. You would be able to add at the same time that you attach some value to knowing the ideas of Austria on this matter, as that one among the Powers whose opinion is by no means immaterial to you. Nowhere are they as impressionable with regard to the form of diplomatic relations as in Vienna. Count Kálnoky, in this respect, is an agent eminently useful, especially if he were given opportunities for some intimate conversation from time to time."

I availed myself of this opportunity to state with what scrupulous loyalty we had up to now maintained the secrecy agreed upon about these pourparlers.

[1] Kálnoky, Count Gustavus Siegmund (1832–1898), Austrian statesman, began his career in the army. Entered diplomacy in 1854, and after serving in junior posts in Munich and Berlin, he acted as Secretary of the Embassy in London where he spent ten years, during which time he rejoined the army. He was, however, sent as Minister to Copenhagen and in July, 1879, as Ambassador to St Petersburg. He succeeded Haymerlé as Austro-Hungarian Minister for Foreign Affairs on 21 November, 1881. He resigned in 1895.

Berlin, 12th May, 1880.

To Baron Jomini.

I hasten to reply to the questions put in your letter of
8th May. In the first instance, let me say a word on the
psychological law which you deduce from the events of history. You say that the habit of peace makes men peaceful,
and that the habit of war makes them warriors.

That law seems to me too absolute. Between history and
politics there is this difference that in the one, passions are
dead, and ideas play a preponderant rôle; whilst in the other
we have to deal with living beings who try to impress their
will on the march of events. Thus it is after all men, and not
ideas, which guide the world. History only produces philosophy after it is all over, arranging in a system that which, in
its origin, was only the product of the fortuitous clash of
individuals wills. History will endeavour to show that the
unification of Germany came about because it was fated to
come about in virtue of a higher law which governs human
affairs. But the contemporaries think otherwise. They know
that this event was the fortuitous product of the genius of
a German, combining with the mistakes of a Frenchman.
Two such factors may be seen in all events. Men bring on
the clash of nations without caring about the habits which
these latter have formed. Rightly or wrongly, they always
guide them. Ideas are only of service to them as munitions.
They load telegrams and speeches with them just as you load
muskets and cannon with powder.

Some one has said before me: "The European Concert is
only the dream of the idealists. There is no Europe; there is
a Russia, a Germany, a France, an England". In order that
there may be a Europe, there must be a Confederation obey-
ing a single will. But there are five of them.[1] To arrive at an
era of lasting peace there must be victors and vanquished.
That is the law of the world. In 1815 France was the great
vanquished one. A European Concert was set up; but what

[1] *Sc.* Austria.

was its character? It was a Concert of satisfied victors, which could last just so long as was necessary for the vanquished to recover and work for revenge. It lasted forty years.

To-day the situation is not so very dissimilar. The vanquished is the same; there is a European Concert, but in the given situation, is it possible to find in it the stamp of sincerity? I do not think so. Under the appearance of general agreement is concealed the lack of real alliances. For want of the reality, one clings to the shadow, and the seeming Concert only serves as a transition to groupings, as yet unknown, but at which the best advised will know how to arrive sooner or later.

I hesitate to attach the importance to the reaction in England which you seem to give to it. The English elector does not make history; he yields much rather to a very common impulse, the love of change. If he helps thereby to mark the end of a bellicose period, he is like the "bourgeois gentilhomme"; he makes prose without knowing it. He assures peace to us, not for one or two generations, but till the time when some gamester of genius, or some clumsy individual, will be willing to engage in some high play on the gaming-table of Europe.

I think that in this way I have answered your first question,—whether the desire to maintain the Concert of Europe is sincere or if it is a masque. I have no hesitation in thinking that it is a masque for every one; that no one believes in its continuance; that for Gladstone himself, who labours for it in the front rank, this Concert has only the value of a clever introduction; and that we are right to make use of it, not to delude ourselves with the dream of a universal peace, but in order to arrive at some practical result in connection with the pending questions which interest us in the East.

Gladstone's idea seems to be this—to show the English nation that he will succeed in securing results where the blustering policy of Lord Beaconsfield failed. In other words, to bring peace in the East out of that same Treaty of Berlin which his predecessors signed without knowing or wishing to understand its importance for the well-being of the Christian populations.

That is why I think that we shall be able to arrive, on this ground, at satisfactory results with England. We shall be able to induce her to carry out a naval demonstration which will probably be sufficient to settle Montenegrin and Greek affairs to our mutual satisfaction; after which Gladstone's "idea" will without doubt be to resume his insular policy, and we shall be able to take courteous leave of one another.

As to your second question on the subject of Bismarck's "idea", I have still less hesitation in answering it. He does not easily let go of his ideas. Through that nebula which they call the Concert of Europe, he will continue to pursue the solid elements of real alliances. Till now I have no reason to suppose that he has modified his way of thinking, and the Dreikaiserbund remains the favourite object of his contrivances.

We shall make a great mistake if we act differently. Let us take from the European Concert whatever is useful to us now, but not throw aside the real for the shadow.

With regard to the Anglo-French sympathies for the Greeks, I have studied them a very great deal on the spot. Have an easy mind; their sympathies will never take them to Constantinople, and we have no need to irritate the amour-propre of the Greeks by repeating to them that we forbid them from having so chimerical a dream. Like all idle fancies, it is a harmless "grand idea". In our time a Byzantine Empire suits nobody—Austria no better than us. Besides, France and England do not think of going beyond the Treaty of Berlin for love of the Greek.

During the last war, when every question was still outstanding, I had submitted the idea of a Confederation of all the little States, created, and to be created, in the peninsula. It would have been, in my opinion, the best contrivance to put an end to the jealousies of race, and remove the influences which are hostile to us. This idea was lost in the conflict. Our negotiator at that time had sacrificed all other considera-

tions to the creation of a Greater Bulgaria. I had made sure
of the co-operation of the leading political elements in Greece,
in order to win over that country to the idea of a Confederation, by means of an enlargement of territory. But all that
is past, and it is no longer the time to discuss these great
problems of the future. They will present themselves some
day or another; let us hope that it will not be soon. For, as
you say, quietness is not for us of mere theoretical use, but
a practical need of the first order. Therefore, let us thank the
Emperor for leading us in the paths of peace. Kindest regards.

At Gladstone's accession to power, several clauses
of the Treaty of Berlin had not yet been put into
execution. The Turks made difficulties about sur-
rendering the territory which had been awarded to
Montenegro. The promise given to Greece about
extending her frontier on the Thessalian side equally
remained in suspense. Finally, Armenia still awaited
the reforms promised under one of the stipulations
of the Treaty. Gladstone resolved to take in hand the
initiative in the settlement of these different questions
by inviting all the great Cabinets to agree to joint
action. The whole summer of 1880 was taken up with
negotiations which ended in a naval demonstration
at Dulcigno in order to compel the Turks to hand
over the territory promised to Montenegro. Later, a
Conference, held at Berlin, settled the matter of the
Greek frontier in Thessaly. As the result of all these
circumstances, our secret negotiations at Berlin necessarily came to a halt for the time being, and were not
resumed till September, at the time of an interview
between Baron Haymerlé and Prince Bismarck at
Friedrichsruhe. In the interval, I saw the Prince

the day before his departure for Kissingen on 14 July to ask him if I might speak in full confidence with Prince Hohenlohe during his absence, in the event of circumstances arising which would be favourable to a resumption of our confidential pourparlers.

The Chancellor replied that he had confidence in the discretion of Hohenlohe, and that he saw no objection to my making use of that means, in case of necessity.

This preamble naturally led to our discussion of the chances which might present themselves of inducing Austria to accept our programme. At first the Prince renewed his assurance to me that if, as the result of unforeseeable events, the question of the Straits happened to come up, we should find him on our side. He passed in review the circumstances which could give this question a character of present interest.

"We do not know", he said, "where the political campaign inaugurated by England will lead. If it were to lead to coercive action against Turkey, that action will take the form of an Anglo-French expedition, for neither Austria nor Germany will follow them on that ground. But an Anglo-French combination will produce an effect on Austria such as my arguments by themselves have been unable to do. Austria will throw herself into your arms however little you may be disposed for that, and it will be easy then for us to make her espouse your point of view about the Straits. Our accord on that point will then acquire the character of a preservative measure, for the absolute closing of the Straits will be the most efficacious means of maintaining the Sultan in Constantinople, and preventing a catastrophe which neither you nor Austria desire at this moment. The Straits are the most vulnerable spot where England can strike Turkey, and under the pretext of carrying out the Treaty of Berlin, Gladstone might well be led to demolish the whole structure. Austria will not wish this, and that will be the moment to dwell on this point in order to make her adopt our idea."

I replied that this seemed to me indeed realisable, nevertheless there was one preliminary condition to be fulfilled, namely the settlement of the Montenegrin affair, which interests us most. Then we shall be able to place ourselves frankly on the side of the Powers that are guardians of Turkey. Till then we have no other choice except to associate ourselves with the action of England who works for that end.

The Prince admitted that from our point of view we could not do otherwise. He continued thereafter to develop his favourite argument. In his opinion, Russia, Austria and Germany are interested in allowing the Sultan the force necessary to keep the key of the Straits, and to make of him, according to his expression, "a faithful porter", assuring him that position by their common support. In short, our idea has taken such good root in the mind of the German Chancellor, that he even finds sides to it that fit in completely with his way of looking at things, and he sees in it a connecting link destined one day to rally Austria to us in our Eastern policy. "Then", said he, "we shall be able at last to create this monarchical square, and no longer be concerned about the internal convulsions of the Western States. The three Em-

perors united are sufficiently strong to defy all agitations from without, and sufficiently lordly to live
satisfied with the patrimony of their ancestors."

While listening to this conservative profession of
faith, I said to myself that there was a time when this
very statesman had not disdained to make use of the
services of the leaders of the Hungarian revolutionary
party. Nevertheless, these words have the merit of
proving to us that his distrust of us has really disappeared. So, I find it very useful to take up with
him again the thread of our conversations of last
winter, whenever the opportunity arises. That is a
method of keeping him in our wake, of preventing
his restless mind from wandering elsewhere, and even
if these conversations were to end in no practical
results, they secure the immediate aim of keeping our
relations on the cordial footing which we desire at
this moment.

Bismarck does not believe that the Gladstone Ministry will remain long in power. According to his
information, there is already a reaction in England
which springs from the noticeable agitation going on
in the working classes.

"If only", I remarked, "this Ministry remains in
power sufficiently long to settle the Montenegrin
affair."

Berlin, 16 August, 1880.

Hohenlohe, who recently saw Prince Bismarck after
his cure at Kissingen, made me acquainted with their
conversation. The ideas are the same with some further developments.

An entente necessary between Austria and us, with regard to eventualities in the East. Without her, the triple accord will never have a solid basis.

In this entente, the question of the Straits must be settled in a manner favourable to Russia. It is necessary to entice Turkey into this scheme, which is the best safeguard of her sovereignty on the Bosphorus. But previous to that, Turkey will have to set her house in order. She will have to yield on the Montenegrin question, and later, to put up with the union of the two Bulgarias, and the definite surrender of Bosnia and Herzegovina.

However pleasing the prospect offered to us by the goodwill of Prince Bismarck concerning the Bulgarian union, we must carry out that affair in such a way as not to spend our blood and money a second time. Do not let us forget that this affair is still a question of *force* between Turks and Bulgarians, and that an agreement on paper with Austria and Germany will not settle it. We must be very sure of the success of a Bulgarian move before authorising it. Let us bear in mind the experience of the Serbian war. At that time, also, we believed that the Serbian move would succeed without our assistance, and that the teeth of the Turk were rotten! That mistake involved us in a great war. If we repeat the same miscalculation, the same voices which but lately accused Bismarck of having instigated us to war in order to weaken us, will make themselves heard afresh amongst us. Whether this calculation was a fact or not, it rests with us to foil it by acting with prudence.

Accordingly, to arrive at a practical conclusion, I shall sum up in two points:

(1) It will always be advantageous to us to make sure, first of all, of Austria's eventual assent to the union of the two Bulgarias.

(2) As for the carrying out, it will be necessary to adjourn this to a time when the weakness of Turkey, whether as the result of a struggle with Greece or from some other cause, would assure the Bulgarians the means of bringing it about without our material assistance.

CHAPTER VII

HAYMERLÉ AT FRIEDRICHSRUHE

Berlin, 31 August/12 September, 1880.

COUNT LIMBURG-STIRUM[1] has just conveyed to me, on behalf of Prince Bismarck, the following communications on the subject of his interview with the Austrian Minister of Foreign Affairs at Friedrichsruhe.

The Prince, in the absence of more detailed data with reference to our views, was unable to take up the general question of eventualities in the East, not being sufficiently prepared to set his finger on all the points where our interests and those of Austria collide or agree.

The question of the union of the two Bulgarias was broached.

Baron Haymerlé began by expressing his lively satisfaction at learning that it was not our intention to hasten that union. He was then brought to recognise that Austria would eventually be able to agree to it without her interests suffering thereby. Passing next to the question of "compensations", he said that he attached no importance to the idea of an ultimate annexation of Bosnia and Herzegovina. In other

---

[1] Limburg-Stirum, Count Friedrich Wilhelm, German diplomat, b. 1835. Entered diplomacy in 1860. After holding various junior posts, he returned from Constantinople in 1871 to work in the Ministry for Foreign Affairs, acting as Interim Director from September, 1880. In 1881 his diplomatic career ended, and he entered home politics.

words, he made it clear that Austria looked on these
provinces already as indisputably hers, even if she
still lacked the formal title to possession. So, giving
up the idea of entering on the discussion of compensations, Haymerlé preferred to examine the most
appropriate means of protecting Austrian interests in
the eventuality of a Greater Bulgaria. These means
he divided into two categories—those of the future
and those of the present.

With regard to the future, it would be understood
that the frontier of Roumelia will not be extended,
in the event of annexation, either to the south or to
the west.

With regard to the present, Austria would wish an
end put to the Bulgarian propaganda in Macedonia.
She attaches to this the importance of a vital interest
for her. This propaganda will finish one day by insti-
gating Turkey to an armed conflict, which in its turn
will call for the intervention of Russia in defence of
Bulgaria. Austria would like to avoid this double
eventuality at whatever cost. Therefore she wishes
the Bulgarians to confine their ambitions to Eastern
Roumelia, and definitely renounce claims to Macedonia.

The second wish with regard to the present is to
see Russia give proof of her goodwill by advising the
Serbian Government to be more tractable in the
negotiations pending with the Cabinet at Vienna.

Finally, with regard to the Sanjak of Novibazar,
Haymerlé does not regard this point as distinct from
the Bosnia and Herzegovina matter. The eventual
occupation of this Sanjak has already been approved

of by Russia in virtue of an agreement signed at Berlin by Prince Gortchakov and Count Andrassy.

Such is the general tenor of the explanations which Prince Bismarck caused to be conveyed to me, without the addition of any comments of his own upon them.

I begged my interlocutor to thank the Prince for these confidences. Nevertheless, I considered it my duty to make some observations to prevent the formation in the mind of the Prince of certain points of view which might be in danger of not being in agreement with ours.

As to the extension of the limits of Roumelia, dreaded by Haymerlé, I said that on this point an agreement seemed to me clearly indicated. Since we were speaking of the present Roumelia, there was no question of a Roumelia without definite boundaries.

As to the Bulgarian propaganda in Macedonia, I did not think that an entente between Austria and us would present any difficulties. Moreover, it would be possible to prevail on the Bulgarians to consider Macedonia as the nucleus of a future autonomous province, if they were made to understand that in renouncing Macedonia they would be able the more easily to acquire Eastern Roumelia. One must not run after two hares at the same time.

As to Serbia and the proof of goodwill which Austria asks of us, I said that I could not prejudge the degree in which my Government would consider it opportune to give practical application to it.

The point upon which a divergence of views could arise, was the question of Novibazar.

I asked Count Limburg-Stirum whether Baron

Haymerlé had expressed the intention of effecting this occupation in the near future, and if there had been talk about this at Friedrichsruhe?

The Count replied in the negative. In his opinion, this occupation was only expected in the event of the Turkish administration being unable to maintain itself there.

I went on to state the difference between our points of view, whilst admitting that, since Austria has no intention of carrying out that occupation in the near future, the question was not a burning one.

Austria considers the question of Novibazar inseparable from that of Bosnia and Herzegovina,—in other words, as definitely settled. She believes she has the right to take possession of that province when she wishes; she considers that Russia has already given her consent to this through the notes exchanged between Prince Gortchakov and Count Andrassy at the close of the Congress.

We consider, on the other hand, that this question is distinct from that of the two other provinces. This distinction springs from the very tenor of Article XXV of the Treaty of Berlin relative to Novibazar.[1] Whilst the occupation of the two northern provinces has the

---

[1] The text of the Article was as follows: "The provinces of Bosnia and Herzegovina shall be occupied and administered by Austria-Hungary. The Government of Austria-Hungary, not desiring to undertake the administration of the Sanjak of Novibazar...the Ottoman administration will continue to exercise its functions there. Nevertheless, in order to assure the maintenance of the new political state of affairs, as well as freedom and security of communications, Austria-Hungary reserves the right of keeping garrisons and having military and commercial roads in the whole of this part of the ancient vilayet of Bosnia".

character of a complete occupation, militarily and politically, in the case of the Sanjak the Treaty only contemplates the establishment of some garrisons for the security of the roads. The civil administration remains Turkish. There are indeed some stages to be traversed in order to compare the position of this Sanjak with that of the two provinces bordering on Austria. These stages cannot be passed through without modifying Article XXV of the Treaty of Berlin.

As to the agreement between Prince Gortchakov and Count Andrassy, Austria appears to be remembering it very late, after having forgotten it for two years! This is so true, that last year it was I who recalled its existence to Prince Bismarck in order to show him the sound basis of our complaints against Austria, when she continually voted against us in the Executive Commissions formed on the spot under the Treaty of Berlin. The engagement was binding on the two parties. Can Austria assert, with her hand on her heart, that she has strictly carried out her obligations? Has she helped us in the application of the clauses which interested us in particular? The antagonism of her agents and ours proves the contrary. It is then much better to speak of that agreement as little as possible.

Such are the remarks that I made, whilst informing Count Limburg-Stirum that I undoubtedly shall be compelled to explain myself in a more authorised manner.

One fact remains secured: Austria accepts the union. This admission is a fresh stroke of the pen-knife to the Treaty of Berlin. In virtue of this, the interview at Friedrichsruhe has not been without result.

Berlin, 14/26 September.

It would be of great interest for the harmony between the three Courts, and above all in view of their future accord, to give to the Friedrichsruhe pourparlers a form *satisfying* to everybody, whilst preserving their strictly contingent character. On this ground we can avoid disputes, and confirm points of agreement.

In this order of ideas we would be able to reply almost in these terms:

"The Imperial Government is grateful to Prince Bismarck for having succeeded in securing from Austria the important admission that she would not eventually oppose the union of the two Bulgarias.

"It agrees to the condition which Austria attaches to this union, namely, that Bulgaria does not extend beyond the present boundaries of Eastern Roumelia.

"With regard to the point relative to Serbia; if Austria wished to express the desire that the policy of the Imperial Cabinet should not be inimical to her on that matter, it was useless to draw up that request, granted as it was in advance. But Austria cannot expect to see Russia exercise her influence in order to guide an independent State in negotiations which do not concern us at all. Serbia is the sole judge of her own interests. We would voluntarily give Austria a proof of goodwill in refraining from advising resistance at Belgrade. But we can hardly take upon us to decide for the Serbians what best suits their economic interests.

"As to the Bulgarian propaganda in Macedonia, if it came to assume proportions disquieting to peace, we should be disposed to join with Austria in making the Bulgarians listen to counsels of prudence".

A reply in this sense, establishing an eventual agreement between the three Courts, would serve as a conclusion to the pourparlers at Friedrichsruhe.

The question of Novibazar having only been touched upon incidentally, I consider it to our interest not to mention it in this reply. This question contains the germ of a serious disagreement, and it is of importance to us not to multiply the number of questions on which we differ with Austria. It would be sufficient for us to have let Bismarck understand, as I have done, that we do not acquiesce in the Austrian interpretation. This disagreement will remain in a theoretical state so long as Austria does not propose to extend her occupation. It is even probable that the fear of letting a disagreement break out will induce her to postpone this occupation indefinitely. In any case, since Haymerlé himself has not wished to get involved in the matter of "compensations", it will be much better not to mix up the question of Novibazar with that of Bulgaria.

The interview at Friedrichsruhe has had one other important result for us—that of throwing a stronger light on the aims and ambitions of Austria.

They betray themselves in each of the points mentioned by Haymerlé; Novibazar, which he would like to accustom Europe to consider as already belonging to Austria; the Danubian Principalities, which he wishes to hold in chains by means of commercial agreements; further, the transaction which he proposes in order to help him to overcome the resistance of Serbia would not suit us. The care he exercises in opposing the extension of the frontiers of Roumelia towards the south and towards the west, and so keep the road open in the direction of Constantinople and Salonika, indicates to what degree Austria has already changed her centre of gravity. There are unavowed ambitions there which betray themselves in spite of themselves, and which are the more dangerous in that they can find friendly support in Germany. If the Austro-German Alliance, concluded last year, had not had as an immediate corrective a lessened strain in our relations with the German Government, our position in the East would no longer have been tolerable. To-day Bismarck feels the need of preserving a certain balance between our interests and those of Austria.

The Germany of our time pursues the same policy that the Prussia of Frederick the Great adopted when he proposed the partition of Poland. Turkey is a body more difficult to divide; but the tendency at Berlin is the same as a hundred years ago—to create between the three Empires bonds of mutual connivance. Frederick the Great was "honest broker" before Bismarck!

It would be dangerous to-day to engage in that struggle with Austria for the East which a future generation will perhaps see, but which we can only pursue at present with any success on pacific lines, by being satisfied with the compromises which Germany offers to support, each time that the opportunity of doing so presents itself.

Berlin, 23 September/5 October.

The reply has come from St Petersburg. It is expressed in the terms that I suggested. I have communicated it to Limburg, requesting him to send it to Friedrichsruhe.

At the part relative to Serbia, Limburg interrupted me to say that Haymerlé did not urge pressure on our part on the Serbian Government, but that he confined himself to expressing the hope that our Minister at Belgrade would not adopt a hostile attitude to Austria, and that from time to time we would agree to give the Serbs some simple friendly advice.

After the reading, he asked me if I had not something to say about Novibazar.

I replied that "this point having only been touched on incidentally, my Government had thought that it ought not to mention it. In my correspondence I had given an account, it is true, of my remarks on the subject of the document signed by Prince Gortchakov and Andrassy. Although I had not received any instruction, I have good cause to believe that I had exactly represented the point of view of my Government. But I was sure beforehand that Prince Bismarck would appreciate the motives for our silence. The thing is to establish the points of *agreement*, and not the points of *divergence*. That is the reason why we wished to avoid a polemic with Austria at this moment—a needless polemic moreover, since the Cabinet at Vienna was not thinking then of occupying Novibazar. So, it was simply in personal confidence, and without being charged with any communication, that

I had gone into these details. In our opinion a considerable difference exists between the question of Novibazar and that of Bosnia and Herzegovina. I was persuaded, moreover, that when the time came, Prince Bismarck would find the means of putting us in agreement".

Next day, Count Limburg called on me by order of the German Chancellor. The latter charged him to say to me that he had read our reply with very great interest, and a lively thankfulness for the manner in which his efforts were appreciated by the Emperor. So he was anxious to convey the assurance to us that he would always be ready to work for the reconciliation of our interests with those of Austria.

CHAPTER VIII

THE QUESTION OF THE STRAITS

Berlin, 23 September/5 October, 1880.

THE language of my English colleague betrays the anxieties of his Cabinet, which is placed to-day in the most difficult of situations.

These anxieties are apparent in every attempt made by Mr Gladstone to bring about an entente with the other Powers on the questions which he has raised in Turkey. This impetuous statesman is compelled to go on, for, like a bicycle, if he stops, he falls.

Already the English Ministers have deliberated on the project of a European naval action located in the Dardanelles, because there they might attack Turkey at the most vital point.

Strange reversal of human affairs! After she had got the Treaty of Berlin signed by us in order to arrest the break-up of the Ottoman Empire, England takes this same Treaty as a starting-point to continue the work of demolition which we had begun!

Besides, one can never predict the line that public opinion in England will follow. My British colleague quoted to me the following saying of Lord Derby, who is paying the price of having always wished to be Minister of Public Opinion—"When the Government wishes to keep out of Eastern complications, something happens unexpectedly, and John Bull cries out: 'We won't stand it!' Then the Government hastens to intervene, and after a little while John Bull gets angry and says: 'Could you not have left it alone?'"

Berlin, 28 September/10 October, 1880.

Prince Bismarck sent me this morning, through the medium of Count Limburg, an unexpected communication, though satisfactory in the highest degree.

At the time of the visit of Haymerlé to Friedrichs-ruhe, he had obtained the personal assent of the latter to the subject of the question of the Straits. To-day Haymerlé formally authorised him to say to us that the Cabinet at Vienna was prepared to commence pourparlers with Russia and Germany with a view to giving a practical form to our idea. Haymerlé adds that in his opinion these pourparlers could be begun whenever the questions of the day, which are the object of the European action in Turkey, shall have been settled.

I lost no time in supporting this opinion, feeling how much it would embarrass us to resume the pourparlers of last winter at a moment when we are involved with England in a common action. I said to Count Limburg that since it is a question of enticing Turkey into an agreement which has, as aim, to assure the inviolability of the Straits, it is clearly necessary to wait till the termination of the action in which we are at present engaged, and which is, as a matter of fact, directed against Turkey.

Count Limburg agreed with this point of view.

The following are the motives which have exercised so favourable an influence upon our secret conversations:

At Berlin, as at Vienna, they are afraid that we shall let ourselves be carried along by Gladstone to the point of bringing about the fall of Turkey, without wishing it. They want to save Turkey, and the best way of doing so is to interest us in her preservation. Helped by this situation, Bismarck has succeeded in securing the agreement of Austria to the plan drawn up between us. Our line of action is perfectly clear; let us continue to co-operate with England for the settlement of the Montenegrin and Greek affairs. These points gained, the European action will be finished, and we shall then be able to resume the negotiations with our two neighbours for the settlement of our permanent interests.

I sent to Prince Bismarck the following note:

Dear Prince,

I am most anxious to tell you how very happy and grateful I am for the communication which you were good enough to forward to me by Count Limburg-Stirum. When so important a step has been made towards the accomplishment of a political system, destined, I hope, to revive with us the good old traditions under the shade of which our two countries have grown and prospered, I cannot refrain from a feeling of pride in seeing myself associated, by the chance of circumstances, with one of your fruitful undertakings. Therefore, the modest workman wishes to lay aside for a moment his diplomatic trappings to do homage to the master.

In giving this note the form of an impulse as coming from the heart, I wished to remove from his suspicious mind any fear that we had changed our ideas in the interval under the influence of the action instigated by England. I was bound then not to have any hesitation in my personal attitude, which was invariably favourable to the system of alliance with Germany.

The Prince replied in the following note:

Friedrichsruhe, 12th October, 1880.

My dear Ambassador,

I thank you sincerely for the kind words which you were good enough to address to me.

I hope that we shall be allowed to reach the goal which, in the common interest of our Monarchs and of our countries, we have proposed to attain. The valuable support of your influence and the mutual confidence which unites us, are the best guarantees for the successful fulfilment of our wishes.

Please accept, my dear Ambassador, the repeated assurance of the sentiments which animate me, and the expression of my very high consideration.

Bismarck.

Berlin, 1/13 October, 1880.

The situation has been modified as the result of the resolution of the Turks to indemnify us in the Montenegrin matter by abandoning Dulcigno.

It is easy to see in this the action of the German Chancellor. He saw that the foolish resistance of Turkey offered us too strong a temptation to attack her conjointly with England. Therefore he will have used all his influence at once, at Constantinople as at Vienna. At Constantinople Hatzfeldt[1] will have been

---

[1] Hatzfeldt, Count Paul von, Prussian statesman (1831–1901). Entered the diplomatic service and worked directly under Bismarck, whom he accompanied during the Franco-German War (1870–1871). He was appointed Extraordinary Ambassador at Madrid 1874 and transferred to Constantinople in 1878. In 1881 he became Secretary of State and deputy for Bismarck in the Ministry of Foreign Affairs, Berlin. He was appointed German Ambassador in London in 1885.

instructed to use language almost in these terms: "It is no longer Russia but England who is now your real enemy. It is she who can penetrate with her fleets to the walls of Constantinople. Indemnify Russia, and a situation will be created where Austria, Germany and Russia will be able to agree to give you security in the Straits".

At Vienna, where the preservation of Turkey has always been an interest of the first order, Prince Bismarck will have employed the same arguments to overcome the last hesitations of Haymerlé, and bring him to our point of view on the question of the Straits.

The result that Bismarck proposes to attain now becomes realisable—to prevent England from pursuing an action which would prematurely bring up the big Eastern questions on which Austria and Russia are not yet in agreement. These questions will serve, in his eyes, as a means of equalising matters and facilitating the Triple Alliance which is, there can no longer be any doubt, the object which the German Chancellor has sincerely followed since his confidence in us has been restored.

Berlin, 16/28 October, 1880.

During my short stay in Paris last week, I had a very interesting conversation with Radowitz.

My former relations with this diplomat, sent to Paris on a temporary mission, made me attach a quite particular value to checking my Berlin impressions by the retrospective confidences which he could give me. He had been, besides, the first intermediary between Bismarck and myself the previous winter;

he was kept informed as to our first confidential pourparlers, and had confided to me formerly that his
chief had charged him to make a written record of
our various conversations.

I asked Radowitz if he was still in the know with
regard to these pourparlers. Without being con-
versant with all the details of them, he knows that
they are progressing favourably.

He then related to me all that he knew about the
last phase of the Montenegrin matter. His confidences
confirm at every point what I had only been able to
guess at Berlin.

According to him, Prince Bismarck started from
the point of view that, in order to check the events
in Turkey, it was necessary at all costs to induce
Russia to stand aside. The critical moment had arrived.
England was going to seize Smyrna in concert with
us; a cannon shot could kindle a new war and set
Russia on a plane opposed to that of Austria, upset-
ting the whole political combination projected last
winter. It was at this moment that Bismarck decided
to intervene directly, and ordered Hatzfeldt to use
every effort to obtain from the Turks the unconditional surrender of Dulcigno to Montenegro. At
the same time, Radowitz was charged with informing
the French Cabinet of the mission enjoined on Hatzfeldt, and with asking whether France was disposed
to support this procedure with the object of rendering
the expedition to Smyrna unnecessary. The French
Government hastened to signify its agreement.

It is curious to observe with what dexterity Bismarck succeeded on this occasion in conjoining the

action of France to the advantage of the German policy. It was necessary to avert the danger of a very eventful expedition, which would perhaps have involved Russia in an isolated alliance with England, at the same time estranging her from Germany and Austria. Well, it was France who aided him in this! The short-sighted Ministers who rule in Paris did not suspect that at this critical moment they themselves were working for the object pursued at Berlin —that of re-establishing the Dreikaiserbund which every Frenchman ought instinctively to dread as the greatest obstacle to the claims of his country!

To Baron Jomini, at St Petersburg.

Berlin, 24th October, 1880.

Your letter of 17th October gives rather a gloomy picture; but I only find in it more reasons to persevere in the efforts for an understanding with Germany and Austria along the lines outlined for me in my instructions.

When one abandons oneself to despondency, one is lost. We are there, not to lament the mistakes of the past, but to try to neutralise their consequences. You say that Austria is spreading her net over Serbia and the Danube; you answer this yourself by adding that she will make herself the more hated for this, and that our influence in these countries will profit thereby. It is then an evil which corrects itself, and since we are not asked to renounce our political traditions and assist Austria in her disputes with the small Principalities, this is not a hindrance to the realisation of the programme with the bringing about of which I am entrusted. They only ask one thing of us, namely, not to adopt a hostile attitude to Austria in Serbia. But, does this request not fit in with our intention to put an end to our contest with Austria in the East? I would understand that struggle, if we were prepared to accept all its consequences. But what good is there in a dull struggle that leads to nothing? In the present situation, our best chance of stemming Austria's action would be the way of the Triple Entente which was decided upon last winter, after mature deliberations. To-day it is on the way to succeed. At least there are reasons for hoping so—and we shall make a big blunder if we change our mind at the last moment by preferring isolation—isolation which perhaps will not bear upon us too much, so long as Gladstone's Ministry lasts, but of which we shall quickly experience all the inconveniences when England becomes again unsympathetic to us. For Gladstone is only a shining meteor—a meteor which will pass.

Continual divagations in our course will only discredit us in the eyes of Europe. Frequent change of our programme would simply be equivalent to realising nothing at all. It is not thus that I have interpreted the task entrusted to me, and I can only continue to persevere in it with all the zeal of personal conviction, at least as long as the Emperor considers it advantageous to keep me at Berlin. With the "Minotaur", as you call him, it would be a very dangerous game to turn up one's nose at his alliance after having proposed it to him; and I should become the most noxious of agents if I ceased to be sincere in my relations with the German Government. I can render service only on the condition that that sincerity be not suspect.

I have wished, dear Colleague, to tell you all my mind, and I heartily hope that you will appreciate my frankness.

Kindest regards.

CHAPTER IX

RELATIONS WITH AUSTRIA

To M. de Giers, at Livadia.

Berlin, 1/13 November, 1880.

I have at last received your letters of 14th October. They have enabled me to continue our confidential exchange of ideas with Bismarck....

I have communicated the substance of both your letters in the form of extracts, while introducing some changes in wording in order to convey the shades of meaning I had in view. I herewith enclose copies of them. In delivering them to Count Limburg, I requested him to ask Prince Bismarck to regard the second of these letters as a confidential communication, personally intended for himself. We have no intention to recriminate with the Cabinet at Vienna; but in our confidential explanations to the Prince, we prefer to speak frankly with him, without subterfuge, in order to avoid misunderstandings later.

After this preamble, I entered on the following details: Our position in the East has more points of contact with Austria, since the last war, than was the case formerly. If, as the result of the desire to go in agreement with Germany, we feel the more the need of acting in concert with Austria, the task becomes also the more difficult in proportion as these points of contact multiply. It is up to Prince Bismarck to come to our assistance. I stated thereafter precisely those points of contact which are to-day in danger of degenerating into points of disagreement. There is the question of the treaty of commerce with Serbia: there is that of the Danube: there is the matter of the Bulgarian railways. Assuredly the balance would not be held with an even hand if Germany ranged herself on the side of Austria in all these questions.

With regard to the Bulgarian railways, for example, Austria maintains the thesis that the new Principalities are bound to assume the responsibility for all the obligations contracted by Turkey at a time when these Principalities were not yet in existence. That is a proposition which is, to say the least, open to dispute. The Bulgarian Principality, reduced by the Treaty of Berlin to her present dimensions, has too limited a budget to make it fair to compel her to carry out engagements entered into before her creation. She will be better prepared to fulfil them when the two Bulgarian provinces form a single state. The German Cabinet would be able to exert itself usefully in moderating the action of the Cabinet at Vienna in this direction, if Germany specially, as I think, has not yet taken up a strong position on this question.

Count Limburg confirmed this last reflection. He promised to convey to the Prince all that I had just said to him.

Direct explanations, such as those which I have just undertaken, are, in his opinion, infinitely preferable to the action of local agents who are always inclined to make more than is necessary of the questions in their province. "It is in this way", he added, "that the affair of the Mixed Commission of the Danube has been disproportionately exaggerated. I tried to explain repeatedly to the Rumanian Minister that it rests entirely with the three Principalities to put Austria always in a minority by voting together, and that automatically the question of the casting vote of Austria loses the importance which is attached to it."

It seemed curious to me to see a German Minister develop an argument of this nature, and show the little Principalities the way to resist Austria!

The day before this interview, a telegram from Vienna gave the news of a conciliatory overture made by the new Serbian Ministry. I made use of this news, which had arrived so opportunely, to say to Limburg that it was the best proof that the wish expressed by Haymerlé had been taken into consideration at St Petersburg, and that our attitude at Belgrade was not hostile to Austria.

To M. de Giers.

Berlin, 1/13 November.
(Extract.)

The foregoing analysis leads me to the conclusion that we have no cause to be excessively alarmed at the "encroachments" of Austria. In any case, the facts reported in my preceding letter are not of sufficient weight to call again in question the reconstitution of the Triple Entente upon the bases which take ample account of our principal interests in the East. Moreover, they are not the last word. They suffice us, so long as we need quietness to recover our strength, to give our rouble time to rise, to reconstitute our naval forces in the Black Sea, without which we cannot attempt anything of a decisive character. And, by a fortunate coincidence, every one needs peace as much as we, without excepting even Austria. This breathing space is far from excluding future eventualities, and we know sufficient to be able to judge of the scope that the Triple Entente holds in store for us. Bismarck said to me on two occasions: "I do not share the prejudices of the other Cabinets on the subject of the danger of giving up Constantinople to Russia". If our intention to establish an alliance with Germany remains firm, there is no reason to apprehend a change of opinion at Berlin.

Radowitz, who has just made a quick journey to Friedrichsruhe before leaving for Greece, confirmed me in every respect with regard to the impressions which I have just reported to you. He found Bismarck completely won over again to his old sympathies for Russia. In speaking of the Dreikaiserbund, the Chancellor had repeated to him that he saw no objection to the realisation of Russia's boldest dreams in the East, on the sole condition that she lets Austria subsist, and does not contend for her sphere of influence in the western part of the Balkan Peninsula.

No combination of European alliances would be able to assure a more advantageous situation for us on the day when we shall be ready for action. It will be the glory of the present reign to have prepared for it.

To M. de Giers, at Livadia.

Berlin, 3/15 November, 1880.

Two days after the interview of which I sent you an account in my letter of 1/13 November, Count Limburg-Stirum called on me to convey the thanks and reply of Prince Bismarck to my recent communications.

They have been received, I must say, in the most friendly spirit. The Chancellor conveys to me the assurance that he will continue to use every effort to remove the causes of friction in the East, the dangers of which to the Entente of the three Empires he acknowledges.

Admitting the profound change occasioned in the East by the creation of the new independent Principalities on the frontiers of Russia and Austria, he nevertheless could not infer from that circumstance that the interests of these two States have become more difficult to reconcile. In his opinion, it is not so much their *direct interests* which are at stake in the present case; it is rather the character of their relations with these Principalities, which constitutes a new element. The Prince recognises that Austria ought to exercise much tact in this, so as not to estrange Russia. As a general rule, he does not think that Austria, whilst endeavouring to extend the sphere of her commercial relations, can injure our political interests, or prejudice in any way whatever, future settlements; still, the Prince will not fail in making the Cabinet at Vienna attentive to the considerations developed above, and recommend to it a course of action which will prevent it from offending public opinion in Russia. In deferring in this way to the justifiable susceptibilities of the Imperial Cabinet, he will nevertheless need to take account of the interests of Austria, where these interests seem to him just.

In conclusion, Prince Bismarck renewed to me his firm hope that with the spirit which at present animates both the Cabinets of Russia and of Germany, we shall arrive sooner or later at our common object, even if some secondary difficulties should retard its realisation.

The result of these explanations is that your letter of 24th October produced the desired impression on the mind of the German Chancellor.

To Baron Jomini.

Berlin, 11th November, 1880.

I have just received your letter of 8th November. The controversy in which we have become engaged is one of those that is better settled by word of mouth. The occasion for this will probably present itself in the course of the winter, for, in order to keep myself always in tune with St Petersburg, it is indispensable for me to make brief appearances there.

For the moment, I will confine myself to saying to you that your arguments in favour of a policy of isolation have not convinced me. Since we are flanked by a great Germany, it is probable that we can only live beside her either as allies or as enemies. There is no middle course; or else it is a middle course in which one could only learn to maintain oneself by miracles of balancing, as on the blade of a knife. For my part, I prefer a system of sincere entente, especially if it assures us real advantages for the present, as well as for the future....

To M. de Giers, at Livadia.

Berlin, 16/28 November, 1880.

Lord Odo Russell, whom I had not seen since his errands to Friedrichsruhe and London, has come back to Berlin.

He did not fail to give me interesting details on the subject of his conversations with Bismarck, as also with Gladstone and Granville.

At the time of his stay in London, he said repeatedly in every sort of way that it would be a mistake to rely upon the participation of Germany in a European action which would go beyond diplomatic pressure on Turkey. He added, however, that neither would Germany hinder the other Powers from taking executive measures if they considered it necessary to have recourse to them. Therefore, he said, England can persevere in her line of action without coming up against the opposition of Germany.

These facts did not seem sufficient to the English Ministers to encourage them to action. Ireland is to-day their principal anxiety; whence the moderating speech of Gladstone at the Lord Mayor's Banquet.

Nevertheless, according to what Lord Odo Russell says, this speech has been wrongly interpreted on the Continent. Gladstone has in no way given up the Greek affair, nor the matter of Armenian reforms. At this very moment he is investigating the means of assisting the Greeks, if they decide to act. It is probable that the British Cabinet will not go beyond the combination of protecting the Greek ports and perhaps hindering the Turkish means of revictualling by sea.

During his stay in England Lord Odo Russell became convinced that Gladstone is, still at this moment, much stronger and more popular than people generally think, and Lord Beaconsfield, who has just written a new novel, will have time to write a second one!

On the testimony of my British colleague, Lord Granville is absolutely pleased with the present relations between Russia and England, and in general with the attitude that he finds in us in connection with all the questions which he handles. He wishes and hopes for the conclusion of an agreement with us on the subject of affairs in Afghanistan. So far as I have been able to understand, the English Government is desirous of a like agreement to facilitate it above all in the evacuation of that country, a thing which it cannot do at this moment without exposing itself to the attacks of the Opposition, which would reproach it with having evacuated that province without having obtained guarantees for the future. But, the best guarantee for the security of India would be, in his opinion, a friendly agreement with Russia.

I now arrive at that part of his account which is the most interesting for us.

At Friedrichsruhe, Prince Bismarck confided to him the

real reason why he wished the maintenance of peace in
Turkey at the present moment, and was unable to associate
himself with any action, even of a joint character, which
might have brought about a revival of the whole Eastern
question.

Germany wishes to reconcile the interests of Russia and
Austria in order to prevent a quarrel between these two
Powers. It is a laborious task which takes time. It would be
upset by a premature catastrophe in Turkey. Here Prince
Bismarck made a remark which deeply impressed Lord Odo
Russell. He said to him that he wished to remain, as through
the past, the friend of Russia; that his alliance with Austria
offered no hindrance to this, and that he intended, if the case
arose, to support very fully the interests that Russia possesses
in the Eastern question. Touching thereafter on the questions
that could divide Russia and Austria, the Prince added: "For
Germany, the dimensions of Bulgaria are a matter of complete indifference. Such is not the case in Vienna. But I
believe that Austria maintains an exaggerated point of view
on this question. I do not think that an enlarged Bulgaria
menaces her interests".

Prince Bismarck in this way raised a portion of the veil
which covers our present relations; he has done so just enough
to show that there is no longer anything to reckon on in the
way of a supposed hostility between Germany and Russia,
but yet without revealing the secret of the combination
towards which we are tending.

His language to the English Ambassador has, besides, in
my eyes, the importance of furnishing a further proof of his
perfect good faith with regard to us.

There are limits to mistrust, as to everything else, and I
wonder what other proof could still be demanded by those
amongst us who persist in dreading being taken in, and de-
nounce the German Chancellor as a Minotaur devouring all
those who have the temerity to treat with him as an equal.
As for myself, I have a nobler idea of Russia, and of the
respect which her power inspires, as a defence against the

clever tactics of others. The same Odo Russell said to me one day: "The only man in the world who has inspired respect in Bismarck is the Emperor Alexander".

Therefore, in the course of the pourparlers which we shall have with the German Chancellor, let us pay him in his own coin. When he has been distrustful, we have been so also; to-day he seriously desires an Entente, because he is convinced that the Emperor desires it also. Let us remain vigilant—it is our duty; but do not let us remain distrustful *indiscriminately*; that would be a sign of weakness.

Schweinitz has gone to Friedrichsruhe during these days. In an intimate conversation with him, I acquainted him with a reflection which appeared to strike him, and which he doubtless repeated to his chief. "I would like to know", I said to him, "if Prince Bismarck clearly realises the extent of the services which he renders every day to Austria by his Alliance. For Austria, that Alliance has become a matter of safety, for could she be at rest a single day with on the one hand the Italian aspirations, and on the other those of the Slav populations, towards whom she has not the ability to know how to make herself sympathetic? Assuredly the Prince has the right to be exacting, and to make himself obeyed at Vienna. If he desires to keep the balance equal between our interests and those of Austria, he certainly has all the means for it."

Schweinitz returns to-morrow to St Petersburg.

Please accept, etc.

CHAPTER X

RESUMPTION OF THE GREAT AFFAIR

My conversations at Friedrichsruhe,
27 and 28 November, 1880

PRINCE BISMARCK said to me that from the very beginning of the joint action in Turkey, he had never been in favour of the naval demonstrations. Therefore it was only unwillingly that he had agreed to take part in them. "These demonstrations", he continued, "placed us in the dilemma either of compromising the dignity of the flags, or of having recourse to acts of war, an alternative which did not suit Germany."

He had said to Lord Odo Russell that instead of being always invited to take part in joint measures, he would much rather have England pursue her campaign without the co-operation of Germany, and that she rest satisfied with her moral assent. "Let England act alone, or let her come to an arrangement with Russia to carry out her programme with her aid—I shall not object to this at all, and nobody in Europe will oppose it. I shall wish for the success of the enterprise, provided that no one asks me to take part in it positively."

Concerning the Greek affair, the Prince thinks that at Athens there should be no going beyond what can be obtained by pacific measures. Certain of his reflections lead me to suppose that at Vienna they suspect us of looking upon a Greek complication with complacency as a favourable pretext for starting the union movement in Bulgaria. The Prince, to tell the truth, never said that to me, but he did say that Haymerlé suspected us of trying to come to an arrangement with Rumania for the eventual passage of our troops through her territory. Bulgaria was evidently implied by these words.

I answered that I was quite unable to explain to myself what could be the cause of this suspicion.

The Prince then gave me a retrospective account of his interview with Haymerlé. In order to get the latter to take up our point of view on the subject of the Straits, he had made use of the following line of argument: "Austria, by the Danube, has a commercial and defensive interest in the Black Sea. What would she say if that sea was thrown open, and English gunboats came and paid visits in the Danube or blockaded its mouth? So Austria has the same interest as Russia that the Black Sea should not become an English battle area. It would be equally advantageous for the two Powers to prevent the great ocean tempests from entering this sea ".

I put two questions to the Prince. I asked him in the first instance what he thought of the terms laid down by Haymerlé concerning the time at which the pourparlers between the three parties could begin, —namely, after the settlement of pending questions. Is he really in earnest, or is it indeed only an evasion on his part?

The Prince does not consider Haymerlé dishonest, but he is timid; he is not accustomed to high politics;

he fears responsibilities. A newspaper article produces more impression on him than the great advantages flowing from a political plan maturely contrived. He has agreed to the pourparlers, but he will never take the initiative in them. "When he was here, in that very seat, he seemed like a school-boy impatient to get out of school, and thinking of nothing but how to extricate himself as well as possible, without losing too many feathers."

These words show me that Austria scents the danger of a slackening of her ties with Germany, ties which she believed she could make exclusive, until she saw that Bismarck had other strings to his bow. Provided that we persevere in our way, our action will not fail to act as a solvent on the Austro-German Alliance. It seemed a favourable opportunity to explore once again the importance of that Alliance. So I expressed the opinion that Haymerlé did not perhaps wish to enter into our plans, seeing that he believed Austria to be sufficiently protected by the Treaty of Alliance with Germany. Sure of that protection, she would like to put off the new combination to the Greek Kalends, whilst avoiding offending the German Government by a direct refusal.

The Prince answered me with a certain animation: "Austria would be much mistaken, if she thought herself completely protected by us. I can assure you that this is not the case. Our interest orders us not to let Austria be *destroyed*, but she is not guaranteed against an attack. A war between Russia and Austria would place us, it is true, in a most embarrassing position, but our attitude in such a circumstance will be dictated by our own interest and not by engagements which do not exist.[1] Our interest demands that neither Russia nor Austria should be *completely* crippled. Their existence as Great Powers is equally necessary to us. That is what will guide our conduct in such an event".

I inferred from these words that in the event of war, Germany is not unconditionally bound by an offensive and defensive alliance, but that she reserved the right to intervene, whether after the first battles, or in the peace negotiations.

The Prince finished by saying that he did not think that Haymerlé wished to put off the pourparlers to the Greek Kalends, but that he would be content to keep silent so long as no one spoke to him about the matter. "It will be necessary", he added, "to appeal personally to the Emperor Francis-Joseph in order to get this matter going."

The second question which I put to the Prince was to learn whether a treaty on the projected bases could remain secret, and whether at Vienna and at Berlin it would be possible to avoid the communication of it to Parliament.

As far as Germany was concerned, the Prince was very categorically of the affirmative opinion. The Treaty of Alliance with Italy in 1866 had not been submitted to the Houses. The article in the Constitution is very elastic on this matter. It requires the presentation to the Houses of a treaty which would

---

[1] In view of the text of the Treaty, this hardly seems an accurate statement, and the next paragraph shows that Saburov was misled by it.

lay any "burdens" on the nation. This word leaves a large margin of interpretation.

As for Austria, the Prince thinks he remembers that the article of the law in question is framed in the same sense. But he will need still to verify this point.

I had taken with me the draft of the project covered in February last with the approving annotation of our August Master. Up to this I had not thought it prudent to return to the discussion of the details of the draft, not being sure that the Prince would consider this discussion opportune during the events of last summer. The sight of His Majesty's handwriting at the top of the document made a lively impression on him. Convinced as he is of the serious character of these pourparlers, he is none the less very sensible of every fresh proof of sincerity which is given him. He said to me: "Since the Emperor wishes it, we can be sure of carrying out this task successfully". It was then that he asked me to submit to our August Master the plan of action, of which I shall have the honour to give an oral account to His Majesty.

He readily adopted the changes which we had made in the original draft. We spent an hour discussing the project afresh as a whole and in its details, and there resulted some amendments which I have provisionally accepted, subject to approval.

This talk led us to touch on future eventualities, and to ask how far the arrangement now planned will facilitate the future settlement of the Eastern problem. The Prince, far from evading this subject, was, on the contrary, quite open-hearted. He said that if there were really perspicacious statesmen at Vienna, he would not have hesitated to undertake to draw on the map of Turkey a line of demarcation between the interests of Austria and ours, and that to the satisfaction of both parties. But the Austrian Ministers are the most timid in Europe; they are afraid of every question which is not a question of present interest, and one would not arrive at any result with them by a premature discussion. He went on: "To-day we must be satisfied with the projected arrangement which gives us the great advantage of keeping Austria better under control, and of forcing her, should occasion arise, into an entente. When that arrangement has become an accomplished fact, suppose a situation like that which brought about the Crimean War. If Austria were tempted to join England against Russia, would she dare to do so without asking us if we shall remain neutral? Our reply will be dictated by the present understanding, and Austria will not be able to think of budging. Suppose then that a fortunate campaign takes you to the Bosphorus. I have already told you my way of thinking. I flatter myself on having been the first, in Europe, to break with that old tradition with which the Western Powers have inoculated all the Cabinets, namely, that Constantinople in the hands of Russia would be a European danger. I consider that a false idea, and I do not see why an English interest must become a European interest. As for the interests of Germany, they will decidedly not be affected by that eventuality, and I believe, on the contrary, that the Russian nation will become more seriously converted to the cause of peace when their ambitions at last have reached their goal, and when, having attained possession of Constantinople, they are convinced von der Nichtigkeit aller irdischen Dinge[1]—as I am ", he added, with a sad smile.

I did not think that I ought to push this exchange of ideas further. It is always something to have secured a declaration of such import from a leading German Minister, who would never know how to take shelter behind the inability to make his will prevail at Vienna.

To attempt to turn explanations of this nature immediately into articles of treaty would have been an awkward blunder, for sound treaties only arise under the influence of necessity; to-day that would only have been a theoretical treaty, to which moreover Austria would never have been able to bind herself beforehand.

The following is the text we agreed on at Friedrichsruhe :[2]

Article I. The three Courts agree that if a difference or grievance were to arise between any two of them, this difference would be referred to the mediation of the third, in order to be afterwards removed by a triple agreement.

In the event of one of them finding itself compelled to be at war with a fourth Power, with the exception of Turkey, the other two will maintain a friendly neutrality towards her, and will see to the localising of the conflict.

In the special event of one of them obtaining from one of its two allies more practical co-operation, the obligatory value of this article will remain in all its force for the third one.

[1] Of the vanity of all earthly things.
[2] For Prince Bismarck's exposition of the draft, see his letter to Prince Reuss, D.G.P. III, 158–161.

Article II. Russia, in agreement with Germany, proclaims her firm intention to respect the interests which follow from the new position assured to Austria by the Treaty of Berlin, and defined lately by her convention with Turkey, concerning the occupation of certain parts of the Ottoman territory.

The three Courts agree that any new modifications in the territorial status quo of Turkey in Europe shall only come about in virtue of a common agreement amongst them.

None of the Powers will send troops into Turkey in Europe, Rumania, Serbia or Montenegro without concerted agreement with the other two. If one of them were to feel compelled to go to war with Turkey, she would consult together with the other two with regard to the eventual results of that war, before entering on the campaign.

(Here is the origin of the last paragraph of this article: Bismarck thinks he knows that Austria is uneasy about a possible invasion of Rumania by Russian troops. I objected that we could also have anxieties with regard to a possible invasion of Serbia by Austrian troops as a result of the constant disputes of Austria with that Principality. In consequence, the Prince proposed the amendment in question.)

Article III. The three Courts recognise the European and mutually obligatory character of the principle of the closing of the Straits of the Bosphorus and of the Dardanelles, founded on international law and confirmed by the Treaties.

They will watch in common that Turkey does not make any exception to this rule in favour of the particular interests of any Government whatsoever, by lending the part of her Empire which constitutes the Straits to the war operations of a belligerent Power.

In case of infringement, or in order to prevent it if such an infringement can be foreseen, the three Courts will warn Turkey that they would consider her, should it so happen, as having put herself in a state of war with regard to the party injured, and as having deprived herself from that time of the benefits of security assured by the Treaty of Berlin to her territorial status quo.

In the beginning of December I left for St Petersburg, carrying with me the projected articles with the amendments agreed on at Friedrichsruhe. This draft was submitted to a new examination, under the presidency of the Emperor, and the following modifications were introduced into it.

In *Article I*: The second paragraph was expressed thus:

In the event of one of them finding itself at war with a *fourth Power*, etc.

In place of the words "a fourth Power" it was decided to put "a fourth *Great* Power".

This change was introduced in order not to bind us by an engagement of neutrality in the event of Germany making war on a little State, like Denmark or Holland.

In *Article II*: With regard to the entry of troops into Rumania, we wished to preserve our liberty of action in certain circumstances. Therefore we introduced the following addition, which later compelled Prince Bismarck to give up his amendment:

It is understood, however, that if the political status quo guaranteed to certain provinces of Turkey happened to be endangered, and was the cause of an armed intervention by one of the three Powers, the other two will not oppose the necessary means of execution.

At the end of Article II, we have introduced further the following paragraph:

In order to facilitate the settlement provided for by the present article, a settlement of which it is impossible to foresee all the circumstances, the three Courts will state henceforth, in the confidential communications between them, the points on which an entente has already been established in principle.

This last addition seemed necessary to us in order to confirm by writing the consent of Austria to the union of the two Bulgarias, and above all in order to serve as a starting-point for a more general entente on the eventualities of the future in the East.

I returned to Berlin the first days of January (n.s.). Prince Bismarck had returned the day before my arrival. He was anxious to arrange with me what course to follow, before making the Emperor William acquainted with all our labour.

CHAPTER XI

CONTINUATION OF THE SECRET NEGOTIATIONS

Berlin, 29 December, 1880/10 January, 1881.

I HAVE succeeded in re-establishing Article I in its
original form, and in applying its stipulations con-
tingently to a war between us and Turkey. This
is the argumentation that I made use of with Bismarck:

"We bind ourselves", I said to him, "to see to the
localisation of a war between Germany and France,
between Austria and Italy. It is a very possible
situation that England ranges herself on the side of
France, if, for example, on strategic grounds you
violate the neutrality of Belgium.[1] Italy, also, can
become the ally of France. In both cases, we shall
have to see to the localisation of your war with France,
and assist you in a material manner if England or Italy
happened to stir.

"Where is the advantage of the reciprocity for us?
The event of a war between us and France, between
us and Italy, is not to be thought of. With England
we can be at war only as a result of a conflict with
Turkey. You will prevent France or Italy from joining England, well and good; but already we shall have
two enemies on our hands. Besides, according to
Article II, we can only be at war with Turkey after

---

[1] The fact that such a line of argument could be openly employed in conversation with Bismarck in 1880 is very significant
in view of long-subsequent events.

a preliminary entente with Austria with regard to the results of that war. Such an entente supposes reciprocal advantages, stipulated for us as for Austria. Therefore, in practice, we shall engage in battle with Turkey and with England while it is Austria who benefits with folded arms, and without risking anything if we were beaten! That is not admissible. It happened once against our will, but we will not allow it a second time. If ever we agree with Austria upon a solution of the Eastern question, she must move on with us, and England must take it for granted!"

Prince Bismarck seemed struck by this line of argument. So he showed himself disposed to include Turkey in the category of Powers envisaged by Article I, and to re-establish the original text, such as I had brought it to him at Friedrichsruhe. "As soon", he said, "as you will have established a programme in common with Austria, equity demands that you should not be the only one to bear all the cost and sacrifices resultant upon it."

It seems to me that this is the most important result that we have obtained. It remains to be seen if Austria will subscribe to it. But it is already much to have won Bismarck over to the defence of this thesis.

In passing to the discussion of Article II, I said to the Prince that it was repugnant to the Emperor to contract an unconditional engagement as to non-intervention in Turkey, and to give up the power to make our troops advance through the Principalities except after a preliminary entente with Austria. We must foresee situations like that which led to the last war. We cannot lessen our moral position in the East, and bind ourselves to ask Austria's permission to succour our co-religionists. Moreover, in tying ourselves in this way, we would give carte blanche to Turkey. What will always prevent her from re-occupying Eastern Roumelia is the fear that a Russian army should come back. That is the reason for the addition which we propose, and which I read to him.

Here the Prince replied that this addition would encounter unsurmountable opposition at Vienna, by rousing Austria's distrust. She will be convinced that we are preparing the way for a new campaign to bring about the Bulgarian union.

It was in vain for me to explain that that was only a precaution for the future, and not at all a desire to hasten the Bulgarian union. As far as he is concerned, he believes this willingly. But he considers that it would be dangerous to rouse Austrian distrust in so delicate a negotiation. It is important on the contrary to allay it.

As I did not give way, he finished by saying that he would prefer to suppress the whole of his amendment relative to the non-entry of troops into Rumania, Serbia, etc. At St Petersburg, the Grand-Ducal heir also declared himself for the suppression of this troublesome engagement. I then consented to it, subject to approval, for I had in view the importance of our coming forward at Vienna with a programme in which we should be in agreement with Bismarck on all the points. The thing will be, then, to suppress the whole paragraph which the Prince had added at Friedrichsruhe to Article II.

Our other amendments were adopted without objection. After this meeting, the Prince went to the Palace to submit all our work to the Emperor.

At Friedrichsruhe, Prince Bismarck asked me to submit to the Emperor Alexander the suggestion to select the Grand-Duke of Saxe-Weimar as intermediary between our two Sovereigns and the Emperor of Austria, thinking that in this way we should arrive at our object more quickly.

The Emperor consented, and entrusted me with a letter which I was to forward to the Grand-Duke of Saxe, as soon as I should be informed that the Emperor William approved of this plan.

In the interval this is what happened. It had been agreed that Prince Reuss, the German Ambassador, should leave Vienna to inform the Grand-Duke, his father-in-law, of the mission which it was proposed to entrust to him.

Reuss then wrote to Bismarck that he would be in an extremely false position if the matter was carried on unknown to Haymerlé. What would he answer, if the latter were to ask him how the matter stood? He could not allege ignorance, for his journey to Weimar would betray him.

Reuss wrote, moreover, that Haymerlé was plying him with questions on the subject of my visit to Friedrichsruhe. He had become very nervous, and seeing that the matter was becoming urgent, he no longer tried to put it off by a passive attitude, and asked on the contrary that Bismarck make proposals to him.

These considerations, joined to the personal objections of Reuss, were the reason of Bismarck's preferring to-day the regular method of a diplomatic negotiation to that of the Grand-Duke of Saxe.

As for myself, being furnished with a letter from the Emperor for the Grand-Duke, it was essential to maintain the first plan in order to be able to send this letter a little sooner. I explained to Prince Bismarck that if the text of our draft passed first through the hands of Haymerlé before reaching the Emperor Francis-Joseph, we ran the risk of injuring the matter by the comments in which Haymerlé could envelop it. I suggested combining the two methods of procedure.

Bismarck accepted this idea and promised to propose it to the Emperor William.

Berlin, 29 December, 1880/10 January, 1881.

The following is a résumé of Reuss's correspondence which Bismarck read to me.

Haymerlé kept coming back on my visit to Friedrichsruhe, without Reuss being able to satisfy his curiosity, seeing that he was forbidden to reveal the existence of the rough draft worked out between Bismarck and myself.

For one moment Haymerlé became bitter, and reminded Reuss of the advantages which Germany had derived from her alliance with Austria. According to him, it is thanks to this alliance that the relations between Russia and Germany have improved.

At the reading of this passage, the voice of the Prince hesitated a moment. He had evidently started on a phrase which he would have preferred to skip. But like a sensible man, he quickly made up his mind, and finished the reading of the passage with a firm voice.

I did not wish to be behindhand, and I interrupted him to ask him to remind Haymerlé, when the opportunity occurred, that the interview at Alexandrovo had taken place *before* there was any question of an Austro-German alliance.

Bismarck resumed his reading. Haymerlé called attention to the hostility with regard to Austria which was shown in the language of the Russian consuls, the press, and public opinion in Russia.

With these notions, it is impossible to have a sincere alliance. Hatzfeldt will, without doubt, have informed Prince Bismarck that Russia had tried to indemnify Montenegro at the expense of Austria.

"Hatzfeldt has never written me anything of the kind", observed the Prince. He made on the whole passage the following comment: "The opinion of the Emperor of Russia and of his Heir, constitute, in my eyes, 99/100 of public opinion in Russia".

"There is only one real influence in the East", continued Haymerlé,—"that of Russia. We are conscious of it at every step. Whenever we wish to turn an Austrian interest to account, we clash with the hostile action of the Russian agents. Under these conditions, we risk becoming permanently the dupes of Russian diplomacy, if we let ourselves be fascinated by a Treaty of alliance."

Here Bismarck commented: "They will risk it much more without the Treaty than with it".

"Is Prince Bismarck himself really sure of the sincerity of

Russia?" pursued Haymerlé. "Would it not be better to stop at the object agreed on last year at Vienna—that of working to remove every cause for conflict or for war between Russia and Austria? To confine ourselves, in short, to preventing blows, without running after an alliance which will not, for all that, bring to an end the latent rivalry of our interests in the East? Austria would be able to work quietly to surmount the difficulty of the Bulgarian union. The bases of the Entente are laid. They will do away with the danger of a conflict when the question arises. Afterwards, if new problems force themselves on us, we could agree on a line delimiting our influences?"

Yet this idea of partition was only mentioned by the way. As a practical question, Haymerlé did not go beyond the Bulgarian union.

"That is just like Haymerlé", remarked Bismarck. "He sees nothing beyond that. He thinks that is the only thing, and does not even dream of the European side of the projected transaction."

In one of the last letters from Reuss, Haymerlé was still saying: "It is necessary as a Vorbedingung[1] to every negotiation that the attitude of the Russian agents be modified".

Annotation by Bismarck: "Nicht als Vorbedingung, sondern als Consequenz".[2]

"There must be", added Haymerlé, "a change (*Umkehr*) of Russian political views in the East and more calmness in their application."

Annotation by the Prince: "Umkehr nie; Ruhe ja".[3]

[1] Preliminary condition.
[2] Not as preliminary condition, but as consequence.
[3] Change, never: calmness, yes.

This reading was to me very instructive. For a year
an Austro-German alliance has been spoken of, and
yet, curious confidences are going on between St
Petersburg and Berlin. In short, all my impressions
are excellent.

Berlin, 29 December, 1880/10 January, 1881.

In our conversation of to-day, Bismarck made me
acquainted with his work of the previous day with
the Emperor William. His Majesty felt keen and
profound joy on learning all that had been done
between us and his Premier during the course of the
year. It was the crowning of all his desires. With
his practical mind, the Emperor and King pointed
out that we must agree completely on every point in
the draft, before attempting anything at Vienna.

The King much appreciates the idea of bringing
in the Grand-Duke. He was only afraid that the
latter might refuse so delicate a mission. But having
learned that I had a letter for the Grand-Duke, the
King said: "Oh, in that case, I am sure he will accept:
a letter from the Emperor Alexander will work on
him better than anything I could have said to him".

So the plan of making use of the Grand-Duke was
definitely adopted. On his arrival here, Bismarck will
initiate him in the details, and has asked me to help
him in this task.

As to the mode of procedure at Vienna, this is the
plan he proposes. He considers that the most effective method of acting on the mind of Haymerlé would
be to present the project under the form of a proposal
made by Germany. A refusal of it by Austria would

become more difficult, and on the other hand, as the proposal did not come from Russia, the refusal, if it takes place, will not produce the same unpleasant effect on our direct relations with Austria, as if the initiative emanated from us. The form of a joint Russo-German proposal would perhaps have a threatening character, and since we do not wish to displease Austria, but, on the contrary, to attract her into the Triple Entente, it is better to choose the form most appropriate to that end.

I could only assent to all these reasonings, knowing how much the Prince prides himself on his tact, and, being easy as to the spirit of it, the form matters little to me.

We agreed that Bismarck should send his instructions to Reuss the following week: Reuss will act in such a way as to give Haymerlé priority in learning this piece of news. As to the text of the project itself, the Grand-Duke will communicate and explain it first to the Emperor Francis-Joseph, and Reuss will pass it on to Haymerlé only on his second visit, when the Emperor will already have become acquainted with it. On his first visit, Reuss will confine himself to saying, "You were enquiring about Prince Bismarck's proposals. Since your stay at Friedrichsruhe he has not been inactive, and to-day I am instructed to make some very reasonable proposals to you. We assured ourselves in advance that Russia would accept them. Are you disposed to examine them with a sincere desire for a Triple Entente?"

After Haymerlé had replied, Reuss would wait until the following day before returning with the project.

The pourparlers would then begin between Haymerlé, Reuss and Bismarck, who will keep me constantly informed. Bismarck would have preferred to deal directly with Haymerlé. I would have preferred this also, because of his personal ascendance. Unfortunately a meeting of the two Premiers would have given the hint to the public. On the other hand, Bismarck has little liking for the Austrian Ambassador at Berlin—who is narrow-minded—and that is the reason why he resigns himself to entrusting the negotiations to Reuss.

I asked Bismarck to inform Schweinitz, as I had myself been a witness of the inconveniences of the ignorance in which he has been kept until now. The Prince promised to do so.

I also drew his attention to the great importance of making sure of the assent of the Prince Royal. He replied: "I am quite as much interested in the matter as you, and I will give it all my attention".

CHAPTER XII

NEGOTIATIONS WITH AUSTRIA

Berlin, 1/13 January, 1881.

BISMARCK had, for a moment, changed his mind and found a multitude of reasons for preferring the King of Saxony to the Grand-Duke as intermediary. To begin with, the King of Saxony is very much liked by the Emperor of Austria, and his words would have more weight in Vienna. Bismarck has often had important business with him in which he had occasion to appreciate his ability. Finally, the King of Saxony, "this flint between three mill-stones", is more interested than anyone else to see that these mill-stones do not clash against one another, and do not end by grinding him. He would work, therefore, as much for himself as for us.

It was then that I had to bring forward my decisive argument in favour of the Grand-Duke, by reminding Bismarck of the letter of the Emperor which I had been commanded to send to Weimar, and thereafter to await the decision of the Grand-Duke.

The project, in its final draft, is so satisfactory that it will be necessary to look out now to avert any essential modification on the part of Austria. The German Chancellor will doubtless have some inclination to make concessions, but if we let him understand that the refusal by Austria will in no respect change our desire to arrive at an Entente, even separately with

Germany, he will not hesitate with Haymerlé, and will be able to say to him that he can take it or leave it.

To M. de Giers.

Berlin, 2/14 January, 1881.

I received yesterday evening at midnight your telegram marked "Private". I deciphered it myself, and have been supremely happy over the approval of the Emperor.

I was getting ready to proceed next day to Prince Bismarck's to discharge the order of His Majesty, when I had a visit from his son asking me to go to him the following day at noon, on an urgent matter.

I went there this morning. This is what the matter was about: the Grand-Duke of Saxony does not appear disposed to accept the mission. He had received almost simultaneously the letter from our August Master and that from the Emperor William, written with the same purpose. He responded to the latter that in spite of all his desire to be of service, he felt great scruples at negotiating a matter of this importance, which did not concern him directly. Bismarck's impression is that these scruples are more "princely" than political, and that the "reigning Prince" would not wish to descend to the rôle of diplomat, especially in the city where his son-in-law acts in that capacity. Besides, the reply of the Grand-Duke gives the impression that his personal relations with the Emperor Francis-Joseph do not seem to him of such a nature as to put him in the position of speaking in a sufficiently persuasive manner.

Passing to another subject, Bismarck said to me that the latest news from England filled him with apprehension. At any moment an accident might happen to the Gladstone Ministry, and lead to a Ministerial combination more favourable to Austria. He fears this eventuality, which might make Haymerlé infinitely more difficult to manage. That is why he is of opinion that no more time must be lost, and that it is much better to give up the Grand-Duke definitely rather than insist on making him reconsider his decision, and get from him his assent reluctantly. For all these reasons he asked my consent to modify the way of proceeding, and to return to the negotiation through diplomatic channels.

Recognising the justice of these reasonings, I consented, but on two conditions: (1) First it is necessary to preserve the idea that the application should be made at Vienna under the form of a *German* proposal. I insisted upon this, for I had just received the assent of our August Master on this matter. (2) Then I made the condition that Reuss should not confine himself to negotiating with Haymerlé, but that he also be charged to treat directly with the Emperor Francis-Joseph, which would compensate for the advantages which we expected from the Grand-Ducal Mission, which it is necessary, of course, to give up, since the Grand-Duke himself refuses it.

With regard to the first of these conditions, Bismarck agreed with alacrity. As for the second, he objected at first, in view of the difficulty which Reuss would feel in negotiating directly with the Emperor without offending Haymerlé. He finished, however, by rallying to my opinion, and for the purpose of making Reuss's task easier, he will ask the Emperor William to send a personal letter to the Emperor of Austria, which Reuss will be instructed to deliver in a private audience.

Under these conditions I think that we have no reason to regret the failure of the scheme centring on the Grand-Duke. Reuss, as a diplomat of great ability, will be able perhaps to speak to the Emperor in a more persuasive manner.

To M. de Giers.

Berlin, 4/16 January, 1881.

In our interview of yesterday, Bismarck said to me that he was now going to send off his despatch to Reuss. That was the moment for me to recall to him that the success of a political plan sanctioned by our August Master and by the Emperor William could not depend only on a "Yes" or "No" from Austria. A refusal on her part ought not to hinder Germany and Russia from making their own arrangements, and formulating between them an Entente of which the bases were already agreed upon—subject to leaving a door open for the admission of Austria.

I was greatly surprised when the Prince replied: "You are stealing my idea; if you had not spoken of it, I intended to make the same proposal to you. Besides, it will be for me a new method of influencing Austria, and forcing her hand by the highly disagreeable prospect for her of a separate Entente between Germany and Russia".

This conversation gives me the firm hope that in his instructions to Reuss, he will introduce a new alteration in the sense of the preservation of the essential parts of the project....

To M. de Giers.

Berlin, 10/22 January, 1881.

...I read to Bismarck the passage from your letter relative to the eventuality of a refusal from Austria, and of an Entente between two parties.[1] He was visibly satisfied with it. He said on this occasion that he was not expecting a refusal, but some evasions. In reading his instructions to Reuss over again, the idea came to him that Haymerlé, seeing Russia and Germany agreeing so well in the preliminary pourparlers, may say to himself: "That is what awaits me in the future triple agreement; Russia and Germany will always agree beforehand, and then impose their wills on me. It is much better to keep out of such an alliance".

We have now sufficient data to judge Haymerlé's attitude exactly. So long as he had no reason to suspect the existence of a real understanding between Germany and us, he gave a cool and discouraging reception to the overtures which came to him from Berlin for the constitution of the Dreikaiserbund. Ignorant of our stake, he did not think that we had anything to tempt Germany with, beyond what Austria had been able to offer her at Vienna last year.

[1] A letter from M. de Giers to M. Saburov of date 2/14 January 1881, is given in D.G.P. III, 156–158.

Since my visit to Friedrichsruhe uneasiness has taken hold of him: and as much as he formerly desired to get away from the Triple Entente, so much he now wishes to enter it, from fear of leaving us alone with Germany.

Austria makes the impression on me of the small gamester who wants to cheat. All goes well, so long as he only risks a few coppers. There comes unexpectedly a bigger gambler, with large stakes. The aspect of affairs changes; and the honest broker of Berlin naturally feels a greater interest in being joined by a more serious partner. There, in two words, is the explanation of the modification of Bismarck's attitude since last year. A promise of neutrality on our part is, for him, a stake of very different importance from all the assurances of a Cabinet as timorous and vacillating as that of Vienna. I think we have done well at the present moment in deciding to make use of this stake as the object of a bargain profitable in every respect. For the benefits which we will derive from it are palpable, whereas if we let uncertainty hover over the alliances, as a perpetual menace hung over the head of Germany, the benefits of such a policy would have remained highly questionable; and who knows whether Germany would not in the end have felt the need of getting out of an intolerable situation at any price, and risking again the chances of war rather than remain indefinitely exposed to the permanent danger of a simultaneous attack on both her flanks?

Two immense forces like those of Russia and of Germany would thus find themselves neutralised in a fruitless struggle, whilst reunited they can govern the world!

A last characteristic trait:

I tried to get at the German Chancellor's ideas about the duration of the Treaty, and in general about the guarantees necessary for its maintenance and faithful execution. I threw out, as a feeler, the idea of an alliance of two Powers against the one that would wish to infringe the Treaty.

"That", he replied, "will come of itself, seeing that we are three. But to formulate such an idea under this form would be mutually offensive. It would be a way of saying that we suspect one another. Frankly, the only Power which would be inclined not to keep an engagement is Austria. That is why, with her, a triple alliance is better than an alliance between two."

It seems to me that we have there the most eloquent funeral oration on what was done at Vienna last year!

Kindest regards.

To Baron Jomini.

Berlin, 11/23 January, 1881.

I am the more flattered by your lines of 6th January that you are the representative of the ideas which have guided our policy during the last quarter of a century.

As you know better than I do, there is nothing immutable in policy, and I am very glad to see that you acknowledge the necessity of introducing certain modifications in the old ideas so that they may be adapted to the circumstances of the moment. Now, the idea of a close friendship with Prussia is older than that of "arbiter between Prussia and France". We owe to the first our preponderance in Europe during the reign of the Emperor Alexander I, and that of the Emperor Nicholas. That of which you speak only dates from the fears which the aggrandisement of Prussia, now Germany, inspired in us. In order to follow up this scheme with success, there is need of extraordinary skill, abundant finances, an army always prepared. Now, let us be modest and confess that "the Minotaur" is cleverer than we, and that before allowing the formation of a Franco-Russian alliance, hostile to Germany, he could defeat us separately.

Therefore it was much better to return to the old idea, clothing it in a new dress to fit its new stature, while asking of it the services which the Prussia of former days was unable to render us. She was not able to guide Austria and impose her will upon her. Germany can do this. In every crisis in the East, this is the essential point for us. The arrangement at present proposed prepares the ground for it, even if it does not yet give us the certainty of it. When the future crisis comes (I hope it will not be too soon), we shall be able to come to an understanding in twenty-four hours.

You ask me what is the reason for the new caresses of the Minotaur. It is very simple; it is precisely because we have decided to give up the scheme of Prince Gortchakov of which you speak,—a scheme during whose existence Germany could not be at rest for a single moment, and which was the true cause of the Minotaur's sleepless nights, of his disordered nerves, and amorous frolics at Vienna. He was missing his legitimate spouse, and he began to run after dancers. Look at him now: he is quite different, even physically: his nerves do not torment him any more, and his health has come back to him. We had to deal with a man subject to hallucinations. We said to him: "'Nothing give, nothing get'; we shall heal you of your nightmares; in your turn put us in better balance; give us some political ballast".

I believe that the bargain is good. It is especially good, because it allows us to reflect and recover our strength.

With all due deference to Prince Gortchakov, one must not make politics à la Richelieu when one is not Richelieu, and the Europe not that of his age.

Let us give up playing at preponderance and rather do something practical. Let us give up luxuries and have necessaries. Ten years of such a régime followed with perseverance—that is what I would have wished.

Kindest regards.

CHAPTER XIII

REPORTS OF PRINCE REUSS

Berlin, 14/26 January, 1881.

P RINCE BISMARCK asked me again to call so that he might read to me Reuss's first report which he had just received. He had forbidden him to telegraph, from motives of prudence.

The report is voluminous. The first eight pages are devoted to explaining all the difficulties in the situation with which Reuss had to struggle, difficulties connected with the internal affairs of Austria, with the Austro-German Entente of last year, and lastly with Haymerlé's personal position. "This long preamble", said Bismarck, "was the usual artifice of the diplomat trying to show off the success of his efforts."

Then comes the account. Reuss began by informing Haymerlé that he was commissioned to forward a letter from his Sovereign to the Emperor Francis-Joseph, and begged him to ask the commands of His Majesty on this matter. He communicated the object of this letter to him at the same time, adding that he would have some formal proposals to make to him afterwards.

The following day, the Emperor, anxious to keep correct as a constitutional Sovereign, requested Reuss to send the Imperial letter to him through the medium of the Minister of Foreign Affairs—which was done.

The day after, Haymerlé invited Reuss to come to see him. He began by saying to the Ambassador that the Emperor had charged him to express the joy which the communication from the Emperor William had given him, that these overtures conformed to his own desires, and that he welcomed them with the greater eagerness since he saw in them at first sight serious guarantees for the consolidation of a general peace. The Emperor added that before replying, he was waiting until he had explained his views on the matter directly to Prince Reuss in a private audience.

At the second interview Reuss, at Haymerlé's request, communicated to him the text of the project with some verbal explanations, putting off the detailed discussion to the following day, in order to give his interlocutor time to study the document.

At the third interview, Reuss did not detect in the language of the Austrian Minister any indication of dissatisfaction that Russia and Germany had come to a preliminary agreement on all the points of the programme before proposing it to Austria. I caught, however, in Reuss's later account, two indications, if not of jealousy, at least of distrust.

In the first place, Haymerlé expressed the desire to know the "genesis" of the different parts of the project. He would like to know especially which parts were suggested by Russia and which by Germany. Naturally, Reuss, not having been present at the different phases of my pourparlers with Bismarck, was not in a position to satisfy this curiosity.

In the second place, Haymerlé, conjecturing that his visit to Friedrichsruhe had been the starting-point of this piece of work, asked why Prince Bismarck had not kept within the confines of the questions discussed with him at Friedrichsruhe? And, on the other hand, why the project contained snatches of things of which they had not spoken at this interview, and passed over in silence questions which they had debated, and which were more specially connected with the interests of Austria?

Reuss was unable to give a reply either to these questions. Bismarck noted on the margin that Haymerlé was making a mistake. But in endeavouring to run over with me the subjects discussed with Haymerlé at Friedrichsruhe, he remembered that the latter had mentioned the question of Novibazar, and that he had also spoken of his fear of seeing Russia invade Rumania. That was even the reason why the Prince had proposed his amendment relative to the non-entry of troops into Rumania, Serbia, etc., an amendment which we had handled so well at St Petersburg that he had preferred to give it up, and so the mention of Rumania had finally disappeared from the draft.

As to Novibazar, Haymerlé had said to him, after my explanations with Count Limburg, that Russia seemed to wish to withdraw what she had already formally conceded to Austria by the protocol signed in Berlin between Count Andrassy and Prince Gortchakov. "After all", added Bismarck, "I never had any idea of bringing this question into the main body of the project."

I did not think the moment opportune to discuss it then, not being sure that the Prince would side with our point of view; for the terms of the protocol are formal and the wording decides in favour of Austria. Besides, on that question, Austria only holds to the principle, caring very little to apply it and walk into the Novibazar hornets' nest.

I return to Reuss's account. The first impression produced on Haymerlé's mind seemed quite favourable. Above all he mentioned with pleasure the character of the project, which, by generalising the questions, brings them back to certain fundamental principles, thus avoiding touching on certain delicate points, difficult to formulate. At Berlin, as at St Petersburg, they had taken into account his wish not to try and foresee all the possible eventualities which no foresight could exhaust in advance.

For his part, Haymerlé does not ignore the value of the guarantees of peace which Austria can get from this arrangement either. "I only entreat you", he added, "not to hurry me; to give me time to study it more in all its aspects, and if there result some amendments which I would like to propose to you, to have the kindness to take them into consideration. Don't be afraid of my analytical mind; your project will not suffer from it; you will even see that I will go further"—here Bismarck interrupted the reading to say to me, "You presume that he is going to say, 'further than you'" and catching himself up again, he continued—"further than you think!"

To this Reuss replied that the project in its present form was the result of long and laborious negotiations; that, consequently, it was not a simple draft which one could easily modify without running the risk of compromising the whole matter, and that he ought to put Baron Haymerlé on his guard against the danger of too marked amendments.

"Reuss", remarked the Chancellor, "has gone here beyond my instructions. With a man of Haymerlé's temper, there is danger in offering him a dish, and saying, 'You must take it or leave it.' One gets better results by discussing things with him. It does not do to frighten a timid man too much. One must help him along by gentle dealing. Let us see what he will propose. If it is something unacceptable, I undertake to refuse, even without referring the matter to St Petersburg. If it is debatable, I advise you to discuss, and rather than refuse right away, propose some modifications."

All this may be very sound from a psychological point of view, but from our point of view, I am none the less gratified that Reuss spoke in this way.

Haymerlé replied by repeating his assurance that he would confine himself to stating precisely certain points which refer more particularly to Austria, and which, in his opinion leave the door open to misunderstandings. Without more explanation, he confined himself to pointing out, by the way, the stipulation bearing on the pledge of neutrality—"in the event of one of the three Powers being forced to go to war with a fourth one."

"This passage is too vague", he said. "Russia could find herself compelled to go to war with Rumania and conquer her, and during this time Austria would be obliged to observe a friendly neutrality and see to the localisation of the conflict!"

This language shows me that I was quite right in

relying upon Austria herself to define in a more precise fashion this passage from Article I, which I had not thought it wise to touch on at the time of my last pourparlers with Bismarck. Haymerlé, evidently uneasy over the too free attitude which the vagueness of this wording left to Germany in face of small States like Denmark, Belgium and Holland, felt immediately the need of modifying it. But like a wise man, he carefully refrained from naming Denmark or Belgium, and skilfully exaggerated his fears about a possible invasion of Rumania, the only small State which is in our neighbourhood, and which offers him in consequence the only convenient pretext for insisting on a clearer wording without offending the German Chancellor by any sense of mistrust with regard to him! If Bismarck had had any mental reservations, he would certainly have suspected this subterfuge on Haymerlé's part. But to judge from one proposal that he made to me in the continuation of this conversation, of which I shall presently give an account, I must believe that he had no mental reservation at the time of the drafting of this article, and that, in consequence, the true meaning of Haymerlé's subtlety escaped him.

I was pleased with Haymerlé's language for yet another reason. Since he chose, by way of illustration, a possible conflict between Russia and Rumania, and kept silence on the eventuality of a Russo-Turkish war, which may equally be included in the actual wording of Article I, it is a proof that he entirely admits the application of the words, "*with a fourth Power*" to Turkey. If it were otherwise, that is certainly the first objection which Haymerlé would have put forward. We have thus a valuable indication that this capital point will be accepted by Austria, and that she will agree to the pledge of neutrality in the event of a war between us and Turkey. So we cannot sufficiently congratulate ourselves on having refused to agree to the exclusion of Turkey from the category of Powers contemplated by Article I, and on not letting ourselves be influenced by Bismarck's fear of seeing Austria refuse that wording.

But I made all these reflections to myself, without saying a word to Bismarck. I confined myself to feigning great surprise and asking him what, finally, are the causes of these new anxieties on the part of Austria about an invasion of Rumania by Russia— anxieties of which I had never heard before?

The Prince replied to me that he could not very well explain it to himself. He only knew that, some time ago, they had been startled in Vienna by the discovery of a plot against the Prince of Rumania, and that it was attributed to the instigation of Stourdza, father-in-law of the young Prince Gortchakov. This conspiracy is supposed to have had as its object to proclaim Stourdza Hospodar, under the protection of Russia. From that to annexation would not be a long step, always according to the version which has reached Vienna. These rumours might in part explain the anxieties of Baron Haymerlé, according to Prince Bismarck.

"But", I replied, "even if Haymerlé were a prey to such absurd ideas, we have in reserve the variant of Article I which ought to satisfy him, for that variant clearly indicates the *Great Powers* as being alone included in Article I. The contingency of an attack on Rumania by Russia is thus excluded from it."

The Prince pointed out to me that this variant admitted also the contingency of a war between Russia and Turkey—a war which would necessitate, without doubt, the passage of Russian troops through Rumania. Now that is precisely the point on which Austria is sensitive. She would agree to it, should it so happen, as she agreed to it in 1877; but the difficulty is to make her sign this agreement in advance. That is the very difficulty he had in view when he proposed his amendment to me at Friedrichsruhe.

After reflecting an instant he said to me: "One could get round the difficulty by proposing the following wording for this passage of Article I:

If one of the three Courts found itself compelled to go to war with one of the other Powers *signatory to the Treaty of Berlin*, the other two will preserve a friendly neutrality, etc."

"Moreover," he added, "we must wait till Haymerlé formulates his opinion, and it is only then that we shall be able to see what can be done."

I seized at once on this suggestion, declaring it to be perfect, and expressing the certainty that no objection would be found to it at St Petersburg. It answers, indeed, to all that we could wish; it includes Turkey (in the capacity of signatory to the Treaty of Berlin) in the number of Powers contemplated by Article I, and it excludes at the same time all the little States of Europe!

Moreover, this wording, suggested by Bismarck

himself, was, in my eyes, the best proof that he har-
boured no mental reservations with regard to the
little States which border upon Prussia.

Therefore, when Article I will be recast in such a
way as to cover the case of the little States, Haymerlé
will have gained his point, and his fears for Rumania,
whether real or pretended, will be calmed, after
having served our own ends.

But I must return to Reuss's narration. Haymerlé,
whilst expressing a desire for an exchange of ideas in
order to clear up further difficult points in the project,
added that he would like to do so with perfect frankness, without feeling any sense of constraint; to open
his mind in short as one can only open it to the
German Chancellor, the best ally of Austria, and the
most powerful Minister in Europe. In order to be
completely at ease, he would prefer that Russia was
not present at their conference.

Here the Prince interrupted his reading an instant
and looked at me with a sly expression, as if he were
saying to me: "That is why I am reading you Reuss's
report, without sparing you a single line". He annotated this passage to the effect that Haymerlé's wish
was difficult to satisfy, seeing that it would be impossible for him to discuss Russian interests without
Russia.

Haymerlé thereafter expressed his desire to learn
Prince Bismarck's opinion about the change that the
Triple Entente would introduce into the arrangements
concluded at Vienna between their two Governments.
Will their character not be modified by the presence
of Russia in this Entente?

After having read me this passage without the least hesitation, the Prince expatiated at length on this famous transaction, and spoke of it to me as of something about which he had nothing new to tell me since his confidences of September, 1879, the day after his return from Vienna.

"I do not know", he said, "why they are always anxious to let mystery hover over this transaction. At any moment I can make one exactly like it with Russia, without Austria being offended by it. What happened? I said to Andrassy that the maintenance of Austria as a Great Power was in the interests of Germany; that the latter could not allow Austria to be erased from the map of Europe, or else reduced to the dimensions of a State of the third rank. Germany is surrounded by great States; their number makes her strength, for the more numerous they are, the more difficult it is for them to enter into coalitions. At that time the Panslavist tendencies in Russia were causing me anxiety, perhaps quite wrongly; I wondered what would be the direction of Russian policy under the sway of these tendencies; and a Franco-Russian alliance, having as object the destruction of German unity was the particular danger of the future of which I was thinking, and which ended by demonstrating in my eyes the good of maintaining Austria as a Great Power. Andrassy, on his part, gave me analogous assurances. All that I said to Andrassy, I had already said to Oubril in 1877, when Prince Gortchakov had inquiries made of me as to what would be the attitude of Germany in the event of a war between Russia and Austria. Germany's interest indicates to us in a like circumstance a course from which we cannot deviate; we must see that neither of these two Powers is *completely defeated*. They are both necessary to us."

Here the Prince added that he had made it very clearly understood in Vienna that Germany could never bind herself to protect Austria or to espouse her quarrels in wars of aggression.

Haymerlé touched on two other points. He wishes to know Prince Bismarck's ideas as to the *duration* of the Treaty. The Prince made the annotation that this question is still premature. There will be time to come to an arrangement about that.

Then Haymerlé insists particularly on the necessity of maintaining secrecy over this Treaty. He fears the Delegations; he fears the press; he fears the effect which the news of a Treaty signed by three will produce in Paris and London.

The German Chancellor annotated this passage: "If it is necessary we shall keep it secret; but will they keep it themselves?"

I said to Prince Bismarck that, so far as we were concerned, we should keep it secret. We have no indiscreet Houses. I added, however, that there were no such things as eternal secrets; each of our three Cabinets may find it advantageous in certain circumstances, to lift a corner of the veil: Germany, in order to calm bellicose aspirations from France, if such aspirations were in evidence; Austria, in order to make the Italians think; finally, Russia, in the event of a new Beaconsfield Cabinet becoming too aggressive. Therefore we may perhaps agree not to reveal the existence of the Treaty, or any of its stipulations, unless on the unanimous consent of the three Courts.

This question seems a matter of little importance to the Prince.

From our point of view, secrecy seems to me advantageous and even necessary, so long as the Gladstone Ministry lasts. The Opposition would have a formidable weapon against him if the Treaty became known. It would accuse him of having only succeeded in estranging Germany and Austria from England, and of having thrown them into the arms of Russia.

That is the reason why it would be in our interests to begin by coming to an agreement with Vienna and Berlin on the subject of keeping the matter secret. Later, we shall see.

At the end of his interview with Reuss, Haymerlé said to him that despite the responsibility which he assumes for the future, he is ready to take part in this work. He found the Emperor Francis-Joseph more disposed than he had been some time ago to enter into some *fixed* arrangements (*feste Abmachungen abzuschliessen*). All the news which comes from Russia to his Majesty, testifies to the more and more pacific tendencies which show themselves there. He himself is compelled to admit that latterly these soothing tendencies are manifest also in the attitude of the Russian agents in the different places of the East....

Here the Prince remarked to me that it was the first time that he had seen Haymerlé pleased.

In closing, the Austrian Minister of Foreign Affairs

notified also a certain improvement in the attitude of public opinion in Vienna, as also in the organs of the Viennese press. "There is", he said, "no longer the same fear (*dieselbe Furcht*) amongst us of the reconstitution of the 'Dreikaiserbund'."

Here the Prince placed on the margin a mark of interrogation. "I don't understand this passage", he said to me.

"One would really think", I remarked, "that we were lying in wait for Austria in the corner of a wood!"

"And that", remarked Bismarck by way of repartee, "in order to give her our purse!"

In taking leave, we agreed to meet again after the arrival of the communications which Baron de Haymerlé promised to send to Prince Reuss, when he had made a thorough study of the project.

CHAPTER XIV

BARON DE HAYMERLÉ'S OPPOSITION

Berlin, 23 January/4 February, 1881.

BISMARCK said to me that the reply from the Emperor Francis-Joseph to the letter from the Emperor William had just come. The Emperor of Austria had handed it over to Reuss in private audience.

This reply is entirely satisfactory.

The Emperor Francis-Joseph agrees without reserve to a close entente between the three Imperial Courts. He agrees also to all the principles which serve as basis to the project of the future Treaty, and informs the Emperor William that he has charged his Minister of Foreign Affairs to come to an agreement with Germany and Russia over the details. In addition His Majesty said to Prince Reuss that it was absolutely necessary for these negotiations to end in a satisfactory result, and that for his part he would do his best.

In the interval Reuss had had a fresh interview with Haymerlé. They began the discussion of details.

Haymerlé persists in asking why the project contains so many new matters of which he had not been informed at Friedrichsruhe. About this complaint, Bismarck did not give me new details; but I readily understood that the "new matter" for Haymerlé was Article I which contains the benefits to accrue to

Germany. At Friedrichsruhe, the Prince was desirous above all to prepare the agreement between Austria and us. He had secured Haymerlé's agreement to the matter of the Straits (Article III) by means of our promise not to touch Turkey without coming to an understanding with Austria. As for the fundamental principle of the agreement, that of protecting us mutually against coalitions (Article I) the Prince, it appears, had not spoken to him about it. I recognised in this a clever manœuvre of the German Chancellor with a view to compelling Austria to accept this principle, while presenting it to her as having been already definitely agreed to by Germany and Russia.

Haymerlé's objections had reference principally to the wording of this Article I. First of all, what does the word "mediation" mean? How, and in connection with what grievances will this mediation be exercised? If, for example, Russia found fault with some administrative measure of Austria's in her Polish or Slav provinces, the latter could not accept the mediation of a third Power. That would be to open the door to foreign interference in her domestic affairs.

Here Haymerlé's subtle mind was evidently at fault. He believed, according to Bismarck's expression, that he had found out "cunning" in the Russian diplomacy, and directed against it a thorough attack. He did not know that this part of the text was the work of Germany; that the very idea of "mediation" was of German origin, and that he was spending his ardour in contending with Bismarck himself!

He likewise objected to the sentence, "if one of the Powers was compelled to go to war", etc. What does the word "compelled" mean?

I reminded the Prince that the word was his. My first draft had been this: "if one of the Powers happened to be at war", etc. He had said to me at Friedrichsruhe: "Let us make it, '*forced to go to war*'; it is always more proper".

The Prince replied to me, laughing: "I recollect it perfectly. Also I will charge Reuss to explain to Haymerlé that it is a purely ornamental term there —to hide what may offend".

He then proceeded to the most important objection which Haymerlé had brought forward up till then.

It is always Rumania. At the time when she was a vassal principality, her existence was placed under the safeguard of all Europe. To-day this little State is exposed to all the dangers of independence. She can be invaded in two ways; either by engaging in an imprudent war, or by becoming the victim of a crafty policy, like that of the Empress Catharine with regard to Poland, and herself summoning a Russian army on to her territory.

Here the Prince related to me some retrospective details about his interview with Haymerlé at Friedrichsruhe. The latter explained to him the precarious situation of Austria in the event of Russia thinking of absorbing the little independent States which she had created. "What shall we do", he asked, "if Russia occupied Moldavia?"

Bismarck replied to him: "Benedetti once put a similar question to me. He asked me if Germany

would attack France in the event of the latter occupying Belgium. I answered 'No', but that we would
seek our 'Belgium' elsewhere. I had in view the
Germany of the South, from which we were yet
separated by the line of the Main. 'Well', I said to
Haymerlé, 'if Russia occupied Moldavia, seek your
"Moldavia" elsewhere. Occupy Wallachia and hold
it as a pledge'".

"And if Russia occupied Wallachia before us?"
remarked the foreseeing Haymerlé.

"Occupy Serbia, or Novibazar, or something."

"And if Russia attacked us for that?" asked the
courageous Haymerlé.

"Defend yourself", replied Bismarck.

"Will you guarantee us the territories which we
will have occupied?"

"Certainly not", was the reply.

After relating this amusing dialogue to me, the
Prince began to discuss with me the terms of a
draft that would allay the fears of the Austrian
Minister.

"We shall not come to that", he said, "without
putting in again the amendment which I proposed at
Friedrichsruhe."

"Granted," I replied, "only we shall add to it
afresh our counter-amendment, for we cannot close
the road to Bulgaria against ourselves, if that becomes
necessary to us."

We had then to find a new wording by our common
effort, and, strange to say, we arrived at the same
result as in St Petersburg, but in other terms.

This new wording, which the Prince undertook to

put forward in Vienna, is expressed as follows (Article II, between the second and third paragraphs):

"None of the Powers will send troops on to the territory of Rumania, Serbia or Montenegro without having talked it over together with the other two. This engagement will be valid as long as the present status quo in Turkey lasts."

I did not see Prince Bismarck again till 22 February.

On receiving me, he said: "The interval which has elapsed since our last conversation will prove to you that Haymerlé is not an easy dove to tame".

Although he had not yet had a definite reply from Vienna, he did not wish to further postpone taking advantage of his first free day to make me acquainted with the negotiations in their present state.

Haymerlé, pressed to produce his amendments, continued to confine himself within the circle of his criticisms, without formulating anything.

The Prince read me several reports from Reuss which gave me a sufficiently complete idea of the history of these difficult negotiations.

He had sent my letter on the subject of the amendment relative to Rumania, Serbia, etc., to Vienna, charging Reuss to get it accepted.

Haymerlé, in response to this proceeding, formulated the demand that the inviolability of Rumanian territory be placed under the special guarantee of Germany; in other words, that Germany stand guarantee to Austria that Russian troops will not enter Rumania.

The Prince flatly refused.

Haymerlé then concentrated his objections to the Treaty upon two points:

(1) He is afraid that Russia and Germany will always agree more easily between themselves than with Austria about the eventualities in the East. He sees the proof of this in the rapidity with which agreement has already been reached between St Petersburg and Berlin on some points of capital importance— Roumelia, the Balkans, union of the two Bulgarias, the Straits, neutrality, lastly this project of treaty itself. Regarded from this point of view, this Treaty would only serve to tie Austria's hands, and to leave Russia full scope in view of a new campaign in Turkey. Reuss infers from this language that Haymerlé suspects Germany and Russia of having already come to an understanding for this purpose.

Here I interrupted the Prince to say, that having taken part in the discussions at St Petersburg, I could certify that, on the contrary, it is we who thought our hands would be tied up to a certain point by this Treaty, and that we made this sacrifice in order to bring about the alliance of the three Empires.

(2) After having developed this *general* objection to a written treaty, Haymerlé made a second, directed especially against the passage in Article I which is expressed as follows: "If a difference or complaint should arise between two of them, it would be referred to the *mediation* of the third", etc.

Haymerlé sees here a fool's bargain. Between Austria and Russia the mediator will be Germany, and if, as he supposes, Russia and Germany, in the state of their present relations, will always agree easily, such mediation will be equivalent to imposing on Austria a decision favourable to Russia!

In these words, the Viennese Cabinet made an instructive confession of its impotence to reverse the rôles; and that, in its opinion, the friendship of Russia was more necessary to Germany than that of Austria!

Finally, Haymerlé expressed the fear that the principle of *mediation* would only end in altering the relations between Austria and Germany.

Prince Reuss concluded his report by depicting the depressing effect which the feeling of responsibility produces on Haymerlé's mind. The mere thought that the Hungarians will one day learn that he signed a pact with Russia makes him shudder.

In place of applying a brake (*ein Riegel*) to Russian policy, he would be accused of having given her carte blanche.

Finally, Haymerlé began afresh his complaints that Prince Bismarck had not explained to him further the origin and extent of the different stipulations of the projected Treaty, as he had begged him to do.

The Chancellor, out of patience with these evasions, enjoined Reuss to ask an audience with the Emperor Francis-Joseph, in order to invite His Majesty to bring pressure to bear upon His Minister. Reuss was to explain to the Emperor that never had a more favourable occasion presented itself for determining in a lasting way the favourable disposition of Russia with regard to Austria. The Emperor Alexander has a strong desire for this, and has surrounded himself with Ministers animated by the same intentions. If the arrangement happened to fail as a result of Austrian opposition, the Emperor Alexander might quite well think that those who had formerly denounced the Dreikaiserbund to him as contrary to the interests of Russia, were perhaps right, and that with Austria scarcely any agreement is possible. Now, they should understand in Vienna that the relations between Russia and Austria are always liable to deteriorate, and are much more at the mercy of events than those between Russia and Germany. In order to bring on a war between these two last Powers, there must be much desire for it on either side; whilst between Russia and Austria a conflict can break out by the sole force of events, even if their Sovereigns were sincerely desirous of peace. That is why Austria ought to take advantage of this moment in order to assure peace, at least for some years.

Reuss found the Emperor Francis-Joseph animated as always with the best intentions; attaching the greatest value to the present inclinations of the Emperor Alexander and to the necessity of taking advantage of them to realise a combination so useful to the three Empires. Nevertheless it was difficult to get him to emerge from his rôle of constitutional Sovereign, and to induce him to act contrary to his responsible Minister.

At this moment the King of Saxony was in Berlin for the wedding celebrations.[1] Bismarck, who always likes to return to his first ideas, and who was moreover impressed by the difficulties with which he was meeting

---

[1] Possibly the marriage on 27 February, 1881, of Frederick William Victor Albert, eldest son of the German Crown Prince, and grandson of Queen Victoria.

in Vienna, gave some half-confidences to the King of Saxony, and asked him if he would consent eventually to use his personal influence with the Emperor of Austria in order to make a success of the matter in Vienna. The King agreed.

It was, however, only an eventual means of which Bismarck expected to make use in case of necessity; for he sent fresh instructions to Reuss at the same time to make a final attempt with Haymerlé.

In telling me the confidence relative to the King, the Prince added that he did not think he had been guilty of an indiscretion towards us. An eventual appeal to the King of Saxony had been examined in one of our previous conversations; the King was the devoted friend of the Emperor of Austria, as the Grand-Duke of Saxe-Weimar was the devoted friend of the Emperor Alexander. In the present circumstance, the first could be more serviceable than the second in the matter of Vienna.

The King of Saxony will have an opportunity of seeing the Emperor of Austria in April at a capercailzie drive.

Bismarck was kind enough to make me acquainted with the new instructions sent to Reuss. They are indeed the instructions of a man whose patience is exhausted.

"You will say to Baron Haymerlé", he wrote, "that I have promised the Russian Government to secure from Austria a 'Yes' or 'No'. I must have a categorical reply, which the Russian Ambassador has been awaiting for three weeks, and which I am not yet able to give him.

"Tell him also that I am in no way disposed, in the event of a refusal, to share with him the responsibility of the consequences which this refusal may carry in its train. Austria will bear that responsibility by herself. The theme of a cooling of relations between Russia and Germany has already been sufficiently enlarged upon, and, for my part, I shall take care not to give any further pretext for such a supposition. Baron Haymerlé must know, once for all, that if he refuses, he will do so at his own risk and peril."

Taking up thereafter Haymerlé's objections one by one, the Prince authorised Reuss to state that the clause relative to "mediation" was not a Russian idea, but *his own*; that it did not form one of the essential parts of the Treaty; that he does not care for it the moment that any one objects to it; that the two essential principles of the Treaty are the clause on neutrality and that relating to the Straits, and that on these two points he requests a "Yes" or "No".

As a reply to the mistrust expressed by Haymerlé, he leaves him to fix himself the period of duration of the Treaty, and to make it as short as he likes. The Prince mentioned ten, five or three years.

On the subject of its duration, he remarked to me that the essential matter was to get Haymerlé to sign something, even if it were only for two or three years. After having tasted the advantages of this system, no Austrian statesman will take it upon himself to refuse a renewal of it.

In accordance with the good humour of the Prince, I said to him that, for us, the present project is not a matter of a transitory opportunity, but that we see in it the first pledge of a political system of long endurance, such as the august predecessors of the reigning sovereigns have practised for a century, through all the upheavals in Europe. The Emperor, my Master, has taken a liking to this system, above all since he has made sure that Germany is as sincerely desirous as we are that we go hand in hand, and thus give mutual protection against all the perils of an unknown future. "With you", I added, "we shall be able to go very far together. Who knows all the events that may arise unexpectedly in Europe? Who can say how often you will again have need of us and we of you?"

The impression which this language produced, seemed sufficiently strong for me to attempt successfully a suggestion which may be very useful to us afterwards.

"Do you not think", I said to the Prince, "that there would be another way still of influencing Haymerlé? You will doubtless have remarked that for some time we have been adopting on every occasion a more conciliatory attitude to Austria, as Haymerlé himself recognises?"

"I know it", he remarked.

"Well," I continued, "would it not be opportune to show Haymerlé that he will regret it if he refuses? In all the questions which interest Austria—those of the Danube, Serbia, Bulgarian railways—we could suddenly resume a stiff attitude ill-suited to the Austrian Government. But before submitting this means of pressure to St Petersburg, I should like to know if you consider it good."

The Prince replied that at that moment it would still be premature. He expects the definite reply from Vienna at any moment. "If that reply", he added, "was negative or dilatory, the means that you suggest seem to me *clearly indicated.*"

This reply, by which the Chancellor of Germany gives us almost carte blanche to create difficulties for Austria if she refuses the Treaty, is a proof of the great advantage that one can derive from a resolute man like Bismarck, when one has to do with a clumsy adversary like Haymerlé.

The latest report from Reuss gives an account of how he carried out these instructions. He tried to persuade Baron Haymerlé that if the responsibility of signing the Treaty weighs on him, it will weigh on him much more if he does not sign it, and becomes the cause of a change in the attitude of the Emperor Alexander with regard to Austria.

Haymerlé admitted that there was no reply to this argumentation of Prince Bismarck (*er sollte vor Euren Einwendungen schweigen*). He also added a polite phrase for me: "es wäre ihm auch sehr peinlich den Russischen Botschafter auf sich warten zu lassen".[1]

Finally, he asked for twenty-four hours to ascertain the orders of the Emperor.

An hour after my visit, the telegram from Prince Reuss arrived, containing the definite reply from Baron Haymerlé.

[1] It would be very painful for him to keep the Russian Ambassador waiting.

CHAPTER XV

OUR REPLIES

Berlin, 23 February, 1881.

REUSS telegraphs that Haymerlé accepts our proposals with the suppression of the "mediation" of Article I; three years of duration for the Treaty, and some changes in the wording which we shall probably learn to-morrow.

Death of the Emperor Alexander II.

Berlin, 7/19 March, 1881.

I received yesterday the secret letter of 4 March in which M. de Giers announces to me that the Emperor has confirmed the last instructions which had been addressed to me by order of the late Emperor of imperishable memory.

Having repaired the same day to the German Chancellor, I gave him this letter to read, in silence, without comments.

He read it contemplatively, slowly, trying to fix in his memory those words which give the decisions of the new Sovereign of Russia a form worthy of the loftiness of His mind, of the extent of His grief, and of His filial piety.

This important communication placed me in a position to resume with Prince Bismarck our interrupted pourparlers.

The Prince began by expressing a wish,—that we should not be in a hurry to remove Austrian fears about the political consequences of the change of reign. Baron Haymerlé is still making difficulties about the conclusion of the projected arrangement. It would be well to make him feel the danger that would result for Austria from a possible change in the political course of the new Emperor. "*If Austria desires that there be no change, it is necessary for her to deserve it....*"

The Prince then made me acquainted with the amendments proposed by Haymerlé. He said to me that he was refraining from judging them till he knew the view of my Government. However, he wished to know what I thought of them personally.

I said that at first sight the majority of these amendments did not seem to me to exclude the possibility of an entente. I had, however, to make an exception in the case of the changes proposed in Article III relative to the Straits. These changes, in my opinion, cannot be accepted in St Petersburg.

The Prince, while carefully avoiding pleading in favour of the Austrian wording, pointed out to me that the essential was there; that Austria recognised our right to declare war on Turkey in the event of her opening the Straits to a belligerent Power.

I replied that the important thing for us was to *prevent* that eventuality, and that is why we insisted on a common declaration to be sent to Turkey on behalf of our three Courts, relying on the moral effect which such a declaration would produce in Constantinople. Now, it is precisely that eventual declaration which is suppressed in the Austrian draft.

The Prince sided completely with my sentiment.

Without awaiting my return from St Petersburg, he will write immediately to Vienna saying that in his opinion the amendments proposed in Article III will be deemed inadmissible by the Russian Government. As to the others, it will be possible to discuss them.

In running through the text of the project as it has been amended by Haymerlé, I asked what had become of the famous amendment, several times introduced and suppressed, on the subject of Rumania?

The Prince replied that Haymerlé had in the end given it up and replaced it by the term " *Great* Power" in Article I. According to Haymerlé, that is a sufficient guarantee to safeguard Rumania.

So I was right in saying at the time that Rumania was only a pretext, and that in reality Haymerlé was thinking of excluding all the little States from the contingencies anticipated by Article I. Thus we have gained our point with regard to Denmark, Belgium, etc., without having offended the German Government by any manifestation of distrust with regard to it. Austria has performed that task for us. This delicate point of our pourparlers has accordingly been solved in a satisfactory manner, and every embarrassing obligation on the subject of the non-entry of troops into Rumania has definitely disappeared.

The amendments transmitted by Baron Haymerlé were accompanied by fresh laments about the intentions and mental reservations which he attributes to Russia.

He brought down upon himself by that a pretty sharp reply from Prince Bismarck. The latter told him through Reuss that the way in which they were behaving in Vienna at that moment reminded him of his saddest experiences of Austrian diplomacy at the time when he was Prussian Minister at the Diet of Frankfort. There was neither frankness nor good faith—these are his own expressions—in ignoring the advantages which Austria will reap from this arrangement, and in contesting the equity of the Russian demands, her great moderation, and the conciliatory spirit which she had manifested in the course of these important negotiations. "If M. Haymerlé", added the Prince in his letter to Reuss, "would prefer to give up these advantages, let him do so; but then let him also understand that a triple arrangement, however desirable it may be, is not indispensable for us, and that, so far as we are concerned, the friendship of Russia is, perhaps, a more effective safeguard with regard to France, than would be a combination to which Austria would belong."

This is the first time that I heard Prince Bismarck put the situation, so to speak, openly, calling things by their names, without any reserve whatever.

Baron Haymerlé has brought forward the stipulation about the closing of the Straits as of the nature of an "enormous" concession which Austria makes to Russia. Bismarck answered him that the closing of the Straits is as much an Austrian as a Russian interest. What would Austria say, if, under the influence of Republican France, a Rumanian republic were to come into being at the mouth of the Danube, and a French fleet pass through the Straits to support and protect this revolutionary work?

I confess that this hypothesis, somewhat unlikely,

is an argument with little persuasive value, but we must feel grateful to the German Chancellor for his kindness in defending our point of view in these difficult negotiations with the Cabinet of Vienna.

On 10 March I left for St Petersburg in order to be present at the funeral of the Emperor Alexander II, and to take part in the discussions relative to the definitive drafting of the projected Treaty. These discussions ended in the results tabulated on pp. 228–31.

Berlin, 3/15 April.

On my return to Berlin I communicated to Prince Bismarck our counter-amendments with the necessary explanations. After having studied them, he said to me that as for Article III, which interests us particularly, he will insist on its maintenance in the form which we desire. If Haymerlé resists, he will make known to him that in that case he has decided to sign the engagement recorded in that Article separately with us.

As for Article II, I believe I have noticed that it could give rise to some discussions in which Haymerlé might bring Bismarck over to his side, by accusing us of wishing to dispute some day the situation of Austria in Bosnia and Herzegovina. So I said to Bismarck, that in order to avoid discussions, the best thing would be to maintain the original wording which cannot cause any misunderstanding. He will consider the matter further.

In the proposals which will be sent to Vienna I have also restored the original text of paragraph (3) of Article I, which Haymerlé had tried to modify.

15-2

TEXT OF RUSSO-GERMAN PROJECT PROPOSED TO AUSTRIA[1]

Russo-German Project, Proposed to Austria	Austrian Amendments	Russian Replies
Article I.	*Article I.*	*Article I.*
Paragraph (1). The three Courts of Russia, Germany and Austria-Hungary resolve that if a difference or complaint happened to arise between two of them, this difference would be referred to the mediation of the third, to be afterwards removed by a triple agreement.	Paragraph (1). Suppress.	Agreed.
Paragraph (2). In the event of one of them being *forced to go* to war with a fourth *Power,* the other two will maintain in relation to it a friendly neutrality and *will see to* the localisation of the conflict.	Paragraph (2). Suppress the words *forced to go.* Replace the word *Power* by the words *Great Power.* Replace the words *will see to* by the words *will devote their attention.*	Agreed.
Paragraph (3). This stipulation will apply equally to a war between one of the three Powers and Turkey, but only in the event where a preliminary agreement will have been established between the three Courts with regard to the results of that war.	Paragraph (3). *None of the three Powers shall undertake a war of aggression against Turkey. If however one of them were compelled to go to war with that Empire, the stipulation of the preceding paragraph* will apply equally to that war, but only in the event where a	We maintain the original draft.

[228]

Paragraph (4). In the special case of one of them obtaining from one of the two allies more positive co-operation, the obligatory nature of the present Article will remain in all its force for the third.	preliminary agreement will have been established between the three Courts $\frac{\text{conditions}}{}$ on the *territorial limits and* the results of that war. Paragraph (4). Adopted.	Agreed.
Article II. Paragraph (1). Russia in agreement with Germany, declares her firm resolve to respect the interests which arise from the new position assured to Austria by the Treaty of Berlin, *and defined lastly by her convention with Turkey on the subject of the occupation of certain parts of the Ottoman territory.* [229]	*Article II.* Paragraph (1). Suppress the last part of the paragraph from the words "and defined lastly," or add at the end: "Austria-Hungary reserves the right, if the defence of her interests were to demand it, to make changes in the political situation of Bosnia, Herzegovina, and the Sanjak of Novibazar".	*Article II.* We prefer to suppress the last part of the paragraph beginning with the words, "and defined lastly".
Paragraph (2). The three Courts, desirous to avoid all disagreement between them, undertake to take into account their respective interests in the Balkan Peninsula. They further promise that new modifications in the territorial status quo *of Turkey in Europe* will only be carried out in virtue of a common agreement *between them.*	Paragraph (2). *of the provinces of Turkey in Europe at present subject to the authority of the Sultan,* etc. Suppress at the end the words "between them."	We hold to the original draft.

¹ For original text, see Appendix I.

Russo-German Project, Proposed to Austria	Austrian Amendments	Russian Replies
Article II (cont.). Paragraph (3). In order to facilitate the agreement envisaged by the present Article, agreement of which it is impossible to foresee all the limitations, the three Courts will declare, *immediately*, the points on which *an understanding has already been established* in principle.	*Article II (cont.).* Paragraph (3). Suppress, or modify thus the words italicised "will state the points on which a previous exchange of ideas has demonstrated an agreement in principle".	*Article II (cont.).* We hold to the original draft.
Article III. Paragraph (1). The three Courts recognise the European and mutually obligatory character of the principle of the closing of the Straits of the Bosphorus and the Dardanelles, founded on international law and confirmed by the Treaties.	*Article III.* Paragraph (1). Add at the end the words "from Paris, London, and Berlin with indication of the date of the Treaties".	*Article III.* Agreed: but mention also our Declaration at the Congress of Berlin.
Paragraph (2). They *will see to it* in common that Turkey makes no exception to this rule in favour of the particular interests of any Government whatever, by lending to the war operations of a belligerent Power the part of her Empire constituted by the Straits.	Paragraph (2). Suppress the expression "they will see to it" and add at the end, in place of the paragraph following which is unacceptable, the words: "without going to war with the injured Party".	We insist on the maintenance of the original draft.

		Hold to the original text.
Paragraph (3). In case of infringement, or in order to prevent it if such an infringement were foreseen, the three Courts will warn Turkey that they would consider her, should it so happen, as having put herself in a state of war with the injured Party, and as having deprived herself, from that time, of the benefits of security assured by the Treaty of Berlin to her territorial status quo.	Paragraph (3). Suppress.	
	Article IV. Fix the term of three years for the duration of the Treaty.	*Article IV.* Agreed.
	Article V. Pledge to keep the Treaty secret.	*Article V.* Agreed.
	Preamble to the Treaty. State definitely the purpose of this arrangement, destined to provide new guarantees for peace, to the maintenance of which the three Powers are resolved to devote all their efforts.	*Article VI.* Abolish the secret conventions concluded in 1873 with Germany and Austria.

Bismarck will inform Haymerlé that the Treaty in this final form is a thing to take or leave.

As to the term of three years which Austria proposes for the duration of the Treaty, the Prince thinks that at the end of this period the Austrian statesmen will appreciate its advantages, and agree to its renewal. "When Austria", he added, "has worn that flannel for three years next her skin, she will no longer be able to discard it without running the risk of catching cold."

CHAPTER XVI

A CRITICAL MOMENT

Berlin, 25 April/7 May, 1881.

P RINCE BISMARCK, after much trouble, has at
last succeeded in getting Vienna to accept our
draft of the Treaty, with the exception of a single
addition by Haymerlé to Article II. In everything
else, our wording remains intact, and notably the
whole of Article III has been accepted without change.

It seems that the "ribbon of the Order of St
Stephen" played a certain part in this affair. The
Emperor Francis-Joseph, wishing to see the matter
brought to a successful issue, was anxious to gild the
pill for Haymerlé, who complained up to the end of
having been forced to concede points contrary, in his
opinion, to Austrian interests.

The addition in question is made to the first paragraph of Article II. It is expressed as follows:

Austria-Hungary reserves the right, if the defence of her
interests were to demand it, to make changes in the political
situation of Bosnia, Herzegovina and, eventually, of the Sanjak
of Novibazar.

Baron Haymerlé, in agreeing to withdraw all his
other amendments, insists on this one in order to re-
assure Austria on the subject of her future position
in these provinces. He added that if he did not secure
this point, the Emperor Francis-Joseph will not be
able to give his assent to the Treaty. Finally he

appealed to Prince Bismarck's sense of fairness, asking him to show the same warmth in defending this single Austrian amendment as he had displayed in getting Vienna to accept all the Russian proposals.

Prince Bismarck promised to do so. He began by reading to me Reuss's report on that subject. According to that Ambassador, if we refused to set Austria's mind at rest on this point, she would entertain an incurable mistrust, and would suspect us of wishing to dispute the possession of Bosnia and Herzegovina with her later, and free ourselves from our engagement on the subject of Novibazar. She will thus regard the project of the Treaty as a trap, and be unwilling to sign anything.

After reading this report to me, the Prince spoke as follows: "I have had no hesitation in undertaking to bring forward this request of Baron Haymerlé, for I am conscious of asking nothing of you which you have not already granted before. Previous to the Congress of Berlin you had already agreed to the annexation of these two provinces. At the Congress, when the Austrian occupation was decided on, none of the plenipotentiaries understood it to be other than a permanent occupation, equivalent to a taking possession. At the end of the Congress, you gave along with Andrassy your written consent to the occupation of Novibazar. That was a transaction which brought you the support of Austria in the questions of Serbia and Montenegro. To-day Austria suspects you of wishing to cancel that engagement. If you have no such intention, I think that in strict justice you cannot refuse to set Austria at rest on this subject. That is why I believed I could undertake to be her advocate in this matter ".

I felt that the critical moment of the negotiations had come. It was the first time that Bismarck had set himself on the side of Austria against us. The knotty point of the question was Novibazar, which Haymerlé wished to compare to the position of Bosnia and Herzegovina, in order to claim later Austria's right to annex Novibazar as much as the other two provinces. Now, the protocol signed by Prince Gortchakov and Count Andrassy did not go so far.

But I did not think it wise to launch forthwith into a polemic which might have inflamed the dispute; I had to gain the time necessary for my Government to come to a decision at leisure.

On the other hand, I could not confirm, by my silence, Austria's doubts about the loyalty of our intentions. Therefore I said in reply to Prince Bismarck that the suspicions of Baron Haymerlé were unjust; that we have no intention of disputing things which had been granted; but that I was to see that the wording of our project remained such as had been sanctioned by the Emperor; that we could agree on the point in question without touching the Treaty; that this point would find its natural place, like other special questions, in the " current account " envisaged by Article II. In it will figure the union of the two Bulgarias, the prohibition for Turkish troops to occupy the Balkans, in short all the special questions on which we shall come to agreement, but which do not figure in the body of the main Treaty.

The Prince accepted this suggestion and gave orders to recommend it to Vienna.

So the ticklish question of Novibazar will be adjourned to the time when steps will be taken towards drafting a supplementary protocol; as for the main Treaty, it will be signed without any modification whatever. Haymerlé's addition will not be inserted in it.

I proposed to the Prince to leave it to Haymerlé himself to draw up this protocol or "current account". He replied: "I prefer your draftings. Draw up a scheme; Haymerlé will draw up his, and it will then be easier for us to come to an agreement with each other".

I agreed to this, at the same time warning Bismarck that he must consider my project as entirely personal, and intended only to help him in the elaboration of a definite project which I will submit on his behalf to the decision of my Government.

But the difficulty of Novibazar is only postponed, and we shall soon have a renewal of the trouble there. Why did our Chancellor sign that unfortunate protocol of 1878 in any case? The situation is curious in this sense that if we were to say to Austria to-day, "Take Novibazar", she would not do it. She knows that now the Albanians will give her trouble, and that she will be sick of it.

In conformity with the will of the Emperor, I insisted on completing the Treaty by an additional Article, abolishing the military conventions concluded with Germany and Austria in 1873.

This is a great riddance, for we could have had terrible misunderstandings.

I asked the Chancellor if he were not expecting opposition from the Emperor William, who, when speaking to me one day about that Convention, seemed to attach great importance to it. The Prince re-assured me on the subject. He had already spoken about it to the Emperor, and used the following reasoning with him: "What would you have said, Sir, if the Emperor Alexander had taken advantage of that Convention to demand 200,000 men from you at the time of the Turkish war? The Convention was drawn up so as to make such an interpretation possible".

This remark shows that in a reverse situation Germany would have also been able to avail herself of that Convention to her advantage.

Accordingly, it was much better to get rid of an engagement which could have given rise to the gravest misunderstandings.

Berlin, 6/18 May, 1881.

Haymerlé has sent his scheme of protocol contemplated by Article II of the Treaty. The passage relative to Novibazar is worded thus:

Annexation of Bosnia, Herzegovina, and of the Sanjak of Novibazar. Germany and Russia will give their endorsement to this if Austria were to find it necessary for the safeguarding of her interests.

In this new draft Haymerlé calls things by their name, and frankly makes use of the word "Annexation".

Bismarck, in communicating this document to me, said that in our place he would agree to this wording by which Austria will be irrevocably compromised with regard to Turkey and England, by openly confessing her intention of deviating from the Treaty of Berlin. "By this stipulation we shall hold her; we shall take away from her the power of assuming a rôle of virtuous indignation when we ourselves shall be brought to the necessity of stepping outside the limits of the Treaty of Berlin. She will be caught in the network by the scrap which we throw to her; fearing to lose it again, she will have no other resource than to fall in with our future plans."

Here he drew a parallel with the position of Austria in the Polish question. In the first partition, the Empress Catharine had assigned to Austria the largest share of the three, in order to bind her more surely by a community of interests. Maria-Theresa, whilst weeping over the fate of Poland, let herself be caught in the snare by accepting the morsel. To-day half the Austrian morsel is in the possession of Russia! Only Galicia remains to Austria. The Eastern question, which will yet pass through many phases, is of the same nature. In the opinion of the German Chancellor, we should make a mistake if we hindered Austria from compromising herself by formulating *in writing* her appetites which can only set her at variance with the Western Powers and establish a connivance with us in a future Eastern crisis.

The Prince finished with these words: "If you do not accept the Austrian text, I shall undertake, if you wish, to propose yours to them; but I fear that

Haymerlé will end by getting out of the Treaty if the pourparlers are protracted. I see that in Vienna they are already under the influence of the new combination of General Ignatiev".[1]

I replied to the Prince that my wording had some chance of acceptance by my Government. As to the Austrian project, I shall only be able to transmit it to St Petersburg, without giving any hope that it will be accepted.

I transcribe here my proposed wording of the appendix to the Treaty:

(1) *Bosnia and Herzegovina.* Austria-Hungary reserves her right to make changes in the political situation of these two provinces, if the defence of her interests demanded it.

(2) *Sanjak of Novibazar.* The protocol signed in Berlin on the subject of this province remains in force.

While listening to the somewhat Machiavellian arguments of which Bismarck made use in order to incline us to agree to the annexation of Novibazar, I

---

[1] Ignatiev, General Count Nicholas Pavlovitch (1832–1907), a famous Panslavist and able statesman who, along with the publicist Katkov and Baron Jomini, was strongly Germanophobe. He worked to promote Anglo-Russian friendship, coming to London in 1876 in particular for this purpose. As Russian Ambassador in Constantinople, he came to exercise considerable influence on the Turks, and was a signatory to the Treaty of San Stefano. On leaving the diplomatic service he was appointed Minister of the Interior under Alexander III, but his somewhat enlightened, though intensely nationalist, policy brought him into frequent conflict with Pobedonostzev, the reactionary Procurator of the Holy Synod. A proposal of his to convoke a consultative parliament under the old historical name of Zemski-Sobor was considered contrary to the principles of autocracy, and his dismissal by the Emperor followed. His brother Count Alexis was assassinated by Terrorists in 1906.

had the feeling that they would not take this bait in St Petersburg. Therefore the duty remained for me of preventing this disagreement from degenerating into a dispute between us and Germany.

Bismarck withdraws from the Negotiations.

Berlin, 16/28 May, 1881.

The crisis which I foresaw for some time has arrived. As I saw it coming, my principal anxiety had been to make use of Haymerlé as a buffer.

I noticed for some weeks that Bismarck was becoming nervous and irritated with all the discussions about the wording. That one of the two who spoke and objected the most, was certain to get the worst of it. Therefore I adopted the tactics of saying as little as possible, and acting in such a way that the objections came from Vienna.

With this purpose, when Haymerlé had proposed his amendment to the Treaty—knowing that that amendment could not be accepted by us—I had suggested to Bismarck that he should invite Haymerlé to transfer that amendment to the appendix of the Treaty, and draw up that appendix himself. In this way we were spared the inconvenience of refusing an amendment that Bismarck had undertaken to get us to accept; and Haymerlé was compelled to offer a new draft, but such a clumsy one, that it gave us just ground for objection.

Bismarck, while acknowledging the clumsiness of this draft, advised us all the same to accept it, in order to have done with it.

I had for a second time to avoid the inconvenience of replying with a refusal. At this moment I received the letter of 5 May in which M. de Giers informed me of the assent of the Emperor to *my* draft of the appendix. This draft had been a long while in Bismarck's hands.

Without making use of this letter, I said to Count Limburg-Stirum (who often acted as intermediary for me) "that if the Chancellor wished to conclude the matter at once, means were available, namely to adopt my wording, for I was almost certain that they would accept it in St Petersburg. If not, it was necessary to await the reply to my despatch which conveyed Haymerlé's draft to St Petersburg". By speaking in this way, I hoped that Bismarck, anxious to have done with it in order to go and take the cure at Kissingen, would make trial of my draft, and send it to Vienna in order to persuade Haymerlé to accept it.

That is what happened. In this way I compelled Haymerlé to speak and irritate Bismarck a third time, even before we had given a declinatory answer to the successive proposals which the Prince had made to us.

Haymerlé, taking the bait, replied with a detailed and meticulous criticism of each of my sentences. He objects to everything and insists on his draft. Reuss's report, which gives an account of this, arrived yesterday.

Bismarck, who is ill, sent his son to me in order to let me read this report, and say to me that he had reached the limit of his patience and strength, and could no longer continue to serve as intermediary in disputes upon words and turns of phrases. He is going to reply to Haymerlé, inviting him to agree with us without intermediary upon this draft.

Bismarck's son added that his father was very anxious that they should not interpret his decision in St Petersburg in a bad sense. He was always desirous to reach a final agreement, but he was really unable to go on longer.

I replied: "The Prince can be at rest; he knows me sufficiently to be sure that I shall explain the situation at St Petersburg as it is in reality".

In reading aloud Reuss's report afterwards, I entirely agreed with the angry annotations which the Chancellor had made on it in pencil. I said that I did not understand how Haymerlé could dwell upon negligible details of wording, etc.

All this happened two hours after the arrival of the mail from St Petersburg, which brought me instructions to decline acceptance of the Austrian wording. In the new situation created by Bismarck's decision, these instructions were no longer feasible. It was a refusal that I had to transmit, and that would only have been, from that time, to pour oil on the fire, without having the least chance of advancing our affairs. Accordingly, I confined myself to saying to my interlocutor that "if our draft did not give satisfaction in Vienna, that of Haymerlé had no more success in St Petersburg. Besides, I now considered all discussion as suspended, and I was now going to confine myself to telegraphing to St Petersburg what the Prince, his father, had caused to be communicated to me. I was then to await the subsequent decisions of my Government".

Herbert Bismarck asked me by what channel we were to begin direct pourparlers with Austria? I replied that I had not the least idea, and that it was not my business to make any suggestion in this connection.

Although I had succeeded up till now in diverting the complaints of the German Chancellor on to Haymerlé, and maintaining intact our good relations with him, I think that it is not solely Haymerlé's obstinacy which drove him to retire and leave us face to face with Austria. Without saying it yet—because I have not given him the pretext for it—he bears a grudge because, after having got through him all that we demanded, we refuse the one Austrian demand which he undertook to support. That is his feeling. He would have ended by expressing it to us if the negotiations had continued to be carried on by his mediation. So I consider it a fortunate circumstance that his decision had suddenly come to hand before I had time to carry out the instructions which I had received. Perhaps he wished himself to avoid the disagreement which he foresaw between him and us, being brought to light.

Prince Reuss has summed up in three points Haymerlé's various demands about the wording of the supplementary appendix to the Treaty:

(1) That Austria be completely at liberty to do what she wishes in Bosnia, Herzegovina, and also at Novibazar.

(2) That the union of the two Bulgarias be neither instigated nor hastened.

(3) That Bulgarian propaganda be not extended to Macedonia.

As will be seen, we only agreed to the third point.

Berlin, 21 May/2 June, 1881.

Yesterday I received telegraphic instructions to request Prince Bismarck, in the name of the Emperor, to resume the direction of the secret negotiations with Austria.

At the same time I was directed to insist upon *my* draft of the appendix to the Treaty with an addition relative to Bulgarian propaganda in Macedonia, on the lines desired by Austria.

For the moment I was in presence of an unforeseen material obstacle. Bismarck is ill, suffering from a very painful swelling of the veins, and Count Limburg, who makes a daily report to him on current affairs, has not been able to see him for a couple of days. It seems that he over-worked himself this year by remaining in town longer than usual. Last year he was already at Kissingen in the beginning of May. At this moment the doctor urges his departure as soon as he can leave his bed.

This would be very regrettable, for last year it was Prince Hohenlohe who was in charge of the Ministry in his absence; Hohenlohe had the necessary importance and authority to handle the great affair with me. I do not know if Bismarck will decide this time to entrust Limburg with it, who is only a subordinate, and is after all only employed in current affairs. As the Prince was above all anxious to direct the negotiations in person, he desired it to finish sooner. That hope has not been realised.

I have asked Herbert Bismarck to beg his father to let me know when he feels in a condition to receive me.

26 May, 1881.

As the recovery of the German Chancellor is protracted, I have decided to carry out the commands of the Emperor in writing, and have sent to the Prince to-day the letter which follows.

CHAPTER XVII

THE END OF THE NEGOTIATIONS

To Prince Bismarck.

Berlin, 26 May/7 June, 1881.

My Prince,

The Emperor entrusts me with an important and difficult task, and I must appeal to all the kindness with which Your Highness has honoured me up till now, if I am to carry it out with success.

The value which the Emperor attaches to the Entente between the three Imperial Courts, makes him deeply desirous that you should not relinquish the task of carrying through this Entente to a satisfactory conclusion.

Such is the mission which I am entrusted to carry out in relation to yourself. It places me, I frankly confess, in a difficult position, for we cannot agree entirely to the last Austrian proposal which you advised us to accept as a means of closing the matter.

Therefore, my hope of success lies entirely in the firm determination of the Emperor to maintain intimate relations with Germany. This idea has thrown out deep roots in his mind under the very influence of these negotiations, and of the powerful co-operation which the interests of Russia have found in you. This is why the Emperor is anxious to remove from our relations all that might resemble political subtleties. He does not wish to stop at discussions of wording, and he has commanded me to state in a straightforward manner to Your Highness, as to a safe and tried confidant of his Father's ideas, what he thinks he can do and where he thinks right to stop, in his desire to satisfy the last demands of the Vienna Cabinet.

(1) The Emperor thinks he can consent to the definite annexation of Bosnia and Herzegovina.

(2) His Majesty is also prepared to give fresh confirmation to the secret protocol of 1878, relative to Novibazar. This protocol, signed by Prince Gortchakov and Count Andrassy, admitted the eventual right for Austria to extend her occupation to the Sanjak of Novibazar in return for the promise of the Viennese Cabinet to lend us its co-operation in the execution of the clauses of the Treaty of Berlin which particularly interested us.

I should have wished the importance of these two points not to be lessened in Vienna. When I submitted to you, my Prince, my draft project which formulated them, they had not yet been accepted in St Petersburg. I had promised to propose them for the acceptance of my Government, and I have obtained this. I have the right to emphasise the importance of this, for I had to struggle against a feeling shared by all those who knew of the existence of this protocol: we had a grudge against the Viennese Cabinet for having doomed this protocol to oblivion as long as we had the right to cite it in our favour, and for only having remembered it when it was too late! Well, this feeling has been overcome; the Emperor, whilst agreeing to renew this protocol, has conquered himself; and—I have no hesitation in saying it—this victory is your work; it is because you had recommended the last Austrian proposals to us, that the Emperor, taking into account the support which you have given us up till now, has agreed to the two above-mentioned points. It is not an insignificant result for Austria to have removed for ever the causes of disagreement of which this protocol bore the seeds.

I now come to the only point which the Emperor is not inclined to grant. His Majesty does not wish to bind himself forthwith to the *annexation* of Novibazar. He believes that this would go beyond the limits of what the late Emperor Alexander II considered as equivalent for the union of the two Bulgarias. He will keep the engagements entered into by his August Father. Austria will be able to occupy and administer the Sanjak if she comes to an understanding with the Porte. But the Emperor is unable to give his sanction to the *annexation*. He cannot, at the beginning of his reign, assume this new obligation.

It remains for me to await with confidence the decision of Your Highness. You will not allow a work to be endangered which assures you fresh titles to the gratitude of three great nations.

Please accept, etc.

(Signed)   SABUROV.

To M. de Giers (telegram).

Berlin, 27 May/8 June, 1881.

I managed to get Bismarck persuaded to resume initiative in the great affair.

To the same (telegram).

Berlin, 29 May/10 June, 1881.

Affair goes well. Send full powers as quickly as possible. Austrian Ambassador has them already a month ago. Bismarck wishes to conclude before his departure. Details to-morrow by telegraph.

To the same (telegram).

Berlin, 30 May/11 June, 1881.

Have gained principal point about Novibazar. I fight now for the rest. Fight continues by telegraph between Vienna and Berlin to finish sooner. German courier conveys to Vienna this evening final draft which I have just agreed upon with Limburg-Stirum. We shall be able to have Austria's acceptance day after to-morrow. I believe this probable, for Bismarck proceeds this time by ultimatum. He has not given me time to refer, saying that an Ambassador furnished with instructions ought to know to what he can consent without referring. Delay being dangerous, I agreed to make final draft with Limburg, but I have also mercilessly suppressed all the Austrian sentences to which we took exception. For Novibazar we already have assent of Austria. Am happy to announce this success.

Summing-up of the last phase of the Negotiations.

To M. de Giers.

Berlin, 1/13 June, 1881.

Up to the receipt of your telegram of 20 May, I kept quiet, maintaining complete silence with regard to Prince Bismarck. I confined myself to saying to his son that his withdrawal from the negotiations would without doubt make a sad impression in St Petersburg. Two days later Herbert Bismarck confided to me that his father had just telegraphed to Schweinitz ordering him to give the Emperor the assurance that the sole ground for his decision had been the obstinacy of Baron Haymerlé.

For my part, I had not neglected to startle Vienna by letting fall a word to my Austrian colleague. He having asked me how the matter was getting on, I replied: "I believe that it is falling through", and changed the conversation.

Your telegraphic instructions, followed by your two letters of 21 May, having reached me, I had to contrive a plan of action applicable to the singular situation in which I was. I had to negotiate with a Chancellor, sick, invisible and not allowing any business to reach him.

I resolved then to get hold of Herbert Bismarck and make use of him as intermediary between his father and myself. The co-operation of this intelligent young man has been very useful to me; and I ought to say that it is in our talks of the last few days that all the difficulties have been overcome.

I began by asking him to hand to his father the letter of which I send you a copy. This letter was drawn up in a way to exclude a refusal, or at least to make it difficult. I anticipated the objection which the Prince could make to me. He could say to me: "Good, you ask my co-operation, but in that case follow my advice and accept the last Austrian proposal which I have supported". I anticipated that objection by indicating it myself at the commencement of my letter, and then I frankly stated the situation as I saw it myself, without any artifice.

This way of proceeding seems to have been completely successful. I learned, the following day, that a telegraphic application had been made to Vienna, informing Haymerlé of our principal objections, and inviting him to send a new draft of the appendix to the Treaty, resembling ours. I have also reason to believe—although they did not say so to me—that Baron Haymerlé has been strongly recommended to be satisfied with the protocol relating to Novibazar, without demanding the annexation of that province. At least, this is the only way of explaining the prompt conversion of the Austrian Minister to our way of looking at things.

Three days later, Haymerlé's new draft arrived, accompanied by a report from Reuss. The same evening the Chancellor sent his son to me with the two documents.

In order to be brief, I shall only quote to you a single passage from this long report. Haymerlé recalls that it was in anguish of mind that he had consented to Article III of the Treaty relative to the Straits, for, according to him, that Article was equivalent to dooming Turkey (*er hat die Existenz der Turkei preisgegeben*) in admitting the right of Russia to attack her if she allowed a foreign fleet to enter the Black Sea. He had thus exposed and placed at the mercy of Russia an Austrian interest of the first order! That was a great proof of the confidence of Austria in the peaceful intentions of the Emperor Alexander III, and Austria had the right to hope that Russia, in her turn, would take into account her interests in acceding to the new draft.

Indeed, this draft came considerably nearer ours, and I immediately saw in it a possibility of coming to an understanding.

When I had examined these documents, Herbert Bismarck told me that his father had sent him to inform me that he would make his official proposal the following day, through Count Limburg. But before, he wished to apply to me, not as to an Ambassador, but as to a friend, to know beforehand to what it was possible for me to agree. He did so because he wished my definite acceptance by the following day in order to propose my draft thereafter to Vienna *as his last word*. To-day I shall not yet be bound by my word, for this communication of friend to friend will be supposed not to have taken place, and Limburg will not be informed of it. But for to-morrow, he wishes me to agree with Limburg on a definite wording, *without referring* to my Government. He supposes that as Ambassador, I enjoy the confidence of the Emperor sufficiently to take upon me to assent to the wording that suits me without risking disavowal. In short, he wanted to know the changes that I wished to introduce in the new Austrian draft, so that I might be able to give my consent the following day, *at once*.

In other words, the Prince besought me to dictate to him the proposals which he intended to make to me.

I had too many advantages not to avail myself of them. I took a pencil and struck out all the passages which you had pointed out to me in your letter of 12 May. I enclose herewith a copy of the new Austrian draft with my changes marked in red ink. We agreed with Herbert Bismarck that the day following, Count Limburg would discuss the project officially with me, and that we should arrive at a definite draft then and there to be sent to Vienna, by courier, as an ultimatum.

In the discussion next day with Count Limburg, I pretended to be in ignorance of what had happened on the previous day, and we discussed the proposed appendix to the Treaty, article by article. In what concerns the eventual occupation of Eastern Roumelia and the Balkans by Turkish troops, I crossed out the word " diplomatic " which Haymerlé had added in our draft. The entire sentence was expressed as follows: "The three Powers will use their (diplomatic) influence to dissuade Turkey from such an enterprise". I said that we do not ask for more than " diplomatic " efforts from Austria and Germany, but the Emperor of Russia will not agree to bind himself by that word; he intends to conserve his full liberty of action, if it pleased him, to drive the Turks out of Eastern Roumelia, supposing they invaded it.

We agreed to suppress this word.

Then came the last paragraph of the same Article, expressed as follows: "It is clearly understood that Bulgaria and Eastern Roumelia must abstain, on their part, from provoking the Porte by attacks issuing from their territory on the other provinces of the Ottoman Empire".

These lines being almost identical in their meaning with the terms of our draft, I did not make any objection to them.

In the Article with regard to the union of the two Bulgarias I had the two final phrases suppressed, which ran as follows: "They will do nothing to hasten the union, and will endeavour to maintain the present status quo". I said that this was repeating the same thing three times in the same article, and that this insistence could only offend us, seeing that we had stated in every possible way that we will not instigate that union. Baron de Haymerlé cites M. de Giers' letter which was communicated to him last year. Well, that letter must suffice him, and when we have promised a thing, it is not very kind to demand the same promise from us a second and third time.

With regard to the Article relative to the identical instructions to be given to our agents in the East, I have re-established our wording.

Thus, as final result, it is our draft, pure and simple, as it had been approved by the Emperor. The point regarding Novibazar was already conceded by Austria in her new draft.

The courier left yesterday evening for Vienna. To-morrow we can have the reply. Bismarck wishes to sign immediately, as long as he is still here. At Kissingen, a meeting for the signature would have given the alarm to all Europe. Therefore I thought I ought to beg you by telegraph to hasten the despatch of my full powers. Limburg told me that the Austrian Ambassador had his a month ago.

Berlin, 6/18 June, 1881.

The negotiation of the secret Treaty has come to a happy conclusion.

On Tuesday morning, 2/14 June, Reuss sent a first

telegram, announcing the acceptance of all the points with one exception. Baron Haymerlé, meticulous up to the end, did not wish to sacrifice the words: "They will do nothing to hasten the union".

The order was immediately despatched to continue to insist on its suppression.

The same evening, at nine o'clock, Prince Bismarck sent his son to give me the reading of a second telegram from Prince Reuss, announcing the definite acceptance of the German draft planned in concert with me.

Two days later, Thursday, 4/16 June, the couriers of Baron Haymerlé and Prince Reuss arrived with the texts of the Treaty.

Friday, 5/17 June, we met together at Count Limburg's to compare and collate them.

Half an hour before this meeting, the Austrian Ambassador[1] came to me to perform a mission with which he had been charged.

He said to me, on behalf of Baron Haymerlé, that it was by the express command of the Emperor Francis-Joseph that the last difficulties had been removed. His Majesty, placing his trust in the peaceful dispositions of the Emperor of Russia, did not

---

[1] Szechenyi, Emerich, Count von, Austro-Hungarian diplomat (1825–1898). He entered diplomacy in 1845, and after holding various junior posts was sent as Counsellor of Embassy to St Petersburg in 1859 and later to Brussels. He retired for a time from the service, but in 1878 succeeded Count Karolyi as Ambassador in Berlin. It is a remarkable fact, and contrary to usual diplomatic procedure, that he seems to have been kept in complete ignorance of the negotiations connected with the League of the Three Emperors until a comparatively late stage in the proceedings. He resigned in 1892.

wish to put off any longer the signature of this important document.

In dropping the stipulation relative to the "non-acceleration" of the Bulgarian union, Baron Haymerlé expressed the hope that I would be able to give him the assurance that in this respect the intentions of the Emperor Alexander are the same as those of the Emperor, his father, of imperishable memory, and that the policy of pacification in the East will follow its course.

Although this application seemed to me quite unusual, I replied in general terms that the policy of pacification was necessary for Russia for the same reason as it was for the other Powers. The Treaty which we are signing is a proof of this.

At the meeting for collating, Count Limburg proposed to modify the wording of paragraph 3 of Article II of the Treaty.

There it states:

> The three Courts will declare forthwith, in confidential communications between them, the points on which an understanding has already been reached between them.

Since agreement has just been reached on the wording of the document which will serve as appendix to the Treaty, it will be necessary to mention it in Article II and say: "The three Courts declare forthwith, *in the protocol annexed to the Treaty*, the points on which an understanding has already been reached".

I agreed to this with alacrity. This change indicates all the road we have gone since the first draft of the Treaty, where it was only a question *of confidential explanations.* Later, we modified these words into *confidential communications*, and now we have the consent of Austria in *black and white* to the Bulgarian union, in a document annexed to the Treaty, which will have the same force and value.

As agreed yesterday, we met together to-day at 5 p.m. at Prince Bismarck's to proceed to the signing of the Treaty and of its appendix.

At the moment of signing, the Prince recollected that it was a happy date—the day of the battle of Belle-Alliance (Waterloo). I recalled that it was also the anniversary of the first victory in the reign of the late Emperor—the day of the repulse of the great assault under the walls of Sevastopol on 6/18 June, 1855.

And as the Austrian ought also to have his victory, I recalled to him, that it was the day of their victory at Kollin over Frederick the Great.

CHAPTER XVIII

TREATY OF 18(/6) JUNE, 1881[1]

THEIR Majesties, the Emperor of All the Russias, King of Poland, Grand-Duke of Finland, the Emperor of Germany, King of Prussia, and the Emperor of Austria, King of Hungary—animated by a common desire to consolidate the general peace by an understanding intended to assure the defensive position of their respective States, have come into agreement on certain questions which touch more especially their mutual interests.

With this purpose, Their Majesties have appointed [here follow the names of the Plenipotentiaries].

They, furnished with full powers which have been found in good and due form, have agreed upon the following articles:

Article I.

In the event of one of the three Powers being at war with a fourth Great Power, the other two shall maintain a benevolent neutrality towards it, and shall devote their efforts to the localisation of the conflict.

This stipulation shall apply likewise to a war between one of the three Powers and Turkey, but only in the case where a previous agreement has been reached between the three Courts as to the results of the war.

In the special case of one of them obtaining from one of its two allies more positive support, the obligatory value of the present article shall remain in all its force for the third.

Article II.

Russia, in agreement with Germany, declares her firm resolve to respect the interests resultant upon the new position assured to Austria-Hungary by the Treaty of Berlin.

[1] For original text as given in the Memoirs, see Appendix II.

The three Courts, desirous of avoiding all disagreement between them, undertake to respect their individual interests in the Balkan Peninsula. They further promise one another that any new modifications in the territorial status quo of Turkey in Europe can only be accomplished after a common agreement between them.

In order to facilitate the agreement contemplated by the present article—agreement of which it is impossible to foresee all the conditions—the three Courts state forthwith in the protocol annexed to this Treaty the points upon which an understanding has already been established in principle.

Article III.

The three Courts recognise the European and mutually obligatory character of the principle of the closing of the Straits of the Bosphorus and of the Dardanelles, founded on international law, confirmed by Treaties and summarised in the Declaration of the second Russian plenipotentiary at the session of 12 July of the Congress of Berlin (Protocol 19).

They will see to it in common that Turkey makes no exception to this rule in favour of the interests of any Government whatsoever, by lending to warlike operations of a belligerent Power the part of her Empire constituted by the Straits.

In case of infringement, or in order to prevent it if such infringement should be foreseen, the three Courts will warn Turkey that they would consider her, in that event, as having put herself at war with the injured Party, and as having deprived herself, thenceforth, of the benefits of security assured to her territorial status quo by the Treaty of Berlin.

Article IV.

The present Treaty shall remain in force during the period of three years, to date from the day of the exchange of ratifications.

Article V.

The High Contracting Parties mutually resolve on secrecy as to the contents and existence of the present Treaty, as well as of the protocol annexed thereto.

Article VI.

The secret Conventions concluded between Russia and Germany and between Russia and Austria-Hungary in 1873 are replaced by the present Treaty.

Article VII.

The ratifications of the present Treaty and of the protocol annexed thereto, shall be exchanged at Berlin within the space of fifteen days, or sooner if it is possible to do so.

In witness whereof, etc.

(Signed) SABUROV.
BISMARCK.
SZECHENYI.

Protocol.

The undersigned, etc....having recorded in accordance with Article II of the secret Treaty concluded to-day, the points affecting the interests of the three Courts in the Balkan Peninsula upon which an understanding has already been established between them, have agreed to the following protocol:

(1) Bosnia and Herzegovina.

Austria-Hungary reserves the right to annex these two provinces at whatever moment she shall deem opportune.

(2) Sanjak of Novibazar.

The Declaration exchanged between the Russian Plenipotentiaries and the Austro-Hungarian Plenipotentiaries at the Congress of Berlin under date of 1/13 July, 1878, remains in force.

(3) Eastern Roumelia.

The three Powers agree in regarding the eventuality of an occupation, whether of Eastern Roumelia, or of the Balkans, as full of danger for the general peace. Should it so happen, they will employ their efforts to dissuade the Porte from such an enterprise, it being well understood that Bulgaria and Eastern Roumelia must, for their part, abstain from provoking the Porte by attacks emanating from their territory against the other provinces of the Ottoman Empire.

(4) Bulgaria.

The three Powers will not oppose the eventual reunion of Bulgaria and Eastern Roumelia within the territorial limits assigned to them by the Treaty of Berlin, should this question happen to arise by the force of circumstances.

They agree to dissuade the Bulgarians from all aggression against the neighbouring provinces, particularly Macedonia, and to inform them that in such a case they would be acting at their own risk and peril.

(5) Attitude of agents in the East.

In order to avoid the clashing of interests in local questions which may arise, the three Imperial Courts will furnish their representatives and agents in the East with a general Instruction ordering them to endeavour to smooth out their differences by friendly explanations among themselves in each special instance, and in the event of their failing to do so, to refer the matter to their Governments.

(6) The present protocol shall form an integral part of the secret Treaty signed this day in Berlin, and shall have the same force and validity.

Done at Berlin, June 18/6, 1881.

(Signed) SABUROV.
BISMARCK.
SZECHENYI.

The Treaty was ratified by the three Sovereigns two weeks after its signature.

In 1884 it was renewed for three years with the suppression of the last paragraph of Article I.

Political Results of the secret Treaty.

In order to get a clear idea of these, it is necessary to go back to the year 1879, when the first pourparlers began which ended in the present negotiations.

At that time Austria and Germany were closely united, with a view to resisting eventually the Panslavist tendencies which they attributed to Russia. England had morally joined this alliance, whose aims she encouraged. France had ostentatiously taken under her patronage the Greek element in the East, with the avowed intention of strengthening it against the Slav populations whom we were protecting.

So, four Great Powers had come to an agreement to follow the same political line with the common purpose of keeping Russia in check.

They had armed themselves with the Treaty of Berlin! We could not contest a single one of the Articles of this Treaty without calling into being a coalition which, morally, was already formed.

The isolation of Russia was complete!

The Treaty which has just been negotiated modifies the situation entirely.

An Austro-German alliance, hostile to Russian policy, no longer exists. It is no longer England, it is we ourselves, who form part of it. The European equilibrium has been rearranged in our favour, and we have made sure, for a certain number of years, of pacific relations with the two neighbours whose hostility, two years ago, we dreaded.

There is more. We have brought them to invalidate, themselves, several of the most essential clauses of the

Treaty of Berlin—those notably which were especially effective in paralysing our action in the East, and which had compromised the political results of our victorious military campaign.

The Treaty of Berlin stipulated for the eventual occupation of Eastern Roumelia and of the Balkans by Turkish troops.

We have the promise of Germany and Austria to help us in preventing that occupation.

The Treaty of Berlin had cut Bulgaria in two and reduced one half to the state of a Turkish province.

We have the consent of Germany and Austria to their eventual reunion.

The protocols of the Congress of Berlin and the Declaration of the British Plenipotentiaries had given England the privilege to pass through the Straits just when she liked, and had thus destroyed the guarantees of security which we enjoyed in the Black Sea in virtue of the principle of the absolute closing of the Straits.

We have brought Germany and Austria to stipulate with us new guarantees against the violation of the Straits, by subordinating the validity of the Treaty of Berlin itself to the maintenance of the principle of the closing of that important maritime passage.

So, in every respect, the projected Treaty assures us of some indisputable advantages *with regard to the present*. Russia can concentrate on herself, re-estab-lish her internal equilibrium, reform her finances, re-organise all her vital forces, and enjoy the peace which is necessary to her for that task, without external dangers coming to divert her from it.

POSTSCRIPT

(a) PRINCE BISMARCK'S ACCOUNT OF
THE NEGOTIATIONS

B Y a fortunate circumstance it is possible to learn
with a certain measure of exactness the attitude
of Prince Bismarck throughout these negotiations as stated by himself. In Volume III of the
monumental work *Die grosse Politik der europäischen
Kabinette* 1871–1914,[1] is published a certain number
of communications between Bismarck and the Emperor William I and others, which contain direct
references to the matter in question. The difficulty,
of course, is that Bismarck's statements throughout
his life, and even sometimes within short periods,
were often inconsistent with one another and with
his actions.

"Bismarck was a rough man, even in politics,"
M. Saburov remarked on one occasion to the writer,
"but his conservative convictions were very sincere;
he was opposed to Liberalism in any form. 'There
are five Great Powers; I must always strive to be one
of three against two.' These were his simple mathe-
matics and politics. When at one period he saw that
Germany could not agree with Austria, he thought of
Russia and England. Then when he saw that Russia
and England could not agree, he thought of Russia
and Austria. But at one stage at any rate he was not

<hr>

[1] Deutsche Verlagsgesellschaft für Politik und Geschichte
m.b.H. in Berlin W. 8, 1922.

averse to an alliance with England, if it had been possible."

According to the foregoing Memoirs, Bismarck asserts his constant loyalty to Russia even when repaid by ingratitude, yet he was not averse to intriguing against her so as to secure her isolation. He is seen torn between Russia and Austria, even if he had a natural instinctive preference for the latter, and was already committed to her in defensive alliance against Russia under the Treaty of 1879. But it is clear from the secret "Ministerial Declaration of Policy in regard to the Relation of the Austro-German Alliance to the League of the Three Emperors",[1] signed 18 May, 1881—exactly one month previous to the date of signature of the League itself—that the latter was in no way to interfere with or supersede the understanding established between Germany and Austria on the basis of the secret Treaty of 1879.

The first reference in *Die grosse Politik*, strangely enough, contains a confession of a feeling of misgiving on the part, not of Bismarck but of the German Emperor, at the attitude adopted on the German side in the matter of the secret Treaty about to be entered into with Austria vis-à-vis Russia.

No. 495.

Emperor William I at Baden-Baden to the Imperial Chancellor Prince von Bismarck.

Autograph and unsigned.

Baden-Baden, 2–10–79.

...A circumstance has occurred now that can show a way out of the dilemma in which I find myself between my con-

[1] For the text cf. P.S.T. I, 32–33. Cf. also D.G.P. III, 152.

science and my honesty towards Russia, in drawing up the Austrian objections to my views.

In reply to my telegraphic inquiry you telegraphed only yesterday what Saburov expressed to you by order of the Emperor.[1] You infer from these communications that Russia has already got wind of our Austrian negotiations (as is quite natural), and you wish to conclude from the defensive attitude which Saburov has assured you Russia will henceforth take up, that this assurance is no doubt a result of that.

In that case it would be possible to carry out at once my way of communicating our design with Austria...and to put this to Russia as purely general, not only by omitting to mention Russia in the Treaty, and (*sic*) to invite Russia to accede to it.

You yourself have told Saburov that you are wholly desirous of maintaining the Triple Imperial Alliance; in the Memorandum, Protocol and Treaty the same idea occurs—what is then simpler than by this Treaty to confirm now in a real written Treaty, the Triple Imperial Alliance, which till now was only a verbal one, and at most through the Petersburg-Vienna agreement of 1873 had anything to show in writing?

You yourself have further told Saburov that you cannot co-operate in a policy through which Austria would be

[1] At the end of September the Russian Ambassador, M. Saburov, appeared at Berlin on a special mission to the Imperial Chancellor, Prince Bismarck, to ask him whether his sentiments towards Russia were still the same as in 1877. On his part Saburov assured him that Russian policy in future would only be a defensive policy, on the basis of the Berlin Congress. Bismarck replied to Saburov that, if in the future still called on to advise the Emperor William, he would always do so in the same sense as before and during the Congress, but that he was not able to co-operate in a policy through which Austria would be endangered. Towards the Emperor William, who had inquired of Bismarck by telegram on 1 October as to particulars of the conversation with Saburov, the Chancellor expressed himself in a telegram on the same day very sceptically about Saburov's communications, in which he saw an attempt to frustrate the settlement with Austria. (Note in D.G.P.)

endangered. It is as right as it is important that Russia in that way have the first official communication of that of which she has already got wind. I rely further on this that through our Embassy in Petersburg, communication of your Conference with Saburov is made to the Minister Giers, with the question whether Saburov's assurance that Russia instead of this will only pursue a defensive policy on the basis of the Treaty of Berlin is authorised, and whether under it is meant a defensive policy against Germany and Austria. If a satisfactory answer is given and this is immediately communicated to Austria, nothing hinders Austria and ourselves from communicating the projected Treaty to the Emperor Alexander in the above manner, and asking him to agree to it.

He then refers to the modifications that would be necessary, as e.g. the entire omission of paragraph 2, which is directed solely against Russia.

There follow in succession three documents which bear directly on the negotiations.

No. 514.[1]

The Foreign Office Ambassador, von Radowitz, to the Legation Secretary, Count Herbert von Bismarck, at present in Kissingen.

Rough Draft.

Berlin, 15 August, 1879.

No. 14—Absolutely Confidential.

I have had the opportunity of repeatedly broaching the subject of our mutual relations to my former colleague at Athens, M. Saburov, with whom I am on intimately friendly terms, and who has been staying here for two days on his way through.

M. Saburov is precisely informed of the state of affairs through the conversations that he had at Kissingen with the Imperial Chancellor (for which he is particularly grateful),

[1] *Op. cit.* III, 139.

and through his subsequent meeting with Prince Gortchakov as well as with Count Schuvalov. He had also gone through the diplomatic correspondence at the Russian Embassy communicated here on Eastern affairs. The impressions which M. Saburov gained from these various sources of information are of the more importance, because his appointment as Ambassador in Constantinople is confirmed, and he is going straight from here to Petersburg to report himself to the Emperor.

M. Saburov first told me plainly he was astonished and frightened at the present isolation of Russian policy, especially in the Eastern sphere, and that he considered this the consequence of the defective or rather wholly lacking management of foreign affairs for many a long day. He himself personally was convinced of the nature of Prince Gortchakov's mood. But he is still *in the land of the living*, is nominally still the director of policy, and has no intention of retiring voluntarily; as long as this situation lasts, a change in its incoherent desultoriness (*in dem décousu*) is not to be thought of, and it is not at all conducive to the furtherance of affairs that the Emperor Alexander occupies himself personally with details, in some measure tries to be "his own Minister", though it is impossible for him to accomplish the business that at present is more than ever requisite. Count Schuvalov in particular, also indicated this point to him [Saburov] as the most serious in the present situation.

After the conversation with the Imperial Chancellor at Kissingen, he spoke with Count Schuvalov about the relations with Germany, and heard from him the full confirmation of all that Prince Bismarck had said to him of the bearing of German policy before and during the Congress. But Count Schuvalov, as well as he himself, is of the opinion that all explanations on this subject would lead to nothing *now*, so long as Gortchakov is there. The moment will certainly, and, it is to be hoped, soon come when the truth about the services for which Russia has Germany to thank, will gain ground throughout Russia, and when an open mutual explanation between Petersburg and Berlin will have the result of restoring the old intimacy. But for this on the Russian side, a double change of persons in the management of foreign policy and in the embassy at Berlin is necessary. There is little to hope for before this happens.

I told M. Saburov he must admit that this is a circumstance which at least imposes upon us a caution and a reserve towards Russia that we had not known formerly. Germany could not possibly subordinate her own political interests to such incalculable individual considerations as those now determinative in Russia. The friendship that binds both Governments, and their joint interests were surely strong enough to overcome disturbances from personal motives; but that there was also a limit to such trials, and that, it seemed to me, would now soon be reached. I asked him if he knew how systematically for many a long day the view was being instilled into the Russian people that Germany alone was to blame if the Slav hopes and dreams were not fulfilled through the war, and if he believed that the consequence of this long agitation against Germany would vanish all at once, even if Gortchakov were no longer directing it.

On this point M. Saburov also recognised the chief danger, and he said that he could only deplore that the Government had not exercised more influence over the Press. But it was not yet too late for this, and with goodwill much could be done.

RADOWITZ.

No. 515.[1]

Notes of the Imperial Chancellor, Prince Bismarck, on his conversations with the Russian Ambassador Saburov.

Unsigned.

Berlin, 3 February, 1880.

My conversations with M. Saburov on 31 January and 1 February referred to the relations between Germany and Russia, and to the question of the mutual relations between the three Empires.

[1] *Op. cit.* III, 141.

I expressed myself with perfect openness about our position towards Russia, and discussed all the reasons that have given us the impression that in Russia the endeavour to maintain the old friendship between the two countries no longer existed as it used to, as well as the consequences which had necessarily resulted for German policy from this knowledge. At the same time I expressly rendered prominent among other things the Russian flirtations of the previous summer against us in France through Obrutchev[1] and in Italy, without meeting with an objection from M. Saburov. The question of the posting of Russian troops on our Polish frontier was also mentioned and gone into by me.

On the other hand, I expressly emphasised our wish to go on living in peace and friendship with Russia, and repeated that in a Russo-German war there was nothing at all to be gained for Germany. We were solely on the defensive against Russia.

In discussing the mutual relations between Russia, Austria and Germany with which the Ambassador's expressions of opinion were mostly concerned, M. Saburov started from the idea that according to the existing agreement between Germany and Austria, Russian policy was also obliged on its side to seek an understanding in the first place with Austria-Hungary about all the questions concerning Russian interests in the East.

Throughout M. Saburov showed above all the tendency to believe that an understanding of the kind might possibly be brought about through the mediation of the German Government. I admitted this as practicable only for questions in which the German interest preponderates—but there are none such present in the East. In all other Eastern questions, where the Russian and Austrian interests are greater than ours, the understanding would be brought about by direct negotiations between the parties concerned; Germany, however, would then as before adhere to the policy of willingly

[1] General Obrutchev, since 1878, Adjutant-General, 1881, Chief of the Russian Staff. (Note in D.G.P.)

joining the Russo-Austrian Entente, when once that Entente was established.

With this opinion M. Saburov agreed, as well as with what I said about the closer relations between Germany and Austria, and the necessity of the unimpaired continued existence of the Austro-Hungarian Monarchy. From the Russian point of view M. Saburov recognised this as a European necessity.

As to the bringing about of a closer Triple Entente on the basis of the Treaty of Berlin and the stipulations of the Congress, M. Saburov expressed himself in the beginning in a manner that, taken together with his previous communications in autumn, must give rise to the supposition that he was already empowered to open definite negotiations in this direction. His fundamental idea with which I, for my part, agreed, was that the Treaty of Berlin and the stipulations of the Congress should form the basis for the mutual relations between the three Powers. None of them consents to a change in the status quo depending thereon unless the others agree to it. Thus Germany only supports the modification of the work of the Congress to be agreed upon between Russia and Austria.

After the Ambassador had expressed his satisfaction with my readiness to follow him in this proposed course, he did not develop it further, but urged rather the value that the Dual Entente has for Russia especially. He denoted as an obstacle to the agreement with a wider scope the continuance of the official activity of Prince Gortchakov, who would be little disposed to further this combination. But he did not suppose that a change in the position of Prince Gortchakov was to be expected soon, either on his own initiative or on that of the Emperor Alexander.

I also expressed myself in accord with the Dual Entente, so long as nothing was required of us that would include participation in agreements against Austria or without her knowledge.

The neutrality of Germany, which M. Saburov had previously especially emphasised, if Russia, on account of Eastern differences, became involved with England alone, I indicated as almost self-evidently founded in our European position. On the further remark of the Ambassador that the suggestion as to agreements with Vienna did not at present seem indicated, I replied that it was indeed to be recommended that Russian overtures should not be made too hastily to the new Minister Haymerlé, who would be perhaps still somewhat ombrageux (skittish).

Thereupon at the end of our conversation, M. Saburov wanted to sum up the result rather abruptly thus: that I also considered it at present pas encore opportun to develop further the idea of the Triple Entente, and that in the meantime he might discuss it confidentially in this sense with Herr von Giers on his imminent return to Russia. This I decidedly contradicted, and told him that not I but he had hesitated as to the opportuneness of the moment; on my side I was quite ready to enter into further conversations on the points he had brought up.

With regard to definite agreements with Russia, Count Schuvalov said to me on the occasion of his last visit to Varzin that he could not advise coming to any sort of stipulated dual or triple agreement with Russia. Any such arrangement would always form a stumbling-block to mutual good relations between Germany and Russia, which, as was formerly the case, must develop naturally, without a treaty. There was no possible form of a treaty which would be so precise that it would not serve our enemies in Russia as a pretext for the assertion that we had not kept our engagements.

No. 516.[1]

Notes by the Imperial Chancellor, Prince Bismarck.

Unsigned dictation. Taken down by the Reporting Member of Council, Bucher.

Secret.

Berlin, 6 February, 1880.

In the conversation which I had yesterday with the Russian Ambassador, Saburov, he displayed a lively apprehension

[1] *Op. cit.* III, 143.

that the English might some day suddenly occupy Constantinople or even take it away. The fact that the English Ambassador has repeatedly threatened to call out the fleet as a measure that lies within his power at any time, must necessarily direct the attention of Russia to this question. Russia could see without anxiety the key of the Dardanelles in the hands of an independent Government of the Porte, but not in those of a European Power. The Straits were not an open sea, but form Turkish territory, and into such the fighting forces of European Powers may not enter at will whether by land or water. If foreign fleets can enter the Dardanelles at will without Turkey's consent, then the coast of the Black Sea is endangered. Russia is desirous of peace, but also of safety, and her security is endangered by the threatening attitude of the English fleet, especially if the English Ambassador considers himself justified in summoning the fleet to Constantinople without other authority than that of his own Government. It would therefore be quite in the character of a friendly policy to give Russia guarantees against the inroad of foreign fleets into the Black Sea. M. Saburov did not make explicit proposals, and the whole conversation was strictly confidential, so that I do not yet feel myself called upon to make communications about it, and this jotting is only to be taken as a memorandum for the records.

Besides this, concern about a coalition of Continental Powers against Russia came strongly into the foreground. The question of a defensive and offensive alliance between Russia and Germany was put expressly for an instant, but dropped as soon as I declared that we would not conclude such an alliance against and without Austria, that I had been much inclined to such ideas in previous years, but that the events of last summer[1] had no longer left me the measure of confidence necessary for such agreements. I made a counter-proposal by way of sounding him. If Russia feared coalitions, which fear was much more intelligible in the case of Germany because of her geographical position, they could take on a

[1] Compare *op. cit.* III, chap. XIII.

dangerous character only through the participation of France or Germany. Germany was out of the question; but if Russia desired a defensive alliance against France, which would come into force on every attack by France on either of us two, I would recommend this to His Majesty, for by it both Powers would be protected by an alliance against a coalition including France. M. Saburov avoided a direct reply to this by passing to the subject of the Triple Alliance with us and Austria, and proposed giving me a draft of his views in this sphere for further discussion. This draft he has shown me to-day.

There follows immediately the Aide-mémoire on the subject of Russia, Turkey and the Straits drawn up by M. Saburov and handed by him to Prince Bismarck on 25 February, 1880. It runs:

Review.

In 1833 we had assisted Turkey against the victorious army of Mehemet-Ali. The reward for that service was the Treaty of Unkiar-Skelessi, as a result of which Turkey undertook to close the Dardanelles to enemy fleets which might wish to enter the Black Sea.

This stipulation, negotiated to our sole advantage, was modified to our disadvantage by the Treaty of London of 1841, by which the principle of closure, applied up till then to entry, was equally extended to egress from the Black Sea. We were thus closing the outlet for our men-of-war into the Mediterranean.

Later, in 1856, the Treaty of Paris established the same principle, allowing, however, of the entrance of light vessels intended to serve as guard-ships at the mouths of the Danube, and at the Embassies in Constantinople.

At length the Treaty of London of 1871 approved for the first time of the principle of the entrance of entire fleets into the Straits, if the Sultan deemed it necessary. In spite of the subtleties of wording in which this clause was enveloped, it overturned completely the principle of the closure, which, originally, had been intended to serve us on the contrary as a defence.

Finally at the Congress of Berlin, a last security has been taken from us by the declaration of the British Plenipotentiary recorded in Protocol No. 18. England there declared "that her obligations with regard to the closing of the Straits are confined to a pledge made to the Sultan, to respect in this regard the independent decisions of His Majesty".

There follow from this declaration two very serious consequences:

In the first place, England challenges the mutually obligatory character of the Treaty of 1841 which bound all the Great Powers. She only considers herself pledged to Turkey.

In the second place, she will no longer respect the wish of the Sultan if he closes the entry to the Straits at our demand; for then, in terms of the English declaration, the decisions of the Sultan will no longer be independent. In other words, England reserves to herself henceforth the right to enter the Straits when she wishes!

No Power has protested against this new interpretation which makes the principle of the closing of the Straits quite illusory and substitutes the right of the strongest for that of treaties. Russia alone has made a counter-declaration by which she maintains the mutually obligatory character of the agreements of 1841, 1856, and 1871.

Thus, from 1833 to 1878, the successive measures on the subject of the Straits have ended by reducing to zero the guarantees which the principle of the closing of the Straits had assured us at the time of the Treaty of Unkiar-Skelessi.

The next excerpt fills up a gap in the Memoirs.

No. 518.[1]

The Russian Ambassador in Berlin, von Saburov, to the Imperial Chancellor, Prince Bismarck.

Private letter in his own handwriting.

Friday, 6 February, 1880.

Here, my Prince, is a first attempt.[2] I am not very satisfied with the form of the third article, and I count naturally on

---

[1] *Op. cit.* III, 146. [2] See the rough sketch.

your great experience to help me in adjusting it to make it correspond with your views.

I shall await your orders to come and talk the matter over.

SABUROV.

Rough Sketch.

Points on which it would be possible to come to an agreement.

Objects to be attained:

For Russia: to assure her security in the Black Sea—security strongly disturbed by the new interpretation which England seeks to give to the Treaties that regulate the closing of the Straits.

For Austria: for the present, to assure the new position secured by her in the East; for the future, to have the certainty that any change in the status quo of Turkey in Europe can only be brought about if she consents.

For Germany: to set on lasting bases a European system favourable to her security and to the maintenance of the general peace.

Finally,

For the three Powers:

To guarantee themselves mutually against the dangers of coalitions.

Rough Draft of Stipulations summing up the Principles stated above.

I.

The three Courts recognise the European and mutually obligatory character of the principle of the closing of the Straits, as it follows from the existing Treaties. They will be on the watch together to see that Turkey makes no exception to this regulation in favour of the private interests of any Power. In case of infringement, or in order to prevent it if such infringement were foreseen, the three Courts reserve the right to agree later on measures to be taken to recall Turkey to the faithful execution of her duties of neutrality in her capacity of guardian of the Straits. (Or: in case of infringement, the Signatory Powers recognise the injured Party's right of considering that Turkey has placed herself in a state of war with them.)

II.

Russia, in agreement with Germany, declares her firm resolve to respect the interests which arise out of the new position assured to Austria by the Treaty of Berlin in the Turkish territories occupied by her. The three Courts promise that if, as the result of events which no one can foresee, there came about new modifications in the territorial status quo of Turkey in Europe, these modifications will only be brought about as the result of a common agreement amongst them.

III.

The three Courts resolve on a benevolent neutrality in the case of one of them finding itself at war; and they undertake to see to the localisation of the conflict. In the special case of war in which Germany would be engaged, in which the latter secures more material support from one of her two allies, the obligatory character of the present article will not be lessened for the other.

There is only one further unimportant direct reference to the negotiations as carried on between M. Saburov and Prince Bismarck.

On the other hand, many valuable letters and dispatches passing between Prince Bismarck and Prince Reuss, which deal with the development of the situation vis-à-vis Baron Haymerlé, and to some of which reference is clearly made in the Saburov Memoirs, will be found reproduced in Die grosse Politik, III, 165–173.

18-2

The direct reference to the negotiations as between the Russian and German representatives is as follows:

No. 519.[1]

Notes by the Acting Chief of the Foreign Office, the Ambassador Prince von Hohenlohe.

Autograph.

Berlin, 4 August, 1880.

M. Saburov informed me that he has received from M. de Giers a reply to the secret report which he furnished in due course on his conversation with the Imperial Chancellor. According to it the Emperor of Russia agrees with the idea expressed by M. Saburov and approved by the Imperial Chancellor. This idea is as follows:

Should England proceed further in the Eastern question than suits the interests of the Powers, especially if the English fleet prepares to go through the Dardanelles, Germany, Austria and Russia would come to an understanding in order to prevent this design by a joint declaration. When I drew M. Saburov's attention to the contradiction existing between his conception of to-day and that of the 30th of last month, when he told me that if England proceeded in the Eastern question, Russia, inasmuch as the Montenegrin frontier question was not settled, must likewise take action, M. Saburov replied that this action would only be taken if the Montenegrin frontier question were not yet solved. But this would be settled now, so that then only the question des Détroits remained as the most important for Russia.

Saburov asserted in the course of the conversation that Lord Odo Russell had proposed to him, as an agreement between Russia and England, that Russia should leave the Straits open, in exchange for which England would prevent Austria from annexing Salonica!

C. F. v. HOHENLOHE.

[1] *Op. cit.* III, 147.

The final references of general interest deal with the subject of the renewal of the Treaty.

No. 599.[1]

The Secretary of State for Foreign Affairs, Count von Hatzfeldt, to the Ambassador at Petersburg, von Schweinitz.

Rough Draft.

No. 1.
Secret.

Berlin, 6 February, 1883.

Some days ago M. Saburov suggested confidentially the idea of a prolongation of the secret Treaty between the three Imperial Powers. The Ambassador said that the impending coronation at Moscow would offer a suitable opportunity for it; the Russian representatives at the most important posts abroad would probably meet there at that time, and a programme for Russia's foreign policy would no doubt be drawn up there. M. Saburov hinted at the same time, and I beg you to consider this as only intended for your *personal* information, that the tendency at present goes towards satisfying "l'ambition de la Russie" in the East; according to his opinion a diversion of the kind could only have favourable consequences in any crises that might occur.

Whether the suggestion of the Russian Ambassador is occasioned by an official commission or springs from his personal initiative was not to be known from his words; the latter possibility does not seem out of the question if M. Saburov desired to ascertain our way of thinking for his own guidance.

Meantime the Imperial Chancellor cannot bring forward to His Majesty for discussion the question of a prolongation of the secret Treaty before there is an official inquiry from the Russian Government. Prince Bismarck accordingly begs you to find out confidentially, and in a suitable way, whether

[1] *Op. cit.* III, 285.

M. Saburov spoke by order of his Government or on his own initiative. At the same time, please tell M. von Giers that the Imperial Chancellor considers a prolongation of the Treaty very useful; he also counts on the consent of His Majesty, and believes that Austria will also agree to it. I shall express myself to M. Saburov in the same sense.

I beg you to treat the correspondence on this question in strictest confidence, as also the correspondence preliminary to the conclusion of the Treaty, and provide your reports with a particular numbering and marked "Personal" on the outside.

P. HATZFELDT.

No. 605.[1]

Notes by Busch, the Under-Secretary of State in the Foreign Office.

Fair Copy.

Berlin, 25 August, 1883.

The Russian Ambassador called on me to-day, and after the embarrassed circumlocutions peculiar to him, made me the following communication:

The question of the prolongation of the secret Treaty of the 18 June, 1881, he personally has much at heart. He has no sort of commission to mention this now, but he considers it useful on his own initiative to inform the Imperial Chancellor confidentially of the way of thinking on the question that prevails in Petersburg.

During his last stay in Russia, the Emperor Alexander discussed and went into the possibility of a prolongation of the secret Treaty with him, as well as with other influential personages. He, Saburov, gained the impression from these communications that M. von Giers alone is for the prolongation of the Treaty under all circumstances, therefore if need be even in its present wording. But the majority of the rest of the authoritative voices desire a modification of the agreement in a sense more favourable to Russia. The Emperor

[1] *Op. cit.* III, 292.

shares this desire. His Majesty had urged that the Treaty, if it should become known[1] in Russia, in its present form, would not be popular there, and had especially indicated three points which made unaltered renewal of the Treaty serious for him:

1. If the essential stipulations of the Treaty remained a dead letter, then especially the one bearing on the union of the two Bulgarian States (*Staatswesen*).[2]

2. If Russia's freedom of action towards Turkey were more limited than that of Germany and Austria towards France. While the former with respect to proceeding against Turkey would be bound by a previous agreement with Austria and Germany, the latter would have a free hand towards France.[3]

3. That Russia is not sufficiently informed as to the range of the agreement which exists between Germany and Austria, as well as between these two Powers and Italy, and that the concerted action of the three Imperial Courts[4] provided for in the Treaty has actually not been realised in the measure that was expected on the conclusion of the agreement.

He, Saburov, did not wish to enter into a criticism of these points, but he considered it useful to give information here of the existence of this hesitation on the part of the Emperor Alexander. He is not in a position to make positive proposals for the modifying of the Treaty, yet the thought hovered before him that one might have recourse to the Reichstadt Agreement which contained the germ of a farther-reaching understanding between the three Empires with reference to the Eastern question. He is personally so convinced of the utility, indeed necessity of the renewal of the Treaty; his whole position, even his later career, depend so much on the

---

[1] Prince Bismarck's notes in the margin are given in this and the following four footnotes. "Whereby?"

[2] "We are not hindering them, nor is Austria."

[3] "We do not intend to 'proceed' at all. I did not know whither either. Our intentions are only defensive."

[4] "They have not 'acted' either separately or together."

maintenance of good relations between Germany and Russia, that he considers it his duty, even without a commission, to give the impulse to bringing about negotiations for the pro- longation of the Treaty. If this suggestion is met half-way here, he will ask for definite instructions in Petersburg.

With reference to the Reichstadt stipulations, which I have looked into again because of the Ambassador's hints, I note that the greater part of them had in view the attitude of Austria and Russia during the then imminent Russo-Turkish War, and were, therefore, of a transitory nature. On the other hand, in Article 3 of the Supplementary Convention is to be found the following general stipulation, to which M. Saburov points:

"His Majesty the Emperor of Austria etc. and King of Hungary and His Majesty the Emperor of all the Russias have agreed in principle on the following points, in an inter- view which took place between them at Reichstadt:

"In the event of a reorganisation or dissolution of the Ottoman Empire, the establishment of a great compact Slav or other State is excluded; in return Bulgaria, Albania, and the rest of Roumelia might be constituted independent States; Thessaly, a part of Epirus, and the island of Crete could be annexed by Greece; Constantinople, with outskirts whose limits remain to be determined, could become a free city. Their above-mentioned Majesties affirm that they have in no way departed from these views,[1] and declare afresh their desire to maintain them as the bases of their subsequent political action."

As a matter of fact, the League of the Three Em- perors was renewed under Treaty on 27 March, 1884, for a period of three years as from 18 June of that

---

[1] "For us there is nothing impossible in that, but agreements about inheriting Turkey are scarcely opportune."

year, with two slight modifications. The third paragraph of the first Article was suppressed, and in the second paragraph of the second Article the words "of the said peninsula" were substituted for "of Turkey in Europe". The only other change was that in the signatures, the name of Prince Nicholas Orlov replaced that of Saburov, the cavalry general having succeeded him as Ambassador Extraordinary and Plenipotentiary to the Emperor of Germany on 21 March, 1884.[1]

It is matter of history that there was no third renewal of the Treaty. M. Saburov's explanation, so far as it went, was to the following effect. "Alexander III was under the Danish influence and departed from his father's policy, with which many Russians were far from sympathetic. The Russian people had no sympathy with the German people. Germany has always wanted to absorb our commerce and consider us as a colonial outlet for her goods. We must not change our policy again. The trouble is we have little really patriotic spirit here. Every Frenchman was glad to become a soldier and fight for his country. It is not just the same here.

"But to return. After the second renewal, Alexander III originally wished it to be renewed for the third time. But circumstances were too strong for him, and instead there came about the 'Reinsurance Treaty' of 1887 with Germany, which lasted for three years. Then came Caprivi in place of Bismarck, who said it was not necessary to have a separate treaty with Russia because we were on good relations with

[1] For fuller details, cf. P.S.T. i, 90–93.

282 POSTSCRIPT

one another. Then came other Councillors in Russia who began to smile towards France, but whether it started in France or Russia I do not know. Bismarck was clever, and advised Austria not to annex Bosnia and Herzegovina as it would cause irritation in Russia, when Count Kalnoky wanted to do so in 1889–1890. Bismarck said, 'You occupy the provinces: what more do you want?' The Treaty had not been renewed when Aehrenthal[1] annexed these provinces later[2], and Austria had no right to do so. Bismarck had been forward in policy, but became reserved when Gortchakov took up affairs again."

(b) CONCLUSIONS

Theoretically the League of the Three Emperors had in view these principal aims: the consolidation of the general peace, the maintenance of the monarchical principle and so the assurance of political order, and, finally, the regulation of the Balkan question.[3] It had other cardinal eventualities in mind, e.g. war between Germany and France, or Austria and Italy, or Russia and Great Britain, and the attitude of benevolent neutrality to be observed by the remaining parties to the contract. A cursory

[1] Aehrenthal, Count Alois Lexa von (1854–1912), entered the diplomatic service in 1877, and after service in Paris, St Petersburg and the Ministry of Foreign Affairs in Vienna (1888) was appointed Austrian Minister in Rumania 1895. Later he was transferred as Ambassador to St Petersburg (1899), where he remained till 1906, when he was appointed Minister for Foreign Affairs. He was opposed to the aggressive policy of the Archduke Franz-Ferdinand.
[2] 7 October, 1908.
[3] Reference may again be made to section III of Prof. Kratchounof's valuable brochure, *L'Alliance des Trois Empereurs*.

examination of the Treaty, however, suggests that apart from this, Germany got nothing concrete out of it. It is only when considered in relation to the earlier Austro-German Treaty (about which the German Chancellor informed Vienna at the time of the negotiations with which we have been concerned, that whatever happened it would remain in force), the Austro-Serbian Alliance (24 October, 1881), the Triple Alliance (Germany, Austria-Hungary and Italy, 20 May, 1882), and the Alliance of Rumania with Austria-Hungary, and with Germany, and with Italy (30 October, 1883 and 15 May, 1884), that we see how enormously the position of Germany had become consolidated in the international life of Europe as the result of them all—that, in short, they were all interlocking elements in a system of alliances being wrought out, or at any rate turned to advantage, by the master-mind of Bismarck, which had as a common underlying aim to assure the dominating rôle of Germany on the Continent of Europe. The big idea in the League was Bismarck's—the conception of a demonstration to the world of practical and profitable monarchical solidarity in the Dreikaiserbund. On the other hand, two paragraphs of the Protocol favoured Austrian pretensions towards territorial aggrandisement in the Balkan Peninsula.

But now consider Russia in relation to the League. Two paragraphs of the Protocol bore on Russian influence in the Balkan Peninsula. They constituted a sort of recognition of what she deemed to be her historic rights there, and having largely contributed to the freedom of oppressed nationalities in the past, she could not be accused of the same measure of selfish design as underlay the active Austrian programme of annexation which had finally such disastrous consequences for the world at large. Russia certainly hoped to make progress with her dream of Constantinople, and so secure the key to the Russian house, as the Emperor Nicholas I called it. Pathos and tragedy combine in the story of these Russian aspirations, in days before such a resolving and salving idea as Internationalisation of the Straits had risen above the often painfully limited horizon of the diplomatic mind. Time and again Russia has been thwarted in her purposes by her own fatal temperamental indecision. Sometimes it seems as if she had made enormous sacrifices through twice a hundred years at the urge of some instinct that she had never clearly defined to herself. The open Straits exposed her to disasters like Sevastopol; the closed Straits confined her in the Black Sea as in a prison. There were advantages and disadvantages either way. Was she then really envisaging the Straits open to her own fleet and closed to those of other nations? The dream had been temporarily realised during the few years between the Treaty of Unkiar-Skelessi (8 June, 1833) and the Convention of the Straits (13 July, 1841). Manifestly, then, as soon appeared, the League of the Three Emperors did not go nearly far enough for Panslavism, for now she had to be content with the closing of the Straits as an international obligation on the part of Turkey: the matter was not in Russia's hands alone.

Again, it is impossible to believe that if Bismarck

had read the complete text of the Austro-Hungarian-German Treaty to Saburov, the later Treaty would have followed the particular lines that it took, or indeed perhaps have come into existence at all. But further, only ten days later (28 June, 1881), when the ink of her signature to the Treaty of the Three Emperors (18 June, 1881) had hardly dried, Austria concluded a secret treaty of alliance with Serbia, a sister Slav State to Russia, in which she undertook to support the interests of Serbia where other European Powers were concerned, to aid the establishment of the Obrenovitch dynasty, and protect her ally if she were in a position to make territorial gains on her southern frontiers. In turn the Serbian Government undertook to oppose all "political, religious, or other intrigues" directed from her territory against Austria-Hungary, understanding thereby the inclusion of Bosnia-Herzegovina and the Sanjak of Novibazar; to allow no regular or irregular armed force to cross her territory; and to give her ally "all possible facilities" should she find herself threatened or actually at war with one or several other Powers. Indeed, under the political and military clauses of the Treaty, as also in terms of the accompanying personal declaration of Prince Milan, Serbia, a Slav State, virtually became an Austrian vassal or satellite, and so a political enemy of a sister Slav State.[1] In common fairness to Austria it may be added that there is documental evidence to show that later in the same

---

[1] For the full text cf. P.S.T. *op. cit.* I, 50–63. There is a defence of the Austrian position in Count Julius Andrassy's *Bismarck, Andrassy and their Successors*, p. 90.

year the Russian Government armed and despatched volunteers to Bosnia-Herzegovina to raise revolts in these provinces occupied by Austria under the Treaty of Berlin. One other small point may be mentioned, which however is characteristic of the whole proceedings. When on 7 October, 1908, Bosnia-Herzegovina was actually annexed by Austria-Hungary, Russia protested, in spite of having been a signatory to the Treaty that permitted the step. She might, of course, excuse herself and blame Austria by saying that the Treaty had lapsed. The point is that there were many indications going to show how completely that spirit of goodwill was lacking, which alone could have made the League of the Three Emperors a valuable instrument for conciliating the opposing interests of the two rivals in the Balkan Peninsula.

The League of the Three Emperors was renewed, as we have seen, on 27 March, 1884, for three years, so that the spring of 1887 was naturally the period when negotiations might have been supposed to be in motion for reconsideration of the matter, the exact date of expiry being 27 June. The League was not renewed.[1] Instead, on 18 June, Counts Paul Schuvalov and Herbert Bismarck signed the famous "Reinsurance Treaty" (*Rückversicherungs Vertrag*), about the origin of which much still remains to be dis-

---

[1] "In the presence of such a state of affairs, the Tsar deemed it no longer possible to renew the agreement of the three emperors, the pacific purpose of which could no longer be achieved" (Serge Goriainov, "The End of the Alliance of the Emperors", *Amer. Hist. Rev.* XXIII, 330).

closed.[1] Under it Germany and Russia bound themselves to a "benevolent neutrality" in all wars, except in the event of Germany attacking France, or, Russia, Austria.[2] The remaining Articles mainly amounted to acceptance by Germany of the traditional Russian programme in the Near East, as laid down in the League of the Three Emperors, with emendations in the light of recent happenings, and without reference to Austria. As the eventualities foreshadowed in the Treaty were in all probability remote so far as Russia was concerned, the latter did not stand to gain so much as seemed to be set down on paper.

It is quite evident, however, that in spite of the League of the Three Emperors, Austria and Russia had been drifting farther and farther apart, owing to utter incompatibility of policy in the Balkans. Bismarck's line had been to try to get these two Powers to agree to a delimitation of interests there, leaving the west to Austria and the east to Russia. This policy was even more unacceptable to Austria than it was to Russia. Count Julius Andrassy maintains that "the German Chancellor entirely misinterpreted the foreign policy of the Austro-Hungarian Monarchy under Andrassy's direction. Not the division of the Balkan Peninsula, but the very opposite thereof, was our intention.... His (i.e. his father's) chief aim—the

[1] This Treaty, which was likewise for a duration of three years, was not renewed in 1890 by the Kaiser William II and Caprivi, although both Alexander III and Bismarck (recently fallen) were favourable to its continuance.

[2] For the text cf. P.S.T. I, 274–281: also Serge Goriainov, "The End of the Alliance of the Emperors", *Amer. Hist. Rev.* XXIII, 324–349.

elimination of the last remnant of Russian influence
—remained unchanged ".[1] But, surely and admittedly,[2]
this was only in order to substitute Austrian influence.
The differences over Bulgaria (summer of 1887) very
nearly brought the two countries to blows. Bismarck,
seeing the improbability of a permanent understanding between Austria and Russia, and wishing to have
some sort of hold on Russia in view of her possible
affiliation with France, was ready enough to maintain
this direct contact with the Tsar.

On the other hand, Alexander III came to see that
if Russia and Germany were too long or too closely
in alliance, there would be no counterpoise. Germany
and Russia would be too strong for any other combination, in his opinion, and after Germany with the
aid of Russia had succeeded in her aims, she would
then turn on Russia and try to overthrow her. But,
further, the disclosure of the terms of the supposedly
secret Austro-German Treaty of 1879 by Bismarck to
Schuvalov in May, 1887, produced the profoundest reaction.[3] It is most probable that if Germany had not
thus been revealed as having committed herself so
deeply to Austria, Alexander III might have returned
eventually to the policy of his father. The disclosure
of this Bismarckian manœuvre was the main stimulus
in the Russian change of policy. The Slav question
hopelessly separated Austria and Russia. When it

[1] Count Julius Andrassy, *Bismarck, Andrassy and their Successors*, pp. 125, 126.
[2] Cf. his phrase "the dependence of the Balkan peoples on us"
(*op. cit.* p. 181).
[3] We do not read that Bismarck similarly revealed the terms
of the "Reinsurance Treaty" to Austria at any subsequent point!

was abundantly clear from the terms of the Treaty of 1879 that Germany had instinctively determined to support Austria in a policy of which the Bosnia-Herzegovina episode was a later manifestation, Russia "shied off".

The recital of the story of the pourparlers and events leading up to so seemingly important an historical landmark as The League of the Three Emperors carries with it many saddening reflections. The lot of nations, the destinies of peoples, seemed, in the days of their ignorance, to depend in great part on the caprices of secret diplomacy, even on the physical or mental condition, as it might be, of certain individuals on particular days or during definite periods.[1] But if so, how necessary is it now for every individual citizen or subject to take an active and intelligent interest in the internal and external welfare of his country, and, realising that, after all, the Ministers of State are, in a measure, his representatives, endeavour to study along with them the problems that will never cease to arise, and by concerted action endeavour to influence policy where it seems to them with

---

[1] I have heard it seriously argued by a professor of mental diseases in a leading British University that a determining element in the series of events that culminated in the defection of the American colonies was the fact that George III and his Prime Minister, the elder Pitt, were alike subject to the form of mental illness known as Manic-Depressive or *Folie Circulaire*. They were both mentally and physically unfit at certain periods for their high offices. Most unfortunately at a critical time the Prime Minister suffered from an attack of melancholia and lost control of the situation. On the other hand, the conduct of the King indicates that he probably suffered from a mild degree of elation which affected his judgment.

good reason to be directed along lines that will eventuate in more harm than good in the long run. For it is certain that the growing entanglement of Alliances, Leagues and Treaties in Europe during the last quarter of the past century, all based either on fear or hatred rather than on broad community of interests, had disturbing and, in the end, fatal consequences. Events like the secret Treaty of 20 February, 1887, between Austria and Italy, and Bismarck's "Reinsurance Treaty" with Russia, implied the dissolution of the League of the Three Emperors, and the finale to Germany's attempted rôle of mediator between Austria and Russia. The evolution of European political history followed independent laws that not even the genius of a Bismarck could modify. Yet that does not mean that they are altogether unmodifiable. The man who also thinks internationally will have a somewhat different line of conduct to the man who thinks only nationally, and, so far as we can reach a philosophy of history, it looks as if the former stands in the line of progress to-day.

There are two great obstacles to international understanding, Ignorance and Suspicion, and of these the second is the direct offspring of the first. Surely, if anywhere, it is in the Universities of all lands that we must learn to undertake impartial study of the past with a view to the better understanding of the present. Only in that way can we profit from the mistakes of the past, and in that measure be filled with a greater hope for the future.

APPENDICES I AND II

APPENDIX I

TEXT OF RUSSO-GERMAN PROJECT PROPOSED TO AUSTRIA

Projet Russo-Allemand, Proposé à l'Autriche	Amendements Autrichiens	Répliques de la Russie
Article I.	*Article I.*	*Article I.*
Alinéa 1. Les trois Cours de Russie, d'Allemagne et d'Autriche-Hongrie se promettent que si un différend ou un grief venait à surgir entre deux d'entre elles, ce différend serait déféré à la médiation de la troisième, pour être ensuite aplani par un accord à trois.	Supprimer.	D'accord.
Alinéa 2. Dans le cas où l'une d'elles se trouverait *forcée d'être* en guerre avec une quatrième *Puissance*, les deux autres maintiendront à son égard une neutralité bienveillante et *veilleront* à la localisation du conflit.	Supprimer les mots: *forcée d'être*. Remplacer le mot: *Puissance* par les mots: *Grande Puissance*. Remplacer le mot: *veilleront* par les mots: *voueront leurs soins*.	D'accord.
Alinéa 3. Cette stipulation s'appliquera également à une guerre entre une des trois Puissances et la Turquie, mais seulement dans le cas où un accord	*Aucune des trois Puissances n'entreprendra une guerre agressive contre la Turquie. Si toutefois l'une d'elles était forcée d'être en guerre avec cet Empire, la*	Nous maintenons la rédaction primitive.

[292]

préalable aura été établi entre les trois Cours sur les résultats de cette guerre.

Alinéa 4. Pour le cas spécial où l'une d'elles obtiendrait de l'un de ses deux alliés un concours plus positif, la valeur obligatoire du présent article restera dans toute sa vigueur pour la troisième.

Article II.

Alinéa 1. La Russie, d'accord avec l'Allemagne, déclare sa ferme résolution de respecter les intérêts qui découlent de la nouvelle position assurée à l'Autriche par le Traité de Berlin et *définie en dernier lieu par sa convention avec la Turquie au sujet de l'occupation de certaines parties du territoire Ottoman.*

Alinéa 2. Les trois Cours, désireuses d'éviter tout désaccord entre elles, s'engagent à tenir compte de leurs intérêts respectifs dans la Péninsule des Balcans. Elles se promettent, de plus, que de nouvelles modifications dans le statu quo territorial *de la Turquie d'Europe* ne pourront s'accomplir qu'en vertu d'un commun accord *entre elles.*

[293]

*stipulation de l'alinéa précédent s'appliquera également à cette guerre, mais seulement dans le cas où un accord préalable aura été établi entre les trois Cours sur les *limites territoriales* et les résultats de cette guerre.

Adopté.

Article II.

Supprimer la dernière partie de l'alinéa à partir des mots: "et définie en dernier lieu", ou bien, ajouter à la fin: "L'Autriche-Hongrie se réserve, si la défense de 'ses intérêts l'exigeait,' de faire des changements dans la situation politique de la Bosnie, de l'Herzégovine et du Sandjak de Novi-Bazar".

des provinces de la Turquie d'Europe actuellement soumises à l'autorité du Sultan, etc.

Supprimer à la fin les mots: "entre elles".

D'accord.

Article II.

Nous préférons supprimer la dernière partie de l'alinéa, à partir des mots: "et définie en dernier lieu".

Nous maintenons la rédaction primitive.

Projet Russo-Allemand, Proposé a l'Autriche	Amendements Autrichiens	Répliques de la Russie
Article II (cont.). Alinéa 3. Afin de faciliter l'accord prévu par le présent article, accord dont il est impossible de préjuger d'avance toutes les modalités, les trois Cours constateront, *dès à présent*, les points sur lesquels *une entente a déjà été établie* en principe.	*Article II (cont.).* Supprimer, ou bien modifier ainsi les mots soulignés: "constateront les points sur lesquels un échange d'idées antérieur a démontré un accord en principe".	*Article II (cont.).* Nous maintenons la rédaction primitive.
Article III. Alinéa 1. Les trois Cours reconnaissent le caractère européen et mutuellement obligatoire du principe de la fermeture des détroits du Bosphore et des Dardanelles, fondé sur le Droit des Gens et confirmé par les Traités.	*Article III.* Ajouter à la fin les mots: "de Paris, de Londres et de Berlin, avec indication de la date des Traités".	*Article III.* D'accord; mais mentionner également notre Déclaration au Congrès de Berlin.
Alinéa 2. Elles *veilleront* en commun à ce que la Turquie ne fasse pas d'exception à cette règle en faveur des intérêts particuliers d'un Gouvernement quelconque, en prêtant à des opérations guerrières d'une Puissance belligérante la partie de son Empire que forment les détroits.	Supprimer l'expression: "veilleront", et ajouter à la fin, en remplacement de l'alinéa suivant qui est inacceptable, les mots: "sans se mettre en guerre vis-à-vis de la Partie lésée".	Nous insistons sur le maintien de la rédaction primitive.

Alinéa 3. En cas d'infraction, ou pour la prévenir si une pareille infraction était à prévoir, les trois Cours avertiront la Turquie qu'elles la considéreraient, le cas échéant, comme s'étant mise en état de guerre vis-à-vis de la Partie lésée, et comme s'étant privée, dès lors, des bénéfices de sécurité assurés par le Traité de Berlin à son statu quo territorial.	Supprimer.	Maintenir le texte primitif.
	Article IV. Fixer le terme de trois ans pour la durée du Traité.	*Article IV.* D'accord.
	Article V. Engagement de garder le secret sur le Traité.	*Article V.* D'accord.
	Préambule du Traité. Préciser le but de cet arrangement, destiné à donner de nouvelles garanties à la paix, au maintien de laquelle les trois Puissances sont résolues à vouer tous leurs efforts.	*Article VI.* Abolir les conventions secrètes conclues en 1873 avec l'Allemagne et l'Autriche.

TEXT OF THE TREATY OF 18(/6) JUNE, 1881, AS GIVEN IN THE MEMOIRS

TRAITÉ DU 18 (6) JUIN 1881

Leurs Majestés l'Empereur de toutes les Russies, Roi de Pologne, Grand-Duc de Finlande, l'Empereur d'Allemagne, Roi de Prusse, et l'Empereur d'Autriche, Roi de Hongrie,— animés d'un égal désir de consolider la paix générale par une entente destinée à assurer la position défensive de Leurs États respectifs, sont tombés d'accord sur certaines questions qui touchent plus spécialement à leurs intérêts réciproques.

Dans ce but, Leurs Majestés ont nommé (suivent les noms des Plénipotentiaires).

Lesquels, après avoir examiné leurs pleins pouvoirs trouvés en bonne et due forme, sont convenus des articles suivants :

ARTICLE I.

Dans le cas où l'une des trois Puissances se trouverait en guerre avec une quatrième grande Puissance, les deux autres maintiendront à son égard une neutralité bienveillante et voueront leurs soins à la localisation du conflit.

Cette stipulation s'appliquera également à une guerre entre l'une des trois Puissances et la Turquie, mais seulement dans le cas où un accord préalable aura été établi entre les trois Cours sur les résultats de cette guerre.

Pour le cas spécial où l'une d'elles obtiendrait de l'un de ses deux alliés un concours plus positif, la valeur obligatoire du présent article restera dans toute sa vigueur pour la troisième.

ARTICLE II.

La Russie, d'accord avec l'Allemagne, déclare sa ferme résolution de respecter les intérêts qui découlent de la nouvelle position assurée à l'Autriche-Hongrie par le Traité de Berlin.

Les trois Cours, désireuses d'éviter tout désaccord entre elles, s'engagent à tenir compte de leurs intérêts respectifs dans la Péninsule des Balcans. Elles se promettent, de plus, que de nouvelles modifications dans le statu quo territorial de la Turquie d'Europe ne pourront s'accomplir qu'en vertu d'un commun accord entre elles.

Afin de faciliter l'accord prévu par le présent article,—accord dont il est impossible de prévoir d'avance toutes les modalités,—les trois Cours constatent dès à présent, dans le protocole annexé au Traité, les points sur lesquels une entente a été déjà établie en principe.

ARTICLE III.

Les trois Cours reconnaissent le caractère européen et mutuellement obligatoire du principe de la fermeture des détroits du Bosphore et des Dardanelles, fondé sur le Droit des Gens, confirmé par les Traités et résumé par la Déclaration du second plénipotentiaire de Russie à la séance du 12 juillet du Congrès de Berlin (protocole 19).

Elles veilleront en commun à ce que la Turquie ne fasse pas d'exception à cette règle en faveur des intérêts d'un Gouvernement quelconque, en prêtant à des opérations guerrières d'une Puissance belligérante la partie de son Empire que forment les détroits.

En cas d'infraction, ou pour la prévenir si une pareille infraction était à prévoir, les trois Cours avertiront la Turquie qu'elles la considéreraient, le cas échéant, comme s'étant mise en état de guerre vis-à-vis de la Partie lésée, et comme s'étant privée, dès lors, des bénéfices de sécurité assurés par le Traité de Berlin à son statu quo territorial.

ARTICLE IV.

Le présent Traité sera en vigueur pendant l'espace de trois ans à dater du jour de l'échange des ratifications.

ARTICLE V.

Les hautes Parties contractantes se promettent mutuellement le secret sur le contenu et sur l'existence du présent
Traité, aussi bien que du protocole y annexé.

ARTICLE VI.

Les conventions secrètes conclues entre la Russie et l'Allemagne, et entre la Russie et l'Autriche-Hongrie, en 1873,
sont remplacées par le présent Traité.

ARTICLE VII.

Les ratifications du présent Traité et du protocole y annexé
seront échangées à Berlin dans l'espace de quinze jours, ou
plus tôt si faire se peut.

En foi de quoi, etc.

(Signé) SABOUROFF
BISMARCK
SZÉCHÉNYI.

PROTOCOLE.

Les soussignés, etc....ayant constaté, conformément à
l'article II du Traité secret conclu aujourd'hui, les points
touchant les intérêts des trois Cours dans la Péninsule des
Balcans sur lesquels une entente a déjà été établie entre elles,
sont convenus du protocole suivant:

1. Bosnie et Herzégovine.

L'Autriche-Hongrie se réserve de s'annexer ces deux provinces au moment qu'elle jugera opportun.

2. Sandjak de Novi-Bazar.

La Déclaration échangée entre les plénipotentiaires russes
et les plénipotentiaires austro-hongrois au Congrès de Berlin
en date du 1/13 juillet 1878, reste en vigueur.

3. Roumélie Orientale.

Les trois Puissances sont d'accord pour envisager l'éventualité d'une occupation soit de la Roumélie Orientale, soit des Balcans, comme pleine de périls pour la paix générale. Le cas échéant, elles emploieront leurs efforts pour détourner la Porte d'une pareille entreprise, bien entendu que la Bulgarie et la Roumélie Orientale devront de leur côté s'abstenir de provoquer la Porte par des attaques partant de leur territoire contre les autres provinces de l'Empire Ottoman.

4. Bulgarie.

Les trois Puissances ne s'opposeront pas à la réunion éventuelle de la Bulgarie et de la Roumélie Orientale dans les limites territoriales qui leur sont assignées par le Traité de Berlin, si cette question venait à surgir par la force des choses.

Elles sont d'accord pour détourner les Bulgares de toute agression contre les provinces voisines, notamment la Macédoine, et pour leur déclarer qu'en pareil cas ils agiraient à leurs risques et périls.

5. Attitude des agents en Orient.

Afin d'éviter les froissements d'intérêts dans les questions locales qui peuvent surgir, les trois Cours Impériales muniront leurs représentants et agents en Orient d'une Instruction générale pour leur prescrire de s'efforcer à aplanir leurs divergences par des explications amicales entre eux dans chaque cas spécial, et pour le cas où ils n'y parviendraient pas, d'en référer à leurs Gouvernements.

6. Le présent protocole fera partie intégrante du Traité secret signé en ce jour à Berlin, et aura même force et valeur.

Fait à Berlin, le 18/6 juin 1881.

(Signé) SABOUROFF.
BISMARCK.
SZÉCHÉNYI.

BALKAN STATES, 1878

English Miles
0 20 40 60 80 100 120 140 160

NOTE

The boundaries shown are those settled by the
Congress of Berlin

The red line ———— indicates the proposed Bulgarian
boundary of the Treaty of San Stefano

INDEX

302   INDEX

For EU product safety concerns, contact us at Calle de José Abascal, 56–1°, 28003 Madrid, Spain or eugpsr@cambridge.org.

www.ingramcontent.com/pod-product-compliance
Ingram Content Group UK Ltd.
Pitfield, Milton Keynes, MK11 3LW, UK
UKHW020308140625
459647UK00014B/1795